Benoît Henriet
Colonial Impotence

Africa in Global History

Edited by
Joël Glasman, Omar Gueye, Alexander Keese and Christine Whyte

Advisory Board:
Joe Alie, Felicitas Becker, William Gervase Clarence-Smith, Lynda Day, Scholastique Diazinga, Andreas Eckert, Babacar Fall, Toyin Falola, Matt Graham, Emma Hunter, Erin Jessee, Isabella Kentridge, Colleen Kriger, Kristin Mann, Patrick Manning, Conceição Neto, Vanessa S. Oliveira, Lorelle Semley, Ibrahim Sundiata

Volume 3

Benoît Henriet
Colonial Impotence

Virtue and Violence in a Congolese Concession
(1911–1940)

DE GRUYTER
OLDENBOURG

ISBN: 978-3-11-125743-3
eBook ISBN (PDF): 978-3-11-065273-4
eBook ISBN (EPUB): 978-3-11-064909-3
ISSN 2628-1767

Library of Congress Control Number: 2021933298

Bibliographic information published by the Deutsche Nationalbibliothek
The Deutsche Nationalbibliothek lists this publication in the Deutsche Nationalbibliografie; Detailed bibliographic data are available in the Internet at http://dnb.dnb.de.

© 2023 Walter de Gruyter GmbH, Berlin/Boston
This volume is text- and page-identical with the hardback published in 2021.
Cover image: Fruit cutter climbing an oil pam tree, c. 1955, by Henri Nicolaï.
Printing and binding: CPI books GmbH, Leck

www.degruyter.com

To my goddaughters,
Elisa and Kali,
For making the future look brighter.

Contents

Table of figures —— IX

Abbreviations —— XI

Acknowledgements —— XIII

Introduction: "Congo Atrocities!!!" —— 1
    Concessions and colonies —— 5
    Impotence and colonial ventures —— 8
    Contextualizing Leverville —— 14
    A note on the sources —— 19
    Outline —— 25

Chapter 1:
The virtuous enclave —— 28
    Introduction —— 28
    Tropical utopias —— 29
    Colonizing virtuously —— 34
    A clean break? —— 39
    Conclusion —— 45

Chapter 2:
Impotent agents —— 47
    Introduction —— 47
    Agents of empire —— 50
    The shortcomings of power —— 53
    Fiscal impotence —— 59
    Impotence and prevarication —— 62
    Impotence on tour —— 64
    Conclusion —— 68

Chapter 3:
Ordering and evading —— 71
    Introduction —— 71
    Eluding control: the *villages doublures* —— 75
    Deceiving public servants —— 80
    Lukusu and sense-making —— 86

Conclusion —— 92

Chapter 4:
An indescribable ugliness —— 95
    Introduction —— 95
    The many faces of colonial violence —— 96
    Violent recruitment —— 100
    Abuses of power —— 106
    Translucent workers —— 112
    Conclusion —— 118

Chapter 5:
The concession embodied —— 120
    Introduction —— 120
    Embodying colonialism —— 121
    Contested rations —— 123
    The ambivalence of clothing —— 131
    Coercive healing —— 137
    Conclusion —— 144

Chapter 6:
A war against nature —— 146
    Introduction —— 146
    The concession ecology —— 146
    Owning the palm groves —— 149
    Competing for palm oil —— 157
    Fruitless plantations —— 162
    Conclusion —— 167

Conclusion:
The concession experience —— 169
    The unrealized utopia —— 170
    The protean enclave —— 174
    Impotence, in Leverville and beyond —— 176

Bibliography —— 178
    Archival sources —— 178
    Published sources —— 178
    Interviews —— 179
    Reference works —— 179

Table of figures

Figure 1: "Congo Atrocities!!!", 1920 —— 1
Figure 2: View of Leverville, c. 1930 —— 2
Figure 3: HCB circles in Belgian Congo —— 4
Figure 4: Palm oil concessions in the Kwango district —— 16
Figure 5: Annotated map envisioning village displacements —— 84
Figure 6: Mural by Sissi Kalo, Cercle Elaïs, Lusanga, 1989 —— 99
Figure 7: "Friends and Collaborators 1" —— 132
Figure 8: "Friends and Collaborators 2" —— 133
Figure 9: "Waiting to cross the river, Leverville-Soa, 1926–27" —— 135
Figure 10: "My team of rowers and my escort" —— 136

Abbreviations

AAB:	African Archives, Ministry of Foreign Affairs, Brussels.
ABIR:	Anglo-Belgian India Rubber Company.
ABP:	Archives of the Bandundu Province.
AIMO:	Affaires indigènes – main d'oeuvre.
CK:	Compagnie du Kasaï.
GG:	Gouverneur-général du Congo belge.
HCB:	Huileries du Congo Belge.
INEAC:	Institut National pour l'Etude Agronomique du Congo belge.
JAK:	Archives of the Jesuit Province of Central Africa, Kinshasa.
MOI:	Main d'oeuvre indigène.
PLC:	Plantations Lever au Congo.
PLZ:	Plantations Lever au Zaïre.
REPCO:	Régie des Plantations au Congo belge.
RMCA:	Royal Museum for Central Africa.
UA:	Unilever Archives, Port Sunlight.
UMHK:	Union Minière du Haut-Katanga.

Acknowledgements

This book was inspired by my doctoral research at Université Saint-Louis in Brussels under the umbrella of the IAP BeJust 2.0 research project and financed by the Belgian Federal Scientific Policy. I would like to thank my thesis supervisor, Nathalie Tousignant, for her mentoring, friendship, and continuous support. She was the first to introduce me to the fascinating history of Congo and colonialism during my second year of study. In the process of designing my study plan, Nathalie constantly encouraged me to go off the beaten path; to investigate new sources; and to critically approach my archives. I would have been another researcher—and perhaps not even a researcher at all—should I not have the chance to meet her.

I would also like to express my gratitude to the members of my doctoral jury: Alexander Keese, Thomas Hendriks, Pedro Monaville and Pierre-Olivier de Broux. They allocated a significant portion of their precious time to helping me improve my work. Their advice, suggestions, and expertise have profoundly helped me refine my analytical framework and improve my research techniques, both in the archives and in the field. Our paths have continued to cross since then, and I hope we will remain in touch for decades to come. I also have to mention how indebted I am to Thomas for his kindness; for the sharpness of his conceptual mind; and for suggesting that I work around the concept of colonial impotence. As it turned out, I took his advice very seriously!

Countless other people have helped me bring this research to fruition. Many thanks to Pierre Dandoy and Rafael Storme (African archives, Federal Public Service Foreign Affairs, Brussels); Joanne Ruff (Unilever archives, Port Sunlight); and Father Jan Evers (Jesuit archives, Kinshasa), who helped me find my way through the intricate paper trails of colonial institutions. I was also fortunate to be able to count on the support and help of friends and colleagues during my field work in the Kwilu. I am particularly indebted to Katrien Pype, for sharing her time and experiences with me, and for giving me the chance to find a family and a home in Kikwit. I am honoured to count someone as knowledgeable, warm and charming as she among my friends. Thanks also to Pierre Clinquart, Clara Devlieger, Jacob Koster, Emery Kalema, Renzo Martens, Trisha Phippard and Kiangu Sindani for their support and advice and for accommodating me. I am endlessly grateful to the Mbwabala family, Bertine, Noël, Héritier, Florence and Winner, for welcoming me into their home and for taking care of me. Above all, I would like to thank Jean-Claude Lufungula, without whom this fieldwork would not have been possible. Jean-Claude devoted entire weeks to my research and drove his motorbike on hundreds of kilometres of asphalt roads and dusty trails for us to meet the remaining witnesses of Leverville. I am also indebted to his tireless and excellent translation work. Finally, I wish want to thank all of those who were willing to share their memories with perfect strangers and who helped me get a clearer picture of what the concession experience could mean for those who lived through it.

Over the years, this dissertation was progressively turned into a book, a process which brought along another set of invaluable contributors. I want to thank Iris Vandevelde (@Zidiris) for making beautiful maps out of the barely legible ones I found in the archives. I am also forever grateful to Marieke Slovin for her fantastic copy-editing work and for her unfailing vigilance in making sure that I remained consistent in my use of the Oxford comma. Marieke not only patiently corrected all of my idiosyncrasies; she also brought clarity and structure to my often hard to follow streams of thought. I cannot thank my De Gruyter editors, Rabea Rittgerodt and Jana Fritsche, enough for being ever so patient, understanding and supportive during the long writing process of this monograph.

Furthermore, I am endlessly indebted to my colleagues and friends, whose invaluable input and review helped me to significantly improve this present research. Many thanks to Geoffrey Pakiam, Miles Larmer, Reuben Loffman, Iva Peša, Romain Tiquet and Amandine Lauro for reading and rereading my work and allowing me to benefit from their insight and expertise. I am particularly grateful for Amandine's lasting friendship and beautiful intelligence and for the countless projects we designed together, as well as all of those we will pursue in the future. I would also like to thank the two anonymous reviewers' constructive and critical feedback, which helped me improve the book's final outlook.

These last several years, I have had the incredible opportunity to work for and with fantastic academics. I want to express my gratitude to the members of the Comparing the Copperbelt project and the School of Area Studies at Oxford University for trusting and welcoming me into their fold. I am also ever so grateful to my colleagues and to the history students of the Vrije Universiteit Brussel (VUB), from whom and with whom I have learned so much every day.

Finally, I want to thank my close ones for their love and support. Some drifted away while others became closer, but all contributed in no small part to shaping the life experience in which this book was formed. I particularly want to thank my fantastic partner, Kevin, for being the best life companion I could dream of; for our community of minds and souls; and for the future we are building together. I am also ever so grateful that he was the kindest reviewer #1 academia has ever seen during the writing of this manuscript, gently channelling his remarks and suggestions through the warmest chord of care. I look forward to the many adventures ahead of us!

Introduction: "Congo Atrocities!!!"

Figure 1: "Congo Atrocities!!!", 1920. Unilever Archives, Port Sunlight (UA), UAC 2/36/7/1/3

She stands in the centre of the photo, clad in white with a *chicotte*[1] in her hand. A group of men surround her, seemingly posing as either standing adjuvants, kneeling captives, or supine penitents. The staging of the photo sets the men starkly apart; her attire and fair complexion contrast with the darker shades of their bare skin. It is likely a parodic staging, as indicated by the young man in the middle row, who appears to be dissimulating a grin behind his hand. Little is known about the circumstances in which this striking *tableau vivant* was captured. A handwritten note on the back only mentions the year 1920, coupled with a succinct description: "Congo Atrocities!!!".

I found this document among a series of more mundane photographs collected by Elso Dusseljé during his tenure as director of the Leverville concession, Belgian Congo's most important zone of palm oil production in the interwar. Kept among images of buildings, workers, and "tours of inspection" of the company's facilities (see figure 2), "Congo Atrocities!!!" offers a rare glimpse into the

---

[1] The *chicotte*, a whip made of rhinoceros skin, was widely used to punish and discipline Congolese men during the colonial period. Jean-François Bayart, "Hégémonie et Coercicion en Afrique Subsaharienne. La 'politique de la chicotte,'" *Politique Africaine* 2:110 (2008): 123–152; Marie-Bénédicte Dembour, "La Chicote Comme Symbole du Colonialisme Belge?," *Canadian Journal of African Studies* 26:2 (1992): 205–225.

https://doi.org/10.1515/9783110652734-004

daily life of Leverville's inhabitants. This small community pursued a relatively isolated existence on the southwest fringes of the Congolese rainforest; they were connected to the outside world only by company steamboats, which travelled up and down the Kwilu river. Away from Congo's expanding urban and industrial areas, the concession's Europeans had few ways to relieve the monotony of the everyday. Staging mock re-enactments of colonial brutality would, apparently, help them kill time.

Figure 2: View of Leverville, c. 1930. UA, UAC 2/36/7/1/3

A semi-private photograph, intended to only circulate within the close social circle of Leverville's Europeans, "Congo Atrocities!!!" provides an opportunity to learn more about their self-representations,[2] as well as their relation with Congo's then recent, brutal past. Twelve years before the picture was taken, what was to become the Belgian colony was still known as the Congo Free State (1885–1908), the infamous private empire of King Leopold II. This unique polity – a one man colony with no metropolis – is more remembered today for its abhorrent violence than for its institutional peculiarity.

At the turn of the century, the economically struggling "Free State" became a global exporter of widely demanded rubber, which grew profusely in its enormous rainforest. State representatives, agents of concessionary companies,

---

2 For a case-study in the analysis of "semi-private" photographs in colonial Congo, see: Thomas Hendriks, "Erotics of Sin: Promiscuity, Polygamy and Homo-Erotics in Missionary Photography from the Congolese Rainforest," *Visual Anthropology* 26:4 (2009): 355–82.

and their local armed suites attempted to increase rubber collection at all costs, perpetrating countless exactions in the process. They resorted to looting, rape, flogging, and/or kidnapping to mobilize their workforce, capture resources, and control territories. Congolese soldiers and sentries – mercenaries of concessionary companies – would sometimes cut the hands of the living as war trophies and "proofs" that they used their bullets to kill rather than to hunt. A long litany of abuses was first collected by activists in Congo advocating for a regime change, and was later confirmed by an official commission of enquiry set up by the King himself in 1904–1905. The "Congo atrocities" – as they came to be known – also reached a large audience in the West through the tireless campaigning of reformists. In pamphlets and magic lantern shows, the plight of the Congolese was depicted *ad nauseam* with photographic evidences of handless arms, footless legs and severed limbs.[3]

There is no doubt that "Congo Atrocities!!!" directly refers to Free State violence. The photograph's title and its visual repertoire allude to the depictions of Congo popularized by reformist campaigners. The Leverville concession, which will be the topic of this book, was not immediately impacted by the most gruesome aspects of the Leopoldian regime. It was founded in 1911, three years after the transfer of sovereignty over Congo from the aging king to the Belgian state, and stood at the periphery of rubber production zones, where the most gruesome exactions took place.

However, memories of the Free State might have been ever-present in the life of Leverville's inhabitants: in the minds of those who experienced it, in the imaginary attached to Congo, and in the peculiar nature of the structure in which they lived. The Leverville "circle" was a concession, a private extractive monopoly granted by a colonial state, in the direct lineage of the old rubber companies. It also stood on the former grounds of the *Compagnie du Kasaï*, a rubber conglomerate for which Leopold II's Free State was the main shareholder. Furthermore, these traumatic events could not simply be wiped out of existence. Although a legal process handed out in Brussels terminated the Free State to instate Belgian Congo in its place, individuals and communities in Central Africa still had to make do with the long-lasting consequences of its endemic violence. Rubber production zones faced a steep demographic decline, leaving the landscape scattered with ruins of abandoned settlements. Decades after the end of the King's personal rule, survivors of Free State violence could still be spotted

---

3 Isidore Ndaywel E Nziem, *Nouvelle Histoire du Congo. Des origines à la République Démocratique* (Brussels: Le Cri, 2010), 310–18, Kevin Grant, "The Limits of Exposure: Atrocity Photographs in the Congo Reform Campaign," in *Humanitarian Photography: A History*, edited by Heide Fehrenbach and Davide Rodogno (Cambridge University Press, 2015), 64–88.

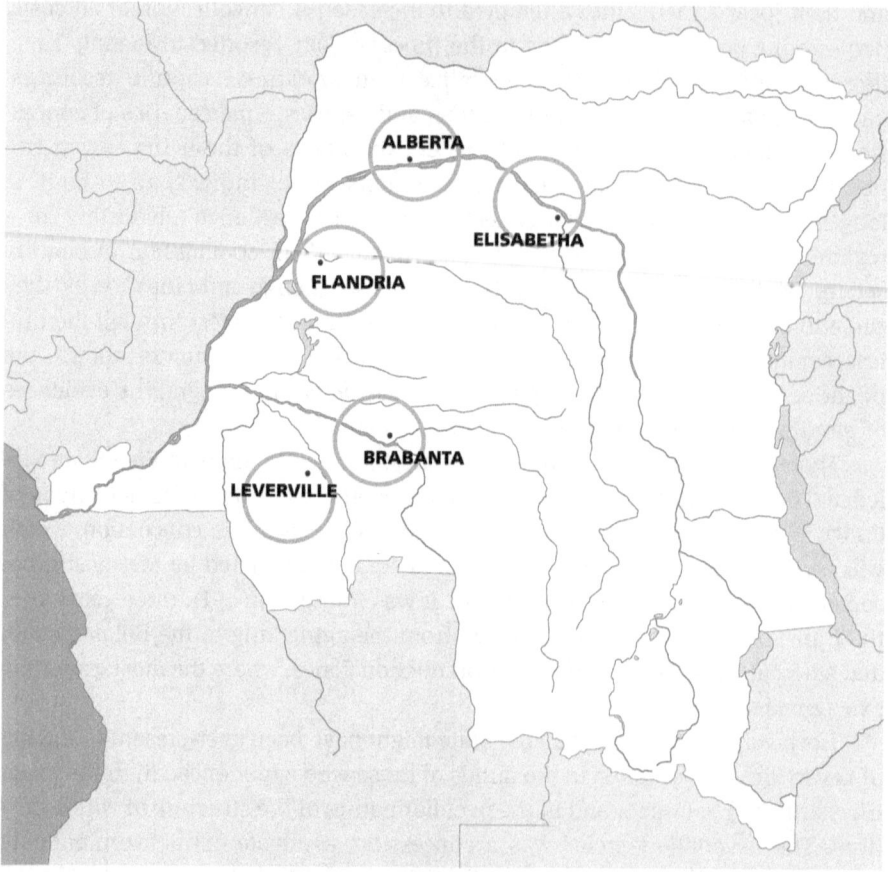

Figure 3: HCB circles in Belgian Congo, Map by Iris Vandevelde.

in villages, missions and colonial outposts, the sight of their amputated limbs acting as daily reminders of past brutalities.[4]

Yet, in 1920, "Congo Atrocities!!!" seemed to become a topic of amusement for Leverville's Europeans. Although the butt of this photographic joke is forever lost, it conveys a sense of emotional distance from the time and practices of King's personal colony. The picture frames accusations of colonial violence as exaggerated, thereby diminishing their lasting impact on Africans. This distancing could be explained in two different, albeit intertwined, ways. First, Leverville

---

[4] On this particular topic, see: Nancy Rose Hunt, *A Nervous State. Violence, Remedies and Reverie in Colonial Congo* (Durham: Duke University Press, 2016), 153–156.

was one of the five "circles" granted by Belgian colonial authorities to the *Huileries du Congo Belge* (HCB) (see figure 3), a subsidiary of the British consortium, Lever Brothers. Makers and sellers of the famed Sunlight line of hygienic products Lever Brothers was at the time known for the paternalistic policies enforced in its English plants for the welfare of its workers. It seems possible to me that the small cosmopolitan community living in the tropical outpost of a company had been imbued with a benevolent ethos and thus felt unconcerned by and unrelated to the woeful practices of the defunct polity. Second, it is also possible that this humorous staging was used to create and maintain distance not only with Congo's brutal past, but also with the daily displays of violence taking place in the Leverville concession itself, turning them into a topic of laughter. Laughter can indeed be multi layered, and its eruption could signal repressed emotions brought to the fore. For Achille Mbembe, it could act as a "refuge" for those who witnessed or participated to acts of brutality.[5] Nancy Rose Hunt found reports of laughter bursting out in the testimonies of victims and perpetrators of Free State violence and suggested that it conveys their anguish, discomfort or shame.[6] Parodies such as "Congo Atrocities!!!" could therefore offer a way to deal with uncomfortable truths, acknowledging their existence without having to seriously face them.

Everyday practices of power and labour in the Leverville concession were indeed much less remote from Free State usages than what could be suggested by "Congo Atrocities!!!". HCB pledged to enforce an ambitious social agenda in its "circles" yet mostly fell short of complying with its own engagements. Rather than relying on a voluntary workforce, it resorted to different strategies of coerced recruitment, comparable to those of Free State rubber companies. In the concession, public and private actors were tied by many informal and sometimes illegal arrangements, not dissimilar to the blurred boundaries between state and capital characterizing the Free State's political and economic governance. King Leopold's personal colony might have lived by the time the HCB came to be, but its legacy stretched deep into Leverville's territory and power dynamics.

Concessions and colonies

Offering a glimpse into the internal tensions and contradictions at the heart of the Leverville project, "Congo Atrocities!!!" provides a fitting entry point for

---

5 Achille Mbembe, *On the Postcolony* (Berkeley: University of California Press, 2001), 203.
6 Hunt, *Nervous State*, 39–41.

the present book. In the following chapters, *Colonial Impotence* uses the Leverville concession as a case study to investigate the discrepancy between the *virtuous colony* imagined in European chancelleries and headquarters of multinational companies and the *violent colony* experienced by those living on the frontier of tropical capitalism. The book illustrates how the Leverville concession provides a unique standpoint to observe colonialism in the field in many of its guises.

Concessions are remarkable nodes within the uneven fabric of colonial rule. As Lauren Benton suggests, empires "did not cover space evenly." Rather, the effective power of colonial institutions of all nature was mostly concentrated along enclaves of strategic and/or economic importance, as well as around the corridors binding them together.[7] Among those enclaves, there were concessions built around the extraction of primary resources – either mineral or vegetal – or the production of tropical cash crops. Whether clearly delimited or not, they are set apart from their surroundings by a significant investment in infrastructure and a markedly higher concentration of colonial agents and indigenous workers. The granting of exclusive rights to extract or produce given to private companies did not necessarily mean that other actors would be excluded from those enclaves. On the contrary, concessions' strategic importance, as well as the various issues posed by the presence of a significant population of colonized wage workers, could induce an increased mobilization of state or parastatal forces. Public servants, policemen and soldiers could be present to prevent conflict. Doctors, nurses and missionaries could be called in to care for the bodies and souls of their inhabitants.

According to Rebecca Hardin, concessions not only define "formal legal acts [enabling] the demarcation of spatial units for utilization and management of ecosystems" but also the "social processes" taking place within their boundaries.[8] Concessions gather a plurality of actors, performing different roles across the racially-structured colonial order, alternately competing and collaborating with one another. They interact in an enclave, which could be both relatively isolated from the rest of the colony while being well connected to the networks of global capitalism.[9] The fluctuation of prices on global markets, for instance, could have dire consequences on the everyday functioning of the concession.

---

[7] Lauren Benton, *A Search for Sovereignty. Law and Geography in European Empires, 1400–1900* (Cambridge: Cambridge University Press, 2009), 2.
[8] Rebecca Hardin, "Concessionary Politics: Property, Patronage, and Political Rivalry in Central African Forest Management," *Current Anthropology*, 52:3 (2009): 115–16.
[9] James Ferguson, *Global Shadows. Africa in the Neoliberal World Order* (Durham: Duke University Press, 2006), 32–6.

These characteristics make concessions peculiar fields of power within the imperial superstructure, microcosms where broader tensions are made more visible and challenged at the same time; for example, between "colonizers" and "colonized"; "state" and "companies"; or "centre" and "periphery."

Concessions were not only nodes within the uneven fabric of empires; they could also "connect" different temporalities with one another. Legal arrangements and social dynamics in the Leverville concession echo for instance the practices of Free State rubber companies (see chapter 1). Furthermore, *fin de siècle* imperial strategies of extraction, recruitment or coercion were still pursued well into the interwar under the veneer of a new, virtuous form of tropical capitalism.

Concession's continuities in governance and resource exploitation were not only stretched in time, but also in space. In the Amazonian rainforest, the commodification of indigenous crops also followed extractive models echoing those enforced in the Congo basin. There were striking similarities between violent labour and extraction arrangements in the Congolese and the Brazilian rainforests during the early 20th century rubber boom.[10] Furthermore, new forms of tropical paternalism appeared in both regions in the interwar. In 1927 for instance, the Ford company purchased a sizeable plot of land in the Amazon to build the concession of Fordlandia. The motor company intended to create a vast rubber plantation attached to a recreated American suburb in the middle of the rainforest. Just as Lever Brothers hoped to emulate its British paternalistic model in Leverville, Fordlandia was aimed at cultivating US middle-class values among its Brazilian workforce.[11] Such echoes and comparisons between Congo and Brazil, stretching from the late 19th century to the Second World War, highlight the relevance of concessions as historical study objects beyond their microhistorical value.

Finally, as unique fields of power and hubs of colonial presence, concessions also provide interesting standpoints to observe the varied interactions between state, capital and indigenous communities. Concessionary companies often held sovereign powers, acting as state surrogates in infrastructure building, policing or the provision of social care to its inhabitants. Studying forced labour in Portuguese Mozambique, Eric Allina-Pisano resorts to the concept of

---

10 Louise Cardoso de Mello and Sven Van Melkebeke, "From the Amazon to the Congo Valley: A Comparative Study on the Violent Commodification of Labour During the Rubber Boom (1870s-1910s)," in *Commodity Frontiers and Global Capitalist Expansion*, edited by Sabrina Joseph (London: Palgrave, 2019), 137–181.
11 Greg Grandin, *Fordlandia. The Rise and Fall of Henry Ford's Forgotten Jungle* City (New York: Metropolitan Books, 2009).

"company rule" to highlight how chartered companies "held what were ordinarily powers of state,"[12] such as legislating, hiring public servants and controlling the entry points of their allotted territory.

Although granted with more limited rights on paper, HCB managers also exerted a form of "company rule" in Leverville, enjoying significant leverage in the daily governance of its zone of influence. At the same time, colonial public servants would still hold their prerogatives on the concession, leading to a flurry of *ad hoc* arrangements between both parties. "Colonizers" also had to make do with the agency of both the Congolese workforce and the communities settled in and around the concession, significantly hampering their hegemonic designs. In spite of the higher concentration of agents of empire and means of coercions, colonial control within concession boundaries was far from sturdy and ascertained. It was fluctuating and negotiated, and it relied on a fragile and ever-shifting power balance. As suggested by Thomas Hendriks in his work on a logging concession in present-day DRC, a "…concession implies both a granted right and a grudging acknowledgement. To concede is both to give away and to give in – to renounce and to yield."[13]

Beyond their strategic importance as "nodes" of concentrated colonial presence within the uneven fabric of empires, concessions could also become spaces of frustrated hegemony. In the face of resistance, competition and a shortage of means or knowledge, it often became impossible for institutions and actors active in concessions to bend land, resources and populations to their will. The discrepancy between principles and practices, between orders and rules on the one hand and their effective enforcement in the other, are this book's main points of investigation. I employ the metaphor of "impotence" to conceptualize how this multifaceted gap lay at the heart of life and governance in the Leverville concession.

Impotence and colonial ventures

Literally speaking, impotence connects several planes. It is first and foremost a male affliction, a process rendering men incapable of sexually performing as they would. Second, impotence alludes to a form of powerlessness, which can impede on both one's self image and social status. Third, it suggests a discrep-

---

[12] Eric Allina-Pisano, *Slavery by Any Other Name: African Life Under Company Rule in Colonial Mozambique* (Charlottesville: University of Virginia Press, 2012), 25–31.
[13] Thomas Hendriks, *Rainforest Capitalism: Ecstasis and Extraction in a Congolese Timber Concession* (Durham: Duke University Press, forthcoming).

ancy between the socially expected behaviours and the lived experiences of impotent men. Figuratively speaking, it is possible to tie these different planes to several theoretical frameworks in colonial and African studies. They inspire and sustain the conceptual ground on which this book is articulated.

Metaphorical resorts to masculinity have led to productive conceptualisations of colonial power. For Achille Mbembe for instance, colonization was "phallic" in both words and deeds.[14] Its omnipresent violence could be evoked as metaphoric and multifaceted sexual aggression. According to Mbembe, discourse paved the way to imperial expansion by hammering the dehumanization of the colonized through the repetition of their unbridgeable "otherness."[15] Colonies were depicted as a series of "hollows" to be filled; lands were *terra nullius* to be appropriated and commodified; "negroes" were depicted as selfless bodies to be exploited and classified.[16] Colonial discourses took the form of a metaphoric rape, a repeated assault against the humanity of their subjects. The exercise of colonial violence could also take a "phallic" guise, for "there is no violence in a colony without a sense of contiguity, without bodies close to one another,"[17] according to Mbembe. He also viewed the dehumanized colony as a place where colonizers could exert their unconstrained lust for flesh, power, violence or gain. "Colonialism frees the conqueror's desires from the prison of law, reason, doubt, time, measure."[18] In short, for Mbembe, "the colonizer thinks and expresses himself through his phallus. […] To colonize is [to] accomplish a sort of sparky clean act of coitus."[19] In the following chapters, I will build on Mbembe's "phallic" conceptualisation of colonialism to demonstrate how the multifaceted limitations faced by agents of imperialism on the field could adequately be perceived as metaphorically "impotent."

Whereas Mbembe delivered a powerful top-down reading of colonialism as an overarching dynamic of "phallic" violence and dehumanization, a recent historiographic stream took a diverging – albeit completing – path to study empires. Offering an outlook into colonialism from the bottom-up, historians reassessed its complexities when observed from the field. By taking local and/or intimate experiences into account, some approaches could nuance visions of colonial empires as "almighty" and of colonizers as "domineering." In his study of the private writings of 19th century British colonialists, Jeffrey Auerbach suggested that

---

14 Mbembe, *The Postcolony*, 175.
15 Mbembe, *The Postcolony*, 178.
16 Mbembe, *The Postcolony*, 179–88.
17 Mbembe, *The Postcolony*, 175.
18 Mbembe, *The Postcolony*, 189.
19 Mbembe, *The Postcolony*, 176.

their daily experience "overseas" was mostly boring, tedious, dull or unfulfilling. Repetitive tasks, isolation, endless waiting and uncomfortable travelling took the lion's share of many descriptions of empire, miles away from the adventurous and exciting life they were promised.[20] In a similar vein, the elaborate display depicted in "Congo Atrocities!!!" also seemed to allude to the desperate means employed by its protagonists to cheat a very colonial type of *ennui*.

Beyond personal frustrations, historians also highlighted how imperial dominance could be frail and how the supposedly rational governance of colonies was pervaded by emotions.[21] Nancy Rose Hunt described Belgian Congo as "a nervous state," ruled by administrators "on edge."[22] Hunt observed "two guises" of the colonial machinery. The first was "biopolitical," which worked to "promote life and health"; and the second was "nervous," which "policed and securitized" and sought to contain real or imagined rebellions.[23] According to Hunt, "nervousness suggest[ed] visceral energy, alarm and fear," shedding light on how uncertainty and anxiety could crystallize into the colonial repressive apparatus.[24] Hunt's take on "nervousness" influenced the present research. It helps shed light on how the affects and dispositions of colonial agents in and around the Leverville concession significantly impacted the region's day-to-day governance, sometimes even more than laws and instructions.

Furthermore, the racial border expected to starkly separate "colonizers" from the "colonized" could be more porous than first expected. Ann Laura Stoler and Frederick Cooper's 1997 outline of a new research agenda in colonial studies, bent on investigating the ever-shifting "grammars of difference" separating imperial social categories have sparked numerous intellectual endeavours.[25] Florence Bernault for instance challenged the idea that "Blacks" and "Whites" belonged to "disparate worlds" in colonial Gabon. She argued, on the contrary, that there were "deeper and more subtle correspondences" between the French

---

20 Jeffrey Auerbach, *Imperial Boredom: Monotony and the British Empire* (Oxford: Oxford University Press, 2018).
21 On the topic, see also: Ann Laura Stoler, *Carnal Knowledge and Imperial Power: Race and the Intimate in Colonial Rule* (Berkeley: California University Press, 2002), Harald Fischer-Tiné (ed.), *Anxieties, Fear and Panic in Colonial Settings: Empires on the Verge of a Nervous Breakdown* (Cambridge: Cambridge University Press, 2016), Will Jackson, "The Private Lives of Empires: Emotion, Intimacy and Colonial Rule," *Itinerario*, 42:1 (2018): 1–15.
22 Hunt, *Nervous State*, 5.
23 Hunt, *Nervous State*, 8.
24 Hunt, *Nervous State*, 18.
25 Ann Laura Stoler and Frederick Cooper, "Between Metropole and Colony. Rethinking a Research Agenda," in, *Tensions of Empire: Colonial Cultures in a Bourgeois World*, edited by Ann Laura Stoler and Frederick Cooper (Berkeley, University of California Press, 1997), 1–42.

and the Gabonese's respective "drives, affects, knowledge and imagination."[26] Bernault saw colonialism as a field of power as well as of transactions, where "myriad of deals, exchanges, and transfers determined each day, major or subtle reordering of hierarchies, status, wealth and knowledge."[27] By conceptualizing colonialism as "transactional," she aimed to highlight "how singular units of exchange arose on the ground, bringing together colonized and colonialists in active and transformative relations […] in processual and dynamic moments of exchange and transformation" within the brutally unequal colony, therefore putting the agency of the colonized to the fore.[28] This book accordingly highlights the existence of mirroring emotional dynamics within both "European" and "African" communities in the Leverville concession's hinterland. These ways of making sense of each other's moves and motives profoundly influenced their respective collective behaviours.

Recent studies nuanced colonial hegemony by weaving frustrations, anxieties and exchanges in its historical fabric; similar approaches have been taken by anthropologists tackling the limits of capitalism in the neoliberal age. Although they focus on contemporary issues, their bottom-up takes on the lived experience of communities living on the margins of the world economy provide stimulating insights to the study of colonial frontiers. James Ferguson has for instance investigated how economic globalization took "inconvenient" forms in Africa, disjointed from general improvements in welfare or governance. Ferguson observed that capital investment remained mostly concentrated in "secured enclaves […] substantially isolated from the wider society," [29] often guarded by security forces blurring the boundaries between public and private affiliations. There seem to be clear continuities between such economic models and the old colonial concessions, allowing a *longue durée* take on the history of economic "valuation" in sub-Saharan Africa.

Anna Tsing has turned her attention to the articulation of non-capitalist and capitalist modes of production. In Tsing's study of the economic networks of the matsutake mushroom, a highly-prized delicacy profusely growing in discarded logging sites, she highlighted both the limits of scalability and the complexities of commodification processes. According to Tsing, scalability, the possibility of applying the same production model to different crops in varying contexts, has "shaped capitalism modernization." It was for long thought that "everything

---

[26] Florence Bernault, *Colonial Transactions: Imaginaries, Bodies and Histories in Gabon* (Durham: Duke University Press, 2019), 5–6.
[27] Bernault, *Colonial Transactions*, 10.
[28] Bernault, *Colonial Transactions*, 8.
[29] Ferguson, *Global Shadows*, 36–8.

on earth and beyond might be scalable and thus exchangeable at market values."[30] However, scalability could sometimes fail. For example, natural resources such as the matsutake could not be produced in man-controlled environments. In order to commodify these resources, capitalist actors then had to resort to what Tsing called "salvage accumulation"; they had to rely on "pericapitalist" modes of production, such as mushroom foraging, in order to gather primary resources later to be commodified and sold on global markets.[31] By studying a frontier of capitalism, Tsing offered a useful take on the complexities of integrating a space such as the Leverville concession into the networks of capitalism. "Unscalable" to a certain extent, the concession's palm groves could only be exploited by a Congolese workforce, mastering skills developed outside of capitalism. The limited control exerted by HCB over both their workforce and zone of exploitation remained one of the main limitations to their hegemonic designs.

In a forthcoming book, Thomas Hendriks reassesses the supposed powerfulness of agents of global capitalism, from the vantage point of a logging concession in the Congolese rainforest. Rather than considering it as an "overwhelming force," he explores how its deployment on the field is "messy" and "murky" and how "any position of power" on the field can be "situational, ephemeral, and often self-destructive." Hendriks aims to shed light on "the often-overlooked vulnerabilities, failures and excesses of corporate power" in his ethnography of a "fragile, permeable, vulnerable" logging company. Hendriks endeavours to think about concessions as "ecstatic" spaces, where "complex feelings of vulnerability, penetrability and relative impotence" arise "in the face of larger forces, structures and histories."[32] Hendriks' field study of an extractive enclave in contemporary DR Congo provides a relevant point of comparison to look at the limits of hegemonic and totalising designs of capitalist ventures in Central Africa.

Colonial Impotence sits at the crossroads of these various approaches. It follows a bottom-up approach to analysing the Leverville concession's history by attempting to see how colonialism and capitalism were jointly enforced within its boundaries and how the different communities inhabiting it made sense of these changes. It highlights the struggles of both the colonial administration and HCB to impose their programs and projects on restive populations and uncontrolled environments. It brings indigenous agency to the fore, in governance as well as in commodification processes.

---

30 Anna Lowenhaupt Tsing, *The Mushroom at the End of the World: On the Possibility of Life in Capitalist Ruins* (Princeton: Princeton University Press, 2015), 40.
31 Tsing, *The Mushroom*, 63.
32 Hendriks, *Rainforest Capitalism*, forthcoming.

If colonialism was "phallic," as Mbembe suggests, observing its deployment from the vantage point of Leverville highlights how it could also be "impotent." According to Angus McLaren, "impotence" has always been a looming threat in the male psyche, for it would "prevent one from providing proof that he could perform as a male should".[33] Impotence merges the personal with the collective, as intimate shortcomings directly impact a man's overall virility and therefore his place in the gendered order of things. Furthermore, impotence is always relational, a person's inadequacy stemming from their inability to "properly" perform during an intercourse. The relational nature of impotence opens doors to discussions about its cause – whether it is rooted in the ailing male or in his partner therefore commands different strands of diagnoses and potential cures.[34] Finally, discourses on impotence also shed light on a given society's values, self-representations and characterization of normalcy.

How to then use the conceptual framework of impotence to think about colonialism in general, and the Leverville concession in particular? First, there were many interconnections between the late 19th early 20th century male ethos and colonial self-representations. Middle-class men were expected to be governed by their reason, to exert self-control, to reign in on their desire. Their adequacy was accordingly based on their ability to perform their manly duties when convenient and expected, in ordered and patriarchal conjugal settings. Their continence and rationality set them apart from both women, thought to be dominated by their emotions, and racial "others," who fell prey to their impulses.[35] "Rationality" and "continence" were also laid at the foundation of the colonial order. "Honourable" colonizers, complying with the higher standards of European prestige were expected to govern and transform colonies on "rational" grounds.[36] The Leverville concession constitutes a prime example of such endeavours: a clearly delimited enclave set up to be rationally organised and exploited, which inhabitants would benefit from the virtuous paternalist policies enforced by HCB. Both male and colonial "potency" could therefore share similar characteristics, where adequacy relied on rationality, restraint and the ability to helm both the relationship and the environment where it takes place.

---

33 Angus McLaren, *Impotence: A Cultural History* (Chicago: University of Chicago Press, 2007), xiii.
34 McLaren, *Impotence*, xv.
35 McLaren, *Impotence*, 102–3.
36 Marie Muschalek, "Honourable Soldier-Bureaucrats: Formations of Violent Identities in the Colonial Police Force of German Southwest Africa, 1905–18," *The Journal of Imperial and Commonwealth History*, 41:4 (2013): 584–599.

Impotent men could not comply with such standards. At the turn of the century, two overarching explanations competed to make sense of their ailment. On the one hand, impotence was justified by emotional excesses. "Neurasthenic" men were crushed under the psychological pressures of a rapidly-changing world in which they struggled to find their footing.[37] On the other, their sexual partners could also be blamed. Either too prude or too demanding, women's "irrational" drives were accused of putting a strain on male's healthy libidos.[38] Interestingly, such explanations mirror what was deemed as inadequate in colonial settings. First, agents of empire could be unable to effectively order the colonial environment as expected. In the Leverville concession, plans were drafted, orders were given, moral endeavours were pledged, and yet they failed to materialize. Second, unruly and uncontrollable colonial subjects did not perform accordingly to what was expected from them. Both the inability of colonialists to master their environment and to exert control on colonial subjects led to frustrations. These were rooted in the inadequacy between principles supposed to command the conduct of colonial affairs, and the unsatisfactory forms colonialism took on the field.

If impotence hampers the male's social standing, colonial impotence threatens the very existence of imperial designs, which led in Leverville to two intertwined responses. Whenever virtue alone could not guarantee the sustained existence of the concession, violence would be exerted to ensure the compliance of unruly "others." However, this very violence should not jeopardise the "adequate" and "virtuous" self-representations of the actors at play. This book tackles the multiple tensions between virtue and violence in Leverville and the manifold ways its inhabitants attempted to navigate the concession's inner contradictions.

Contextualizing Leverville

Before delving into the multifaceted tensions animating Leverville in the interwar, it is indispensable to broadly sketch its cultural and geographic context, as well as its *longue durée* history. All these different elements had a profound impact on the unravelling of events analysed in the following chapters.

The palm groves on which the concession will come to be set belonged to the Kwango-Kwilu ecosystem, which stretches to the southern edges of the central African rainforest (see figure 4). Climate and landscapes in the Kwango-Kwilu

---

[37] McLaren, *Impotence*, 115.
[38] McLaren, *Impotence*, 112.

are no longer those of the rainforest covering most of the Congo basin. The abundant vegetation gives way to an intercalation of savannah and subequatorial woods, stretched in narrow corridors along the region's vast network of waterways.³⁹

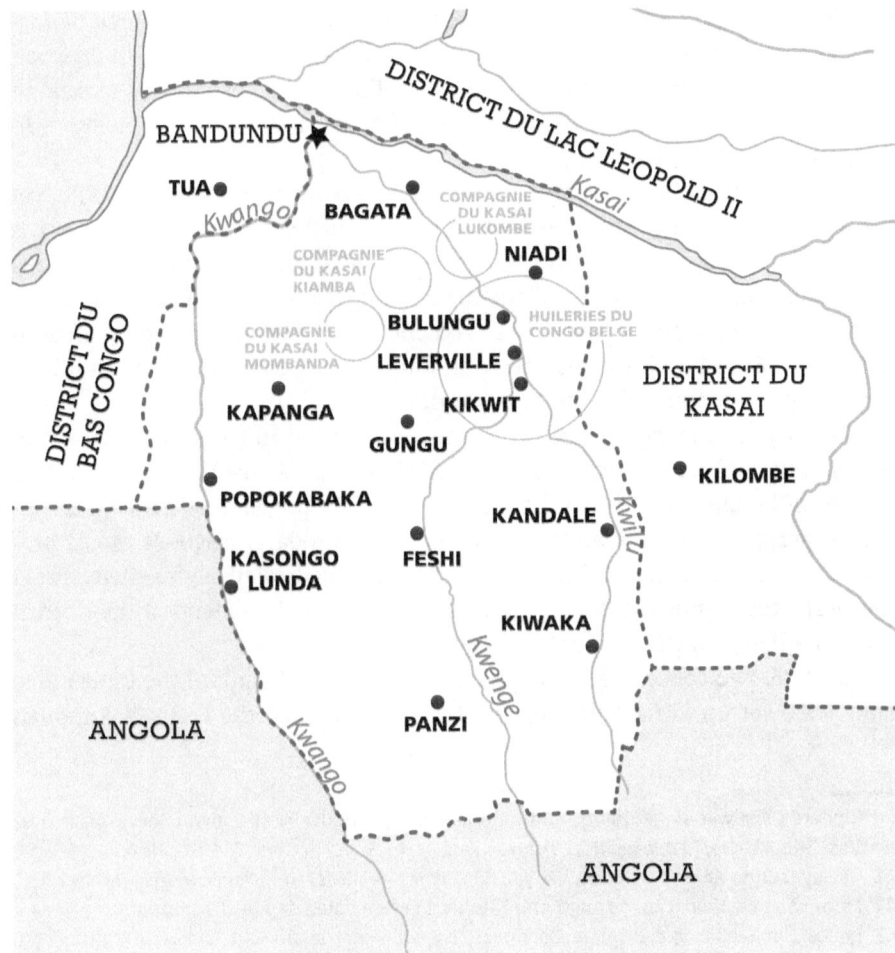

Figure 4: Palm oil concessions in the Kwango district, map by Iris Vandevelde

---

39 Jan Vansina, *Paths in the Rainforest: Toward a History of Political Tradition in Equatorial Africa* (Madison: University of Wisconsin Press, 1990), 45, 47.

Thousands of years of human presence in the area significantly shaped the environment. The presence of long stretches of savannahs and the dense network of palm groves were partially the result of long-term practices of slash and burn agriculture and millennial uses of oil palm (*Elaeis guineensis*) by the region's inhabitants.[40] These trees shared a long history with communities inhabiting West and Central Africa.[41] Beyond providing a crucial resource of vegetal fat for cooking purposes and the often only available spirit,[42] their wood could be used as a building material and their fibres were needed for the making of ropes and fishing nets; both palm oil and palm wine were also key elements in religious of healing practices.[43]

Little attention has been given to the early history of the Kwango-Kwilu, yet the available historiography sheds light on a recurring pattern in its history.[44] The region's often-violent inscription in regional or global economic networks triggered major changes in social organization, through consecutive waves of migration and the foundation of new settlements. To this extent, the colonial domination (c. 1876–1960) was a significant, although not inaugural, step in a long process of encounters with the outer world.

The region first experienced a traumatic inclusion in global economic networks in the 16th century, when Central and Equatorial Africa became prominent sources of human supplies for the Atlantic trade. Fleeing slavers' raids penetrating further and further inlands, communities from today's Angola's coasts progressively settled in the Kwango-Kwilu.[45] It remained relatively sheltered from the flesh trade until the 1680s, when slavers eventually extended their reach up to the banks of the Kwango.[46]

In 1886, two consecutive expeditions organised on behalf of the Congo Free State were set up to map the course of the Kwango and the Kwilu.[47] Although

---

40 Richard Oslisly et al., "Climatic and Cultural Changes in the West Congo Basin Forests over the Past 5000 Years," *Philosophical Transactions of the Royal Society*, 368 (2012): 4.
41 Oslisly, "Climatic and Cultural," 7; Vansina, *Paths*, 58; Ndaywel, *Nouvelle Histoire*, 75.
42 Palm wine or *Malafu* in Kikongo and Kituba, the fermented sap of the oil palm.
43 Janice Henderson and Daphne Osborne, "The Oil Palm in All Our Lives: How this Came About," *Endeavour*, 24:2 (2000): 63.
44 On issues of human development in contemporary Kwango-Kwilu, see: Henri Nicolaï, *Le Kwilu: Étude Géographique* (Brussels: Centre scientifique et médical de l'ULB en Afrique, 1963); Clément Mumvwela, *Le Développement Local au Kwango-Kwilu (RD Congo)* (Brussels: Peter Lang: 2004); Jean-Daniel Mashini, *Le Développement Régional en République Démocratique du Congo de 1960 à 1997: L'Exemple du Kwango-Kwilu*, (Paris: L'Harmattan, 2013).
45 Mashini, *Le Développement*, 40–41.
46 Ndaywel, *Nouvelle Histoire*, 131.
47 Ndaywel, *Nouvelle Histoire*, 268.

King Leopold's private colony had already been diplomatically recognized, most of its colossal territory had yet to be effectively charted, occupied and subjugated. In 1894, fourteen companies were already collecting wild rubber in the Kasaï basin – to which the Kwango-Kwilu belongs[48] – relying on a large set of pressures and acts of violence to maximize the output of local labour. The harsh competition between these commercial actors resulted in a significant decrease of their profits, pushing them in 1901 to merge into the *Compagnie du Kasaï* (CK). Like most ventures active in the Free State, CK was thoroughly intertwined with the monarch and its associates and was officially expected to "second the state and the missions in their work of civilisation" in its 36 million hectares' zone of activity.[49]

In the Free State era, palm oil remained an extremely marginal economic asset. A single industrial oil mill was active in 1896, producing low-quality outputs sent to Europe for the making of candles.[50] This would change in 1908, as Belgian colonial authorities were on the lookout to secure the economic sustainability of their new colony by "valuating" (*mettre en valeur*, following a frequently-used imperial euphemism)[51] its natural resources. Among the different partnerships set up between private companies and the state, it was decided that stretches of the Kwango-Kwilu's dense palm groves would be allotted to HCB and form the Leverville concession (see chapter 1).

Throughout the 1910s and 20s, multiple dissensions rose between the company and the administration on issues such as the exercise of power within the concession or the treatment of their workforce. HCB intended to resort to the *Force Publique* – the colony's armed corps – as a private militia to ensure the compliance of local communities in the supply of workers, and to secure an illegal monopoly on the trade of palm fruits within its zone of influence. In 1915, most of the Leverville area's employees were selected for labour by *chefs médaillés* (i.e., indigenous leaders co-opted by the administration in exchange of a financial compensation).[52] In 1923, a scathing report from one of the administra-

---

48 *La Compagnie du Kasaï à ses Actionnaires. Réponse à ses Détracteurs* (Brussels, 1906), 15–16.
49 *La Compagnie*, 28–29.
50 African Archives Brussels (AAB), AGRI 360, Note sur la fabrique d'huile de palme de l'île de Mateba, 14 March 1896.
51 "Mise en valeur" was an expression borrowed by Belgian authorities from the lexical repertoire of the French empire. It was coined in 1921 by Albert Sarraut, minister of colonies, as he envisioned a vast program of public works in French West Africa (AOF), starting a new phase in France's colonial endeavours. See: Romain Tiquet, *Travail Forcé et Mobilisation de la Main d'Oeuvre au Sénégal. Années 1920–1960* (Rennes: Presses Universitaires de Rennes, 2019), 22.
52 David Fieldhouse, *Unilever Overseas: The Anatomy of a Multinational* (London: Croom Helm, 1979), 514.

tion's medical examiners pinned the advanced state of malnutrition prevailing among the concession's migrant workforce, who only received six insufficient rations of food a week (see chapter 5).[53]

In the mid-1920s, further developments in the global palm oil business threatened the fragile profitability of the company's reliance on the palm groves. The development of large-scale, highly efficient plantations of selected *Elaeis* in British Malaysia and the Dutch Indies hampered the company's future prospects.[54] A slow shift extraction to production, from harvest to plantation, occurred in the Leverville area (see chapter 6).[55] At the same time, Belgian Congo's economy was profoundly impacted by the aftermaths of the 1929 financial crisis. The colonial model of *mise en valeur*, which prevailed throughout the 1920s, was unsustainable on the mid or long term. Indeed, agro-commercial activities based on large-scale gathering of natural products, short-term workforce and artisanal processing resulting in low-quality outputs could not remain sustainable when, as for palm oil, standardised productions became the norm on export markets.

Congolese mining industries were the first to be affected by the global contraction, as soon as 1929, while agricultural prices depleted from 1930–1931 onwards. In 1934, palm oil prices plunged to 20% of their 1929 value.[56] To keep the colony's economy afloat, both the administration and the companies exerted extensive pressures on the indigenous workforce. Between 1929 and 1932, poll tax rates doubled, climbing from 14% to 28% of each "able-bodied man's" income. In the meantime, agricultural production greatly increased in spite of falling prices.[57] Congolese populations, especially in rural areas, were coercively recruited and violently pressured to increase their productivity. In the Kwango district, territorial administrators instructed their "messengers" – local men recruited to act as mail carriers and informal mercenaries – to steal the cattle and hold women hostages in villages were men were reluctant to work for HCB.[58]

Along with exactions and abuses perpetrated in the area by colonial agents during their tours of tax collection, the economic pressures experienced by local

---

[53] 420 gr of rice, 100 gr of dry fish and 50 gr of palm oil a day, with no ration served on Sunday. AAB, AIMO 1654, Hygiène des travailleurs noirs dans les exploitations des HCB dans le cercle de Lusanga, December 1923.
[54] AAB, AGRI 335, Letter from the Director of the Belgian Ministry of the Colonies' Agricultural section to the direction of the *Compagnie du Kasaï*, 6 November 1923.
[55] Fieldhouse, *Unilever Overseas*, 523.
[56] Bogumil Jewsiewicki, "The Great Depression and the Making of the Colonial Economic System in the Belgian Congo," *African Economic History*, 4 (1977): 153–158.
[57] Jewsiewicki, "The Great Depression," 158–160.
[58] Louis-François Vanderstraeten, *La Répression de la Révolte des Pende du Kwango en 1931* (Brussels: ARSOM, 2001), 14.

communities – crushing imposition rates, intensive labour and forced recruitment – proved to be a fertile ground for the emergence of large-scale movements of open resistance against Europeans. A new religious practice – the *Tupelepele* – emerged in late 1930 within the *Huileries*' recruitment hinterland. Leaders of the movement encouraged local populations to embrace a revived worship of ancestors' spirits. They were told to refuse recruitment and taxation, to get rid of all things of white colour in their possession and to burn or bury their money and all official documents they might hold. Followers built *sombolos* – hangar-like constructions – at the edges of villages, in which the spirits were expected to leave food and high-value effects, such as textiles and gunpowder.[59] The *Tupelepele* became the most virulent rural uprising of pre-WWII Congo, and culminated in the murder and dismemberment of a Belgian public servant in May 1931. In the following months, the region was swept by a brutal repression by the *Force Publique* which left hundreds of casualties in its trail. It was nevertheless followed by more subdued manifestations of unruliness. Multiple reports from territorial agents in 1932 mention attacks on messengers, refusal to comply to administrative orders, and the subsistence of a general climate of defiance.[60] *Lukusu*, a secret anti-witchcraft movement also rapidly spread out in the same area in 1932–1933, fostering further angst within the administration about the potential rise of a new insurgency (see chapter 3).[61]

The history of interwar Kwango-Kwilu illustrates the impact of global phenomena and economic exchanges on subequatorial Central Africa. *Longue durée* processes of migration and settlement were disrupted by the region's successive inclusions in trades for which it could provide crucial resources, whether slaves, wild rubber or palm oil.

A note on the sources

Public, and to a lesser extent private, archives constitute my main source of information. They mostly originate from the "African Archives," the written legacy of the Belgian colonial state, which is housed at the Federal Public Service for Foreign Relations in Brussels. Their many documents on Leverville are from various origins and of disparate natures and were written between the 1880s and

---

59 AAB, MOI 1820, Lettre du commissaire général Wauters au GG Tilkens, 2 July 1931.
60 AAB, AI 4739, Rapport mensuel sur la situation du territoire de Kikwit, January 1932.
61 See Benoît Henriet, "Facing the Talking Snake: Witchcraft, Anxiety and Sense-Making in Interwar Belgian Congo," *International Journal of African Historical Studies*, 51:2 (2018): 219–241.

the 1950s. They can be classified into three rough categories: administrative despatches, reports and legislation.

The *Despatches* cover a vast array of topics and connect a broad range of actors with one another. Civil servants, HCB representatives and employees constantly wrote to each other to discuss the concession's present situation and future perspectives. Peripheral actors of relative importance in the Kwango district – such as religious authorities,[62] agents and managers of competing firms or small-scale planters could also intervene – mostly to challenge collusions between the administration and HCB, or to criticize the *Huileries*' recruitment policy. The despatches offer precious information on everyday relations and power struggles in and around the concession. By showing when specific actors intervened on selected issues, for particular purposes at precise moments, they highlight the effective repartition of prerogatives both between the administration and the company, as within their respective hierarchies. Both the colonial state and HCB were supposedly structured along well-defined organisation charts. However, a careful observation of the correspondence tends to redraw the effective repartition of prerogatives between Europe and Africa, between high-ranking and low-ranking actors. These documents hold precious information on the concession's everyday management, on the way workers and local communities were able to challenge colonial rule, as well as on dissensions, solidarities, affinities and animosities animating public and private entities.

The *Reports* are of two different nature. They were either produced for the daily exercise of governance, or were designed to answer and/or investigate unforeseen crisis. For the former – mostly published on an annual basis – different offices inform their superior of progresses in the achievement of their designed purposes. Reports made by HCB,[63] the provincial service of the AIMO (*Affaires Indigènes – Main d'oeuvre*)[64] or the INEAC (*Institut National d'Etudes Agronomiques au Congo*)[65] offer some crucial data on the evolution of the concession's profitability, issues encountered in the recruitment of workers or the introduction of new agricultural techniques in the colony. The latter were produced in times of

---

62 Mgr Sylvain Van Hee (1875–1960), apostolic vicar of the Kwango, was particularly concerned by the recurring issues of workforce recruitment. He participated in an official commission of enquiry, following the uprisings and wrote several books and article on matters of labour in the area.
63 AAB, MOI 3602, AGRI 335.
64 AAB, AIMO 3547, 3548.
65 AAB, AGRI 399.

emergency.⁶⁶ Therein, revolts, labour shortages or lack of profitability were described and explained; possible resolutions were sketched out. The poor health of the *Huileries*' workforce,⁶⁷ the origins of the Kwango revolt⁶⁸ or the recurring reluctance encountered in workers' recruitment⁶⁹ were all the objects of crisis reports.

Finally, *legislation* comprises Congolese laws and a large set of foreign imperial dispositions used by policymakers as sources of inspiration or points of comparisons. These documents are accompanied by extensive exchanges of letters between administrators and civil servants, both in Europe and Africa, who attempted to fine-tune legislation before they were enforced. More marginally, private groups of interests also intervened in the legislative process. As it turned out, rules written for French and British territories had a significant influence on the making of Congolese laws, for they offered ready-made solutions to issues that the debuting Belgian imperial power was just beginning to meet.⁷⁰

Legislative processes offer a fascinating insight on political representations regarding the optimal conduct of colonial affairs, as well as on its negotiated nature. Law-making in Belgian Congo depended of two major influences. First, as Lauren Benton argues, a "shared repertoire" ⁷¹ of legal culture existed between European metropolises. Colonial situations called for specific practices of rule and encountered similar difficulties, such as the issue of dividing land between "natives" and newcomers. To this extent, analogous dispositions were sometimes applied in territories that had nothing common in terms of geography or social organisation, apart from being colonized. Second, private companies and informal groups of interests, such as the Belgian Catholic Church, could have a profound influence on colonial lawmakers. Most legislation related to Congo was already the object of informal agreements between these groups of interest when submitted to the country's bicameral Parliament.⁷²

Along with public archives, I also investigated two separate sets of private documents: HCB's record held at the Unilever headquarters at Port Sunlight, United Kingdom; and the personal documents of Sidney Edkins, Leverville's

---

66 Ann Laura Stoler, *Along the Archival Grain: Epistemic Anxieties and Colonial Common Sense* (Princeton: Princeton University Press, 2009) 31, 141–179.
67 AAB, AIMO 1654.
68 AAB, MOI 1820, AI 4739.
69 AAB, AIMO 1856.
70 AAB, RF 1428, RF 1437.
71 Lauren Benton, *Search for Sovereignty*, 36.
72 Guy Vanthemsche, *La Belgique et le Congo : l'Impact de la Colonie sur la Métropole* (Brussels: Le Cri, 2007), 71.

first manager of the Africa Museum archives in Tervuren, Belgium. Port Sunlight documents contain the personal diaries of Lever Brothers' founder and chairman Lord Leverhulme, where he consigned the impressions left by his 1924 visit of Leverville, as well as his extensive correspondence regarding the HCB's business. These documents shed light on his intention to micromanage as best as he could the company's prospects in Congo. The monopolistic endeavours of the *Huileries'* direction are also much more apparent in these documents. Letters and internal reports reflect their frustration regarding the presence of competitors in their concessions, and their inability to effectively control local communities' uses of the palm groves. The archives of Sidney Edkins are sparse yet crucial to some aspects of my research. For instance, they provide key details on the involvement of the Kwango Jesuits in the everyday management of the Leverville concession, as well as two different histories of the company written by its field directors.

Given the key role played by missionary orders in Belgian Congo, one could be surprised by their quasi absence in this book, both as sources and as actors. Catholic missions have often been considered to have joined forces with administration and big businesses to form the colonial "trinity of power," which presided over the fate of "Belgian" Africa.[73] Missions were a conspicuous presence in the strategic enclaves of colonial activity, and Leverville was no exception. In spite of his own protestant faith, Lord Leverhulme actively supported the exclusive settlement of Catholic missions in HCB concessions. As he wrote in 1916, "if we follow this policy, we can at any time move an intelligent native to the area in which he is most wanted, whereas if some of the natives were Catholic and some Protestant, we might not be able to do this. [...] it would be upsetting to their mentality to know that the white man had many religions".[74]

The Leverville concession would come to host Jesuit brethren, whose main compound was built in Soa in 1917. It was located on the other bank of the Kwenge river, directly facing the Leverville station. Jesuits were responsible for the education of the concession's inhabitants and were also involved in medical endeavours in collaboration with the female order of Sainte-Marie, who managed the company's lazarettos.[75] However, there are few archival traces to denote their long-lasting presence in Leverville. There are no documents of significance to be found in the archives of either the meridional or septentrional provinces of the

---

[73] Crawford Young, *Politics in Congo: Decolonization and Independence* (Princeton: Princeton University Press, 1965), 14.
[74] Unilever Archives, Port Sunlight (UA), LBC/215, W.H. Lever to Henry Moseley, 11 April 1916.
[75] Françoise Van Yve, "Une Communauté Missionnaire au Kwango. Les Soeurs de Sainte-Marie de Namur à Leverville (1923–1940)," *Enquêtes et Documents d'Histoire Africaine*, 7 (1987): 56, 68.

Belgian Jesuits regarding Leverville or Soa in the interwar. A further consultation of the Jesuit archives in Kinshasa yielded a fascinating series of photo albums, of which one has been included in this book (see figure 10), but no other primary documents which could be mobilised in the present research. Therefore, information about missions came from other sources, like Sidney Edkins' private papers, and remains fragmented. This unfortunate shortage of sources is a regular fixture of an historian's craft, which constrains her of him to study the past on the grounds of incomplete sources.

Like many historians of colonization, I found myself facing a complex question: how could I craft a bottom-up history by mostly resorting to what could be called "hegemonic archives," which overwhelmingly reflected the perspective of colonizers? Thankfully, there were recent methodological approaches by scholars in this realm who have paved new ways to tackle the vast written legacy of empires.[76] Ann Laura Stoler, for instance, encouraged "students of colonialism" to read colonial archives both "along" and "against" the grain. Along the grain means paying attention to the structures of archives, to their organisation, to their "uneven densities" and the kind of information they hold or withhold. According to Stoler, such an approach was inseparable from an analysis "against" the grain, on the lookout for fragments of subaltern experiences, colonial powerlessness or indigenous agency.[77]

In this book, I pursued both, by highlighting what archives could reveal about the impotence of agents of colonization both in their content and structure. Furthermore, a systematic reading of these documents "against" the grain helped to shed light on groups and actors who played a crucial role in shaping the Leverville experience even if they have never become a prime topic of scholarly attention. Female and underage workers were, for instance, indispensable agents in the concession's exploitation scheme, but they were rarely mentioned in both HCB and administrative archives. Thankfully, they were not erased from the records; however, I believe that their limited presence designated them as "translucent," or barely visible, as they were only mentioned in passing in a handful of reports and letters (see chapter 4). Finally, the triangulation of public and private written archives with vernacular oral sources brought unexpected stories to the fore. For instance, the regularity with which informants invoked food rations as the prime example of HCB's generosity encouraged me to delve deeper into the subject (see chapter 5).

---

[76] See for instance, David M. Gordon, "Reading the Archives as Sources," Oxford Research Encyclopedia of African History (2018), accessed 13 August 2019, https://oxfordre.com/africanhistory/view/10.1093/acrefore/9780190277734.001.0001/acrefore-9780190277734-e-227.
[77] Stoler, *Along*, 23.

Even if there were no written accounts of the experience of the HCB by its workers and their relatives, remnants of the Congolese experience of the concession were still be found in oral memories. In the summer of 2015, I performed interviews in the Kwilu province, on the former site of the Leverville concession, as well as in and around Gungu, in what used to be the *Huileries'* pool of recruitment. I attempted to meet with elderly individuals, who either personally experienced the last years of colonialism, had relatives who were hired as HCB workers, or who themselves worked for the PLC/PLZ (*Plantations Lever au Congo/Zaïre*), the name adopted by the company after independence. I conducted these visits with my assistant, Jean-Claude Lufungula. We would usually arrive in a village or a small town whose name we had found in the archives. We would introduce ourselves as university students in history, working together on HCB, and we would ask to meet elder members of their communities. Given that I did not speak Kituba, Jean-Claude usually translated questions and answers back and forth between French and Kituba. Without his invaluable help, the present research would not have been possible.

The vast majority of the people we interviewed were children during the colonial era and/or had an older relative who worked for the HCB. My objective was therefore not to collect first-hand memories of the interwar Kwango-Kwilu, but rather to gather sufficient second-hand recollections of the past to be able to see patterns emerge in oral tradition.[78] To achieve this end, I needed to meet as many informants as possible and to ask them more or less the same questions in order to see if their answers would somehow form a broad narrative once taken together.

Some observations can be drawn from the 49 interviews we performed in fifteen different places. They appear to convey an overall feeling of nostalgia for HCB's heydays. Fond memories of times past specifically evoked the *Huileries'* alleged benevolence as a provider of food, work and wages. Such testimonies are by no means exceptional. In former colonies, anthropologists and historians have regularly reported encountering protean forms of colonial nostalgia.[79] However, as underlined by William Cunningham Bissell:

> Colonial nostalgia is not some [...] desire for the restoration of colonialism.
> [Nostalgia] involves the longing for something that cannot be restored, something dead and gone. It precisely marks the distance between the "then" and the "now." [...]

---

78 Jan Vansina, *Oral Tradition as History* (Madison: Wisconsin University Press, 1985), 19–21.
79 Hendriks, *Rainforest Capitalism*; Nancy Rose Hunt, *A Colonial Lexicon: Of Birth Ritual, Medicalization and Mobility in the Congo* (Durham: Duke University Press, 1999), 89–91.

> Nostalgia speaks of [...] deploying sensibilities and values drawn from the past in the context of current struggles, [it] helps us make sense of the world we live in.[80]

By formulating longings for the concession, informants rather spoke of the woes of their present condition; the lack of employment for the younger generations, the scarcity of food, the hardships endured by the Kwango-Kwilu's rural communities. Instead of lamenting on paternalism, they resorted to memories of a remote past as an ideal against which they evaluated their present condition.[81] At the same time, nostalgia was not all-pervasive. Our interlocutors often recalled the brutality of state agents and the overall injustice of the colonial administration. Several of our interlocutors for instance keenly evoked the brutality of state agents, whipping and publicly humiliating the men who could not pay their taxes. In the ruins of Leverville, nostalgia took a peculiar guise. While the archives conveyed the idea that the concession's everyday management enmeshed public and private actors, vernacular memories firmly divided the roles that both parties played. Although fieldwork did not provide first-hand accounts of the concession experience, it both made the complexity of relations between present and past clear and provided a significant counterweight to the overtly European perspective in the written sources I used.

Outline

This book follows a thematic structure. The first chapter traces the conception of Leverville and its emotional, intellectual and historical matrix. It shows the entanglement of profit-seeking and "moral" ambitions as driving forces behind its conception. I highlight how the concession stemmed from the converging visions of the Lever Brothers chairman and of the Belgian government, both ambitioning to implement "virtuous" ways to colonise and do business in Central Africa. I also shows how their shared vision intertwined romantic evocations of tropical otherness and the will to "rationalise" uncharted lands by commodifying their natural resources.

The second chapter details how longings for a virtuous colonialism in Leverville were significantly hampered by the structural weakness of European presence in the field. Lack of personnel, means and infrastructure effectively limited

---

[80] William Cunningham Bissell, "Engaging Colonial Nostalgia," *Cultural Anthropology*, 20:2 (2005): 225–226.
[81] Similar nostalgic longings for a defunct utopia of tropical capitalism have been observed by historian Greg Grandin, in the ruins of Fordlandia. See Grandin, *Fordlandia*, 14–15.

public and private agents' autonomy. Furthermore, diverging visions of how to properly conduct colonial affairs between low-ranking employees and their hierarchy disrupted the chain of command. Isolated territorial public servants and concession employees illegally collaborated and tended to disregard laws and instruction in the daily conduct of their affairs.

The third chapter focuses on the agency of indigenous communities in and around Leverville and how they significantly altered the conduct of colonial affairs. I begin by looking at practices of sense-making through which they coped with the brutal changes brought to the everyday by the concession. I continue by showing how these practices managed to counter public and private attempts to control and constraint local communities, mostly through deceit, dissimulation and elusiveness. The inability of public servants and company agents to grasp the hidden dynamics animating Congolese villages, so close yet still out of reach, marked the sheer limitation of their effective power.

Chapter four deals with the saturation of violence that characterised the concession. I delve into the forced recruitment of its Congolese workforce, and on how waged labour operated in the continuum of previous uses of unfreedom. This chapter also deals with the role played by African intermediaries in the enforcement of public and private endeavours. It finally touches upon the dissimulated participation of women and children to the concession's activities.

The fifth chapter focuses on the company's policies of social engineering, perceived through their impact on the bodies of the concession's workers and inhabitants. It delves into how HCB effectively complied with its legal obligation to feed, dress and cure its workforce. These costly requirements never reached the goals set by Lever Brothers' directorship, hindered by high costs and practicalities. Moreover, diverging visions between management and field agents, as well as the reluctance of workers to abide to the concession's paternalistic agenda also significantly hampered their deployment.

The last chapter highlights how attempts to "rationalise" the concession's existence through legalism and "scientific" means of exploitation failed to generate their expected outcomes. Land laws impeded the concession management's demand of exclusive rights of exploitation, which ultimately led to ad hoc, almost informal legal arrangements designed to trump indigenous property rights. Moreover, standardised means of palm oil production, engineered in public agronomic stations, did not reap their expected yields once implemented in Leverville. These three case studies show how attempts to make colonial and capitalist endeavours "legal" and "rational" could overlook local particularities. They illustrate how projects imagined to be enforced in a vacuum of undiscerned "otherness" bore the fruits of their own failures.

The book's conclusion reflects on the underlying themes of the study, returning to the tensions between virtue and violence in the concession, as well as reviewing the ways each chapter highlighted a different aspect of colonial impotence. It also replaces Leverville's frustrated capitalist utopia in the broader historical dynamic of private tropical paternalism.

Chapter 1: The virtuous enclave

Introduction

Built at the meeting point of two rivers – the Kwilu and the Kwenge – the Leverville concession also occupied more figurative crossroads. It emerged at the intersection of exotic fantasies on Central Africa's "savageness" and of longings for its "rational" exploitation. Leverville's founding act resulted from a seemingly uncanny entente between the young Belgian colonial state and a British soap magnate, the Lever Brothers. Furthermore, both actors endeavoured to jointly pursue two inseparable yet divergent goals: to "value" the concession's natural resources and "civilise" its inhabitants.

Considering that Leverville originated from these diverse meeting points helps us understand its multifaceted nature. The concession not only existed as a physical enclave; it also comprised a legal framework, a set of values and a business model. These facets were all deeply entangled with each other. However, they all originated from a single, grandstanding initiative. Before it came to assume these different guises, Leverville was born as a tropical utopia. It emerged among a continuum of similar initiatives, which spanned across the Global South from the late 19th century onwards. In the time of Western imperial expansion, ambitious men were driven to build their own model societies in landscapes they fantasised as untamed "jungles" and "savannahs." Chosen enclaves became laboratories for private social engineering, where their founders' "virtuous" pursuits were, more often than not, coercively enforced.

This chapter retraces the foundation of Leverville by replacing it in its cultural, contractual and economic frames. It tackles first the concept of tropical utopia, and how the concession could be seen as its epitome. Second, it covers the emergence of Leverville from the convergent moral agendas of Belgian colonial authorities and of Lever Brothers. Finally, it looks at the legal and physical foundation of Leverville. It shows how utopian fantasies and philanthropic goals came to be formalized in Europe, and how they materialised in Congo. These approaches shed light on how imbricated dynamics led to the creation of the concession. Leverville's economic objectives were inseparable from its moral guise, while both were intrinsically linked to a broader cultural framework of exotic fantasies on colonial frontiers.

This overview leads us to two observations that fit into the book's broad argument. First, it calls for critically reassessing the centrality of profit making in colonial private endeavours. The concession survived long after its structural lack of profitability was acknowledged, which indicated that the "virtuous" agenda pursued by the state and company alike was not only destined to cynically cover up their exploitative goals. Fulfilling a moral program "overseas" could very well turn into a genuine incentive for capitalist ventures, not to be systematically subordinated to the promises of short-term financial gains.

Second, although Leverville was framed as a virtuous project, radically breaking with the gruesome practices of the Congo Free State, it still shared many common traits with Leopoldian forms of exploitation. Legal arrangements, resource extraction, and the overall Promethean spirit of the concession directly tapped into Free State precedents. Studying Leverville's emergence therefore brings to the surface how the seemingly clean-cut break of Congo's 1908 transfer of sovereignty actually comprised structural economic and political continuities.

Tropical utopias

Looking for the roots of the Leverville concession requires considering the overall cultural context in which they sprouted. This section accordingly tackles the fantasies circulating on colonial frontiers in the early 20th century and how they stimulated the inception of concurrent experiences of social engineering. These projects, which could be defined as "tropical utopias," shared different characteristics. After having detailed them, I will further delve on how the imaginary of Congo at play in *fin de siècle* Europe has deeply influenced the inception of Leverville as a "virtuous" endeavour.

Landscapes of the Global South have long exerted a fascination for Western minds. For some particularly driven individuals in the age of empires, the rainforests, wetlands and drylands of Africa, Asia and South America were empty pages upon which they could write their own contribution to history. They endeavoured to turn seemingly forsaken places into private utopias, where their ambitions would come to fruition. While deeply entangled with the age of empires, these endeavours would be more adequately labelled as "tropical" rather than "colonial."

Although they were always located in warm climates, such utopias were not systematically related to imperial ventures. For instance, several US corporations created company towns south of the border, including Fordlandia (see introduction). They were conceived as both productive enclaves and laboratories for the inception of American values. These spaces functioned as "New World alternatives to European imperialism," [1] according to Greg Grandin. In both European

---

[1] Grandin, *Fordlandia*, 15.

and American "overseas" enclaves, cultural and economic hegemony went hand in hand.

A form of utopianism was, however, intrinsic to colonialism. For its advocates, colonizing meant improving the social, economic and moral standing of an exotic frontier. It meant considering foreign lands as either blank or chaotic canvasses upon which migrants, companies and states could paint more orderly and therefore better futures. Migrants were susceptible to be inspired by the utopian depiction of settler colonies as promised lands, promoted by their founders and authorities. However, exploitation colonies such as Congo could also become the stage of more seldom and ambitious fantasies.[2] These latter tropical utopias shared three common features. First, they mostly arose in a context of humanitarian urgency. Second, they stemmed from the hubris of colourful characters. Third, they required a certain level of constraint and containment to be achieved. Leverville shared these traits with concurrent prospects, such as Fordlandia and the Haut-Nyong region of French Cameroon, which was autonomously administered by a colonial doctor during the Second World War. These initiatives might seem disjointed at first, given their emergence in varied settings and their diverse points of origin. However, they were all characterised by a blend of exotic fantasizing on Southern frontiers, coupled with a longing on the part of colonists for their radical "rationalisation."

First, these tropical utopias were fashioned as promethean endeavours destined to solve particularly acute plights. Sweeping epidemics, demographic decline, and helpless "natives" left to the mercy of cruel exploiters set the scene for the arrival of ambitious initiatives, which promised to offer all-encompassing answers to these manifold sufferings. These predicaments only enhanced the boldness and heroism of peculiar figures, who took it upon themselves to change the course of these territories' histories. For instance, when Dr. Jean-Joseph David took the helm of Haut-Nyong in 1939, the region was in the midst of a ravaging outbreak of sleeping sickness. The doctor ambitioned to tackle it with structural reforms ranging far beyond the scope of sanitary measures.[3] Similarly, the area chosen by Henry Ford for the building of his Amazonian rubber plantation Fordlandia was reportedly inhabited by destitute, meek, hungry and exploited in-

---

[2] Lyman Tower Sargent, "Colonial and Postcolonial Utopias," in *The Cambridge Companion to Utopian Literature*, edited by Gregory Claeys (Cambridge: Cambridge University Press, 2010), 200.
[3] Guillaume Lachenal, *Le Médecin qui Voulut Être Roi: sur les Traces d'une Utopie Coloniale* (Paris: Seuil, 2017), 28.

digenous rubber tappers, who the company envisioned turning into productive and Americanized planters.[4]

Second, utopias emerged in places depicted in the West as chaotic hells, yet which contained the seeds of prosperous futures should they be correctly organised and exploited. The pursuit of these ambitions was depicted as an almost impossible challenge, which could only be met by an exceptional character: a man gifted with a unique vision, able to foresee and relentlessly pursue a path leading towards better prospects. It required, therefore, an unparalleled hubris to feel up to the task. Haut-Nyong's Dr. David accordingly endeavoured to completely reorganise the territory under his command in domains ranging from alimentation to labour, sports, agriculture and education.[5] Henry Ford seemingly had the ambition to turn a plot of rainforest into both a plantation and an Amazonian remake of an American suburb, complete with white-painted pavilions and red fire hydrants.[6]

Third, these projects relied more on the ambition of their founders than on the consent of their inhabitants. Communities of people living within the boundaries of tropical utopias underwent multifaceted and often coercive processes of transformation. Within these relatively secluded enclaves, workers and inhabitants were "educated," "healed" and put to work; they were then monitored according to their creators' grand designs (see chapter 5). The simultaneous enforcement of new labour techniques, infrastructures, medical therapies or leisure activities might seem unrelated at first sight. However, they participated in an overall process of rationalisation, encompassing both the enclave's human and natural resources. It consisted in implementing a vast array of "standard" behaviours, practices and techniques within the enclave's boundaries to bring "order" where "chaos" was previously thought to prevail. These experiences therefore proposed a radical transformation of all aspects of a given zone through the sheer grid of "rationality."

Fourth, these transformative ventures were, to a small extent, connected with one another. Various utopian projects were indeed envisioned as laboratories of social engineering, where improvement strategies of "Others" could be tried and tested before being potentially emulated in other tropical frontiers. For instance, David envisioned turning Haut-Nyong's medical institutions into experimental centres and training grounds for colonial doctors, who would later be sent to all corners of the French empire.[7] The success of tropical utopias

---

4 Grandin, *Fordlandia*, 86–91.
5 Lachenal, *Le Médecin*, 99.
6 Grandin, *Fordlandia*, 18.
7 Lachenal, *Le Médecin*, 81, 98.

could only be assessed as long as they remained relatively shielded from potentially corrupting outside influences. These ventures therefore had to be significantly self-contained, which included the control of their entry points and a thorough limitation and monitoring of their inhabitants' mobility.

Tropical utopias generally seemed to possess two overarching characteristics. On the one hand, they took the form of rationalising endeavours; they were laboratories of social and economic improvement based on the systematic enforcement of "modern" ways to exploit and to rule. On the other, they did not stem from an extensive knowledge of their target area. To the contrary, the places destined to become Fordlandia or Leverville were hardly charted and documented before the groundwork began to be laid for their creation. They existed, for the most part, in the minds of their makers as fantasies rooted in exotic literature.

Textual production on non-Western lands indeed played a key role in colonisation prospects, both on emotional and rational planes. It simultaneously excited the imagination of its readers and built a body of knowledge to be mobilised for further imperial ventures. For Mary Louise Pratt, sentimentality and objectivity could be concurrently present in travelogues and exploration reports from the mid-18th century onwards. Heroic narrators would reflect on their personal experiences while attempting to convey "objective" descriptions of the places they "discovered."[8] This literary pattern was particularly visible in the written descriptions of Congo circulating in the early 20th century.

For Gaston-Denys Périer, a leading proponent of Belgian "colonial arts" in the interwar, Congo was "born out of literature" and gradually imprinted in European consciousness through the successive reprints of Henry Morton Stanley's oeuvre.[9] At the *fin de siècle*, the explorer's thrilling adventures were still considered as authoritative on Central Africa, which illustrates well the permeability of objectivity and sentimentality in early accounts of the region.[10] Although imposing, Stanley was not the only author musing on Congo at the turn of the century. The Congo was also mobilized in fierce critiques of the Leopoldian rule, penned by prominent figures like Mark Twain and Joseph Conrad. Furthermore, the Congo basin was also the setting chosen by several popular adventure writers

---

[8] Mary Louise Pratt, *Imperial Eyes: Travel Writing and Transculturation* (London: Routledge, 1992), 74–75.
[9] Cited in: Pierre-Philippe Fraiture, *La Mesure de l'Autre. Afrique Subsaharienne et Roman Ethnographique de Belgique et de France (1918–1940)* (Paris: Honoré Champion, 2007), 75.
[10] Kevin Dunn, *Imagining the Congo: The International Relations of Identity* (New York-Houndmills: Palgrave-MacMillan, 2003), 23.

versed in the crafting of fictional utopias.¹¹ These different strands of literary production shared similar visions of Congo as a place of endemic cruelty and savageness, whose future prosperity relied on Western interventions, "less a garden of Eden than an unrealized possibility,"¹² according to Stephen Donovan.

Discourses presenting Congo as a savage yet bountiful land and of the Congolese as helpless prey of slavers, sorcerers, "barbaric traditions" or tropical illnesses set the stage on which the drama of colonization would take place.¹³ Imagined frontiers, compiled in the literary canon that Valentin Mudimbe coined as the "colonial library," ¹⁴ influenced the course of action of Europeans in Central Africa and beyond. It shaped their interventions as Promethean efforts, conjointly bringing the light of civilisation and modernity in allegedly forsaken places.

The colonial library's effective influence on imperial governance could be observed among others in legislative processes. Empires regularly borrowed each other's laws to rule over seemingly unrelated societies.¹⁵ For instance, property laws in the Free State were directly inspired by a South Australian legislation commonly known as the Torrens Act. This body of rules allowed Europeans to formalize their property claims on lands they considered as "vacant." Variations of the Torrens Act were also enforced in territories as disparate as Fiji Islands, French Western Africa, Tunisia and Madagascar, whose sole common features were their coerced annexation to a European empire.¹⁶ In all cases, belief in the "racial" discrepancy between colonizers and colonized was relentlessly echoed in Western literary production and served as the foundation for colonial practices of land encroachment. The belief in an ontological difference between Europeans and undifferentiated "Others" allowed colonial actors to arrogate land for themselves through a process of legal "rationalisation."

Blended discourses of colonial othering and longings for the ordering of tropical frontiers were already at play in the Congo Free State decades before the Leverville concession came to be. The inception of the Leverville concession, however, depended on the emergence of a particular strand of imperial ideology, which derived from converging beliefs from the young Belgian colonial administration and the Lever Brothers that a virtuous form of exploitation could come to light in the marshes of the Congo basin.

---

11 Stephen Donovan, "Congo Utopia," *English Studies in Africa*, 59:1 (2016): 64.
12 Donovan, "Congo Utopia", 64.
13 Dunn, *Imagining*, 53.
14 Valentin Mudimbe, *The Idea of Africa* (Bloomington: Indiana University Press, 1994), 188.
15 Benton, *A Search*, 36.
16 Benoît Henriet, "Colonial Law in the Making: Sovereignty and Property in the Congo Free State (1876–1908)," *The Legal History Review*, 83 (2015): 214–215.

Colonizing virtuously

This ontological change in the governance of Congo closely espoused the disappearance of its infamous first sovereign. Leopold II passed away in December 1909 as a profoundly unpopular monarch.[17] His libertine antics, authoritarian tendencies and controversial African ventures had turned many Belgians against him. The death of the disfavoured king also presented an opportunity for the country's power holders to set a new course in colonial affairs. In the months following Leopold's funeral, both the Minister of Colonies, Jules Renkin and Leopold's nephew and successor, Albert I, publicly acknowledged the "errors" previously committed in Congo and attempted to draw a new way forward for Belgian colonialism, eschewing the "worst excesses" of its predecessor.[18]

This discursive shift also built upon already existing measures. When Belgium officially took over Congo in October 1908, the Belgian Parliament enacted the "Colonial Charter," a body of laws destined to instigate a "righteous" course of action in its new empire. Some of the Charter's main measures were unmitigated responses to the Free State scandal. For instance, the second article forbade forced recruitment for private companies, while the fifth article entrusted Congo's General Governor (GG) with "the conservation of native populations" and the "improvement of their "moral and material living conditions"[19] (see chapter 4).

These initiatives also attempted to deflect the scepticism of other European chancelleries regarding Belgium's colonial abilities. In the light of the Leopoldian debacle and of the new metropolis' lack of previous imperial experience, foreign leaders doubted whether this new colonial venture would fare better than the last. Belgian authorities therefore strived to assert their worth as a major player in the imperial field. They endeavoured to show that Belgian Congo could be efficiently managed and "modernised," while effectively caring for the welfare of its "natives."[20] After the First World War, the administration coined a concept summing up its political goals; Congo was to become *une col-*

---

[17] Matthew Stanard, *The Lion, the Leopard and the Cock: Colonial Memories and Monuments in Belgium* (Leuven: Leuven University Press, 2019), 41
[18] Matthew Stanard, *Selling the Congo: A History of European Pro-Empire Propaganda and the Making of Belgian Imperialism* (Lincoln: University of Nebraska Press, 2011), 52–53.
[19] "Charte Coloniale," in *Codes & Lois du Congo Belge*, edited by Pierre Piron and Jacques Devos (Brussels: Larcier, 1954), 9–14.
[20] Vanthemsche, *La Belgique*, 148–152.

onie modèle, a "model colony."²¹ Although the idea of "model" colonisation remained loosely defined, an earlier occurrence provided a clearer perspective of the objectives originally pursued by the authorities.

The term "model colony" (*Müsterkolonie*) was first used by the German state to boast its achievements in Togoland, which Germany administered between 1884 and 1918.²² Germany and Belgium were both latecomers on the imperial stage, and resorting to such a concept allowed them to affirm their colonial legitimacy. In Togoland, German authorities even managed to win the praise of foreign observers, which seemed to indicate the existence of a loose international consensus on what a "model colony" could mean in the early 20th century. Togoland was applauded for its balanced budgets; its modern infrastructure; and its predominantly "pacified" state. These achievements came at a cost, however, for they necessitated the forced mobilisation of workers; the frequent resort to corporeal punishments; crushing taxation rates and grossly unequal levels of development.²³ These incidences seemed to indicate that the criteria used to define "model" colonialism by the time Leverville came to be mostly depended on a certain level of prosperity. Even before Belgian authorities endeavoured to claim the concept for Congo after 1918, the imperatives of economic success were critical to secure its imperial future. Given the Free State's burdensome legacy, these goals could not be achieved at the cost of a new humanitarian scandal.

The double objective of economic *mise en valeur* and of "civilising" the Congolese was not be pursued by the state alone. Belgium's reprise of Congo happened against the backdrop of a widespread political reluctance to shoulder the costs of colonisation.²⁴ The first article of the Colonial Charter explicitly stated that Congo must remain economically independent from its metropolis. Colonising would therefore require collaborating with private actors who would be both interested in the colony's natural resources and willing to exploit them "virtuously," in stark contrast to the brutality of the Free State's rubber companies. It was in that context that the British soap manufacturer, Lever Brothers, entered the Congolese stage.

Lever Brothers was then heralded by Lord William Hesketh Lever, 1st Viscount Leverhulme (1851–1925), a man famous for advocating philanthropic

---

21 Amandine Lauro, "Maintenir l'Ordre dans la 'Colonie-modèle' : Note sur les Désordres Urbains et la Police des Frontières Raciales au Congo Belge," *Crime, Histoire & Sociétés* 15:2 (2011): 99.
22 Dennis Laumann, "A Historiography of German Togoland, or the Rise and Fall of a 'Model Colony,'" *History in Africa*, 30 (2003): 195.
23 Laumann, "A Historiography," 196.
24 Vanthemsche, *La Belgique*, 208.

forms of entrepreneurship. "It is said that there is no sentiment in business," he wrote in September 1915. "I have always combatted that idea. There is only one phase of life with more sentiment in it than business, that is the home. Business has much more sentiment in it than Art or literature. I sometimes think that business would be impossible without sentiment."[25]

For Lord Leverhulme, capitalism must not only concentrate on profit making; it had to be used as a medium for philanthropic actions. Employers had to care for their employees, as well as for the common good. Benevolence would both secure the loyalty of their workforce and sketch out a path leading to a better society.[26]

The ultimate embodiment of Leverhulme's paternalistic vision still stands today in the outskirts of Liverpool. In 1899, the company founded the garden city of Port Sunlight to house its factory's employees. These rows of suburban pavilions and communal infrastructures such as a hospital, a leisure hall and sports accommodations were gratuitously put at the disposal of Lever Brothers' workforce, expected in return to follow strictly appointed rules of temperance, gendered separation, punctuality and efficiency. Port Sunlight was a utopian reconstruction of the English countryside at the heart of industrial Britain, aimed at fostering middle-class values and habits in the hearts and minds of its working-class population.[27]

Leverhulme was not the only businessman to pursue such goals. Other early 20th century captains of industry endeavoured to firmly weave together social engineering and profit-making. In 1917, Henry Ford decided for instance to grant a 5-dollar daily wage to its workers – the double of what his competitors offered. In return, they were expected to pursue what the company considered as "a wholesome life."[28] Whereas Leverhulme sought to promote bourgeois respectability among his proletarian workforce, Ford attempted to Americanize his migrant employees. It was not coincidental that both men later attempted to propagate their widely praised experiences of social engineering in allegedly "destitute" tropical frontiers.

In their quest for suitable private partners, Belgian authorities sent emissaries in 1909 to Lord Leverhulme, to probe his interest in the colony's vast resources of oil palms.[29] The ever-increasing demand for palm oil on Western markets

---

25 UA, LBC/229, W.H. Lever to Max Horn, 3 September 1915.
26 Brian Lewis, *So Clean: Lord Leverhulme, Soap and Civilization* (Manchester: Manchester University Press, 2008), 20–23.
27 Lewis, *So Clean*, 110–1.
28 Grandin, *Fordlandia*, 38–39.
29 Lewis, *So Clean*, 167.

was at that time sustained by both technologic advancements and new bodily uses. Needed in the first half of the 19th century for the greasing of heavy machineries, palm oil became a staple of soap production from the 1830s onwards.[30] As the social marker of corporal hygiene rapidly spread from the upper classes to Europe's urban proletariat and rural areas, the demand for hygienic products steadily rose, requiring soap makers to find and secure increasingly vast supplies of palm oil.[31]

From 1906 onwards, Leverhulme tried unsuccessfully to found large oil palm plantations in British Nigeria and Sierra Leone, where he faced the opposition of the colonial administration. Public servants feared that the extended concessions Lever Brothers intended to set up would bring havoc to the social fabric of palm oil producing regions, which were divided between local smallholders. They thought that depriving indigenous peasants of their property rights could lead to large-scale unrests.[32] No such issue arose in Belgian Congo, where palm oil production remained in its infancy in the early years of the 20th century, and where the authorities precisely advocated the creation of large-scale exploitation units. Lever Brothers therefore answered positively to the Belgians' offer, and sent two preliminary expeditions to select the five 60-km wide "circles" of rainforest land that the authorities offered them to lease. From the onset, one of those areas appeared to be the most economically promising, for it held the densest and most accessible natural palm groves. Centred on the village of Lusanga at the meeting point of the Kwenge and Kwilu rivers, this area would be baptised Leverville after the company's founder. The four other tracts of land – Brabanta, Flandria, Alberta and Elisabetha – would be granted a name either honouring Belgian's reigning couple or referring to the metropole's geography.

The objectives pursued by Lever Brothers in Congo were loosely similar to those underlying the making of Port Sunlight, and stemmed from the same blend of pragmatism and Protestant, Congregationalist moralism. In Leverhulme's perspective, Africans were granted with resources that they were unable to properly exploit, while Europeans possessed the wisdom and knowledge needed to valorise these neglected assets for the common good.[33] *Mise en valeur* should not happen at the expense of "natives," but must rather be seized as an opportunity to further their civilizational prospects. The Chairman occasionally

---

[30] Henderson, Osborne, "The Oil Palm", 63–64.
[31] Adeline Masquelier, *Dirt, Undress and Difference: Critical Perspective on the Body's Surface* (Bloomington-Indianapolis: Indiana University Press, 2006), 6.
[32] David Meredith. "Government and the Decline of the Nigerian Oil-palm Industry, 1919–1939," *The Journal of African History*, 25:3 (1984), 311.
[33] Lewis, *So Clean*, 177.

shared his optimism with regards to the HCB's ability to durably "civilize" its employee, for whom he fostered a condescending benevolence. "I believe the Congo native is a particularly intelligent man when he is rightly handled,"[34] he wrote for instance in April 1916. According to his personal secretary, Leverhulme even claimed that "the Congo native is [...] the best tropical labourer in the world."[35] To fully reach their potential, Congolese HCB employees had to be properly paid, correctly housed, accordingly fed and cured, like their Port Sunlight counterparts.[36] Leverhulme himself underlined the strong parallels between both ventures in November 1924, a few months before his death. HCB was, according to him, "a business like none other we have. Perhaps Port Sunlight comes nearest to it in social work."[37] At that time, the company had already achieved a global outreach and was active in territories as diverse as the Indian subcontinent, the Solomon Islands, and the Hebrides. Leverhulme's comments therefore appeared to allude to the *Huileries'* uniquely ambitious scope within the Lever Brothers consortium.

Originally, HCB was also depicted and widely supported as a radical break with the woeful practices of the Congo Free State. Leading figures of the anti-Leopoldian campaign actively petitioned for Leverhulme's ambitions in Central Africa, such as Emile Vandervelde, Belgium's historical socialist leader,[38] and Edmund D. Morel, spearhead of the Congo Reform Association (CRA). Vandervelde's advocacy for Belgian imperialism and interest for colonial affairs set him starkly apart from his socialist comrades. He was the sole member of his political group to vote for the annexation of the Free State by Belgium, for he was convinced that a future left-wing government would support the social emancipation of the Congolese.[39] At the height of the Congo scandal, Vandervelde befriended and collaborated with Morel; both men attempted to bring an end to Leopold II's personal rule in Central Africa.[40] Morel would later actively support Leverhulme's prospects in the Congo, for he remained persuaded that the Port Sunlight experience could be reproduced in the tropics by a "decent, honest

---

[34] UA, LBC/215, W.H. Lever to Henry Moseley, 11 April 1916.
[35] UA, UAC 2/34/4/1/1, Diary of T.M. Knox
[36] Lewis, *So Clean*, 168–9.
[37] Lewis, *So Clean*, 177.
[38] Emile Vandervelde (1886–1938), member of parliament, minister of justice (1918–1921), foreign affairs (1925–1927), and health (1936–1937), was the president of the Belgian Workers Party from 1933 to 1938, and the president of the Socialist International from 1923 to 1938.
[39] Janet Polasky, *Emile Vandervelde: Le Patron* (Brussels: Labor, 1995), 58.
[40] Polasky, *Emile Vandervelde*, 54.

and most powerful capitalistic force."⁴¹ Vandervelde similarly asserted that HCB would be beneficial for its Congolese workers after the brutal experience of the Free State.⁴²

Interestingly, Morel's CRA was only disbanded in 1913, five years after the annexation of the Free State by Belgium.⁴³ The Association kept lobbying the new colonial authorities and the British government to make sure that effective reforms would be put in place beyond the formal transfer of sovereignty.⁴⁴ The CRA's delegate claimed to have secured the association's main purposes when they decided to close it down; however, the CRA fell short of reaching all of its goals. First, they could not secure collective land rights for the colony's inhabitants.⁴⁵ Second, Morel ultimately failed in his efforts to emulate the successes of its reform campaign by putting an end to the brutal labour practices in French Equatorial Africa.⁴⁶ Third, workforce mobilisation strategies in Belgian Congo remained widely similar to those in place in the Free State (see chapter 4 in particular). The political climate of colonial affairs in the infancy of Belgian Congo was still significantly shaped by its predecessor. The validity of new capitalist ventures, especially as ambitious as HCB, were widely measured by how they fared compared to Free State practices. This paradigm shift only enhanced the necessity of framing Leverville as a radical, utopian break with the past.

A clean break?

Leverville arose from congruent ambitions to reset colonial endeavours in Central Africa. However, in spite of this meeting of the minds, HCB continued to a great extent in the footsteps of earlier forms of colonialism. I will begin this section by detailing the obligations Lever Brothers pledged to fulfil in the Congo. I will then shed light on how Leverville could be depicted as a tropical utopia. Finally, I will explore the concession's multifaceted roots in the Congo Free State.

On 14 April 1911, representatives of Lever Brothers and of the Belgian government sat down to sign a convention outlining the consortium's future activities in the colony. The corporation had to create a company under Belgian law – the

---

41 Lewis, *So Clean*, 165.
42 Fieldhouse, *Unilever Overseas*, 505.
43 Stanard, *Selling*, 46.
44 Dean Pavlakis, *British Humanitarianism and the Congo Reform Movement, 1896–1913* (Farnham: Ashgate, 2015), 247
45 Pavlakis, *British Humanitarianism*, 235
46 Pavlakis, *British Humanitarianism*, 214

Huileries du Congo Belge – to manage its new exploitations. HCB representatives had ten years to choose up to 75, 000 hectares of vacant lands in each circle, where they could either harvest naturally-growing palm trees or set up new plantations. Within its circles, HCB had to assume the construction of all necessary infrastructures on its own funds – be they roads, canals, railways, telegraph and telephone lines – which could be gratuitously used by state agents. HCB also had to invest in the building of schools and medical facilities, at least one in each circle, to benefit the concessions' workers and inhabitants. In return, the company only had to pay a symbolic loan to the Belgian government – 25 cents per hectare annually – and could come into full ownership of the areas it effectively occupied after 35 years of exploitation. Should HCB fail to uphold its duties, the convention could in term be nullified. HCB would receive a formal warning from the government outlining their shortcomings and be granted a year to correct the course of its operations. Past this deadline, the Belgian state could unilaterally resign their agreement and publically auction all of HCB's colonial assets.[47]

The "virtuous" business venture stemming from the meeting of the minds of Lever Brothers' management and Belgian colonial public elite was utopian in many aspects. Like Fordlandia, it was designed to bring radical forms of social change in a poorly studied and highly fantasised area. The very foundation of Leverville was for instance described by Sidney Edkins – the concession's first manager – as a Promethean effort that would finally bring "civilisation" to destitute indigenous communities. Accordingly, his description of the company's first contingent of workers rendered their alleged helplessness:

> "All this labour was poor, underfed, ravaged by sickness and intertribal warfare and all were cannibals. Sleeping sickness had wiped out 80 percent of the population and human life had little or no value. The Writer during his first visit of exploration inland, saw villages with hundreds of houses abandoned except by a few miserable beings in the last stages of sleeping sickness and others entirely destroyed by fire during a raid by a rival village [...] The remaining population was in such poor physical condition that they no longer had the energy to keep the larger wild animals at bay by attacking them when they approached their villages."[48]

---

[47] "Projet de décret approuvant une convention conclue le 21 février 1911 entre le Gouvernement du Congo belge et la Société "Lever Brothers Limited" et ayant pour objet la concession de terres à une société à constituer sous le nom de: "Société Anonyme des Huileries du Congo Belge", in *Annales Parlementaires* 1911, Document parlementaire n°126.
[48] RMCA EA 54.85.171, Sidney Edkins' notes on the history of the HCB.

This narrative largely resorted to the set of exotic images regularly mobilised in the colonial library.[49] Cannibalism, endemic diseases or continuous inter-tribal warfare were discursive tropes to which explorers, missionaries, colonial writers or filmmakers frequently resorted to justify the necessity of imposing European rule over Africa. Edkin's ample resort to superlatives – *all* workers were cannibals, human life had *no* value – only enhanced the dire need of indigenous inhabitants for initiatives such as Leverville. A titanic effort that the aging Lord Leverhulme attempted to micromanage to the best of his abilities.[50]

The chairman's correspondence regarding HCB regularly alluded to both his very personal concerns for the company and to the colossal challenges it represented. Leverhulme visited his Congolese plants in 1913 and again in 1924, only a few months before his passing at the age of 74. In a letter written shortly before his last departure, he underlined the intimate importance and certain sacrifices that such a trip implied. "I take a personal interest in the success of the HCB and go to the very great expense and rather serious absence of business in England."[51] Furthermore, the interest bestowed upon HCB by King Albert I himself, along with the relationship that the two men developed around the *Huileries*, seems to have only heightened Leverhulme's involvement in his Congolese venture. "My one objective in life today is to prove myself by the success of the *Huileries* to be worthy of [the King's] confidence,"[52] he wrote to an aide in June 1914. This communication expressed a feeling he reiterated ten years later before departing Europe for Congo: "whenever I have visited Brussels I have always found His Majesty, the King, not only to take a very close personal interest in the operations being carried by the HCB in the Belgian Congo, but stimulating in his influence on myself to take a close personal interest and active part in the business of the HCB directly myself."[53] The monarch's attention for HCB also seemed to highlight its importance as a landmark project in the reorientation of colonial affairs in Congo far from its Free State precedent.

Beyond royal favours, Leverhulme's interest in HCB was also linked with the titanic challenge it represented, which he endeavoured to overcome. "It can only be by strenuous hard work, pursued with great persistency over a long number of years, that the scheme will finally win out,"[54] he envisioned in 1916. Six years

---

49 Pierre Halen, *"Le Petit Belge avait vu Grand": une littérature Coloniale* (Brussels: Labor, 1993), 200.
50 Lewis, *So Clean*, 174.
51 UA, LBC/230, W.H. Lever to Max Horn, 18 June 1924.
52 UA, LBC/229, W.H. Lever to Max Horn, 23 June 1914.
53 UA, LBC/230, W.H. Lever to Max Horn, 18 June 1924.
54 UA, LBC/215, W.H. Lever to Henry Moseley, 11 April 1916.

later, he asserted that difficulties encountered would not deter him, which therefore highlighted how the Chairman's personal pride played a crucial role in HCB's continued existence in spite of the many issues it faced. "I have never closed down any undertaking that I have been connected with yet and I am certain the HCB will not cause me to break this good rule."[55] For Leverhulme, HCB's success would be measured by its philanthropic achievements even more than by the profits it could yield. It would "depend upon and be in proportion to the happiness and contentment of the natives, which must be assured,"[56] he wrote in 1912. This ethos would continuously imbue his vision for HCB. "It is up to us to make service so attractive that they prefer to work for us,"[57] he wrote as an instruction to Elso Dusseljé when he took the direction of Leverville in December 1923.

Leverhulme's virtuous designs in Congo, as well as his pride and reputation were deemed important enough for its parent company to keep on investing into HCB, in spite of its limited and only occasional profitability.[58] Throughout its history, the production costs of palm oil in Congo remained structurally higher than its market price (see chapter 6).[59] Enormous amounts of money were nevertheless poured into the *Huileries*, with little returns on investment. In 1911, Lever Brothers had already devolved one million pounds to the company, out of a total capital of 6.6 million pounds at the time. HCB briefly generated profits between 1918 and 1920 – which amounted to less than 72 000 pounds – before generating further losses from 1920 onwards.[60] After Leverhulme's passing and in the midst of the Great Depression, money nevertheless kept on flowing from Port Sunlight. "In spite of the formidable crisis which is currently hitting us extremely hard and forces us to work in pure loss for long months already, our company has not lost faith in the future, and proved it by injecting in total more than 20 million pounds in Congo for the year 1931,"[61] strenuously wrote the HCB's delegate administrator the Minister of Colonies. According to a May 1933 despatch, only 11 million Congolese francs were distributed as dividends

---

[55] UA, LBC/229, W.H. Lever to Max Horn, 24 April 1922.
[56] Cited in Lewis, *So Clean*, 173.
[57] AAB, MOI 3602, Instructions from Lord Leverhulme to Elso Dusseljé, 8 December 1923.
[58] See as well: Reuben Loffman, Benoît Henriet, "'We Are Left with Barely Anything': Colonial Rule, Dependency, and the Lever Brothers in the Belgian Congo, 1911–1960," *The Journal of Imperial and Commonwealth History*, 48:1 (2020) : 71–100.
[59] Charles Wilson, *The History of Unilever: A Study in Economic Growth and Social Change* (London: Cassel, 1970, 1954), 320.
[60] Fieldhouse, *Unilever Overseas*, 508.
[61] UA, UAC/2/36/7/1/2, HCB delegate-administrator to the GG, 9 April 1931.

to the company's shareholders in its 22-year history, against investments amounting to 500 million francs.[62] For David Fieldhouse, "HCB survived [...] only because Lever was willing and able to pour far more money in the Congo than was justified. [...] HCB was always heavily over-capitalised. It could show reasonable profits only when oil prices were exceptionally good."[63] This was another striking similarity with Fordlandia. The Amazonian plantation was built after the rubber boom receded and never became profitable.[64] However, this did not stop Ford to keep investing in it until 1934. In both cases, the success of its utopian vision supplanted profitability as an investment incentive, although Fordlandia closed its door much sooner, after only six years of unfruitful activities.

As a business venture and an experience of social engineering, the Leverville concession was conceived as a virtuous answer to the Free State's abuses. The Belgian government and Lever Brothers worked together to set up the guiding lines for a "philanthropic" capitalism in the Congo. This venture benefitted from the blessing of prominent critiques of the defunct Leopoldian rule and the personal involvement of both the Belgian King and the company's chairman. Lord Leverhulme and his successors also spared no expense to see HCB not only economically succeed, but to fulfil its paternalistic goals above all. However, in spite of the apparent break in colonial affairs that the *Huileries* embodied, HCB remained largely dependent upon Free State uses and practices. Overall, the 1908 reprise did not constitute such a clean break in terms of colonial governance. Many administrators remained in place, such as Théophie Wahis, Governor General of the Free State 1900, who stayed in function until 1912 in spite of his involvement in the "atrocities" scandal.[65] Furthermore, the confusion between public and private interests that infamously characterized the previous era kept on influencing many extractive activities in the colony.[66] The virtuous turn seemingly taken by resource extraction in the newly Belgian colony could therefore not suppress, nor entirely supplant, its pre-existing violent guise.

---

[62] UA, UAC/2//36/1/1/1, HCB delegate-administrator to the Minister of Colonies, 1 May 1933.
[63] Fieldhouse, *Unilever Overseas*, 509.
[64] Grandin, *Fordlandia*, 97.
[65] "Théophile Wahis," in the *Biographie Coloniale Belge*, accessed March 7, 2020, https://www.kaowarsom.be/fr/notices_wahis_theophile.
[66] Jean-Luc Vellut, "Hégémonies en Construction: Articulation entre État et Entreprises dans le Bloc Colonial Belge (1908–1960)," *Canadian Journal of African Studies*, 16 :2 (1982): 326; Julia Seibert, "More Continuity than Change? New Forms of Unfree Labor in the Belgian Congo, 1908–1930," in *Humanitarian Intervention and Changing Labor Relations: The Long-Term Consequences of the Abolition of the Slave Trade*, edited by Marcel Van der Linden (Leiden: Brill, 2011), 375.

On a symbolic plane, the making of Leverville tapped into the practices and uses of the times of the Congo's exploration. Like newly "discovered" lands, HCB's five circles were given new names, symbolically marking their entry into the Western consciousness, and by extension into "civilisation."[67] The concession aimed at becoming HCB's flagship outpost was accordingly christened after Leverhulme, in the same spirit that made Henry Morton Stanley baptise Congolese landmarks after either himself or Leopold II. This recurring trope in empire-building allowed prominent colonial actors to claim foreign lands as their own, and to mark the entry into "history" under their personal tutelage. Asserting a power to name allowed them to "arrogate themselves the power of origins,"[68] according to Anne McClintock.

Furthermore, these circles were concessions, broadly following the legal arrangements enacted between the Congo Free State and rubber companies. Up until the Second World War, the main production scheme in place in those concessions also remained strikingly similar to rubber harvest: indigenous workers were recruited to forage raw materials in forest areas and bring them to the company's buying stations (see chapter 6). In both cases, this business model could only be sustained through diverse forms of coercion (see chapter 4).

Finally, the Kwilu basin being poorly charted and scarcely manned in 1911, HCB would effectively come to play the role of the agent of colonisation in and around Leverville.[69] This pioneering role was a source of pride for its first manager. In his 1936 personal account of the company's history, Sidney Edkins fondly remembered the HCB's beginnings, narrated again in the heroic spirit of 19th century travelogues:

> Neither of the present government stations in the Lusanga area, Kikwit, Bulungu and Niadi then existed. They were created after the HCB had occupied the Lusanga circle and had established firm and friendly relations with the local population. [...] The Kwilu River above Kikwit had never been navigated on until the Writer accompanied by Mr Dusseljé and Mr Moorat, at considerable risk and discomfort, found and marked a passage through several miles of rapids.[70]

HCB agents both opened the Leverville area to administrative occupation, and assumed sovereign prerogatives such as infrastructure building within its prem-

---

67 Pratt, *Imperial Eyes*, 31.
68 Anne McClintock, *Imperial Leather. Race, Gender and Sexuality in the Colonial Context* (London-New York: Routledge, 1995), 29.
69 For similar practices in the Free State, see: Reuben Loffman, *Church, State and Colonialism in Southeastern Congo, 1890–1962* (London: Palgrave-Macmillan, 2019), 85–91.
70 RMCA, 54.85.171, Sidney Edkins' History of the HCB, 31 October 1936.

ises. The blurring of the lines separating state and company within its zone of influence not only constituted another continuity with the Free State, it also became a source of conflicts, frustration and violence. The uncertain prerogatives devolved to private and public actors generated significant frictions between both spheres, as well as within their respective structures (see chapters 2 and 4). The seemingly harmonious meeting of the minds embodied in the 1911 convention held the seeds of the discords to come. Furthermore, it only partially brought an end to Leopoldian forms of governance and resource extraction. As I will detail in the coming chapters, the "clean break" advocated by HCB's metropolitan proponents failed to materialise in the field.

Conclusion

The Leverville concession emerged at many crossroads. In theory, Leverville embodied an institutional and economic break between the violence of the Free State and the virtuous guise that Belgian colonialism ambitioned to assume. The concession's utopian nature was to a certain extent "born out of literature," yet it ultimately took the form of a legally-binding contract, and one that merged the state and the company together. Leverville's prime objective was to foster benefits, yet both its philanthropic goals and the chairman's hubristic will to see them achieved appeared to have prevailed over any form of efficiency.

Seen from the top down, the concession's inception appears as a particularly transformative endeavour. Prominent yet diverse figures – a respected businessman; a leftwing politician; a young Monarch; and a humanitarian activist – actively supported its creation. Lever Brothers and the Belgian government agreed on a plan of action outlining how profit-making in Congo should from then on be bound to a moral straitjacket.

However, once observed from the bottom-up, the radical turn that HCB seemingly embodied rather looked like a thin varnish of philanthropy spread out on old exploitative practices. Leverville was expected to function like a rubber concession, albeit one where Congolese workers would be "humanely" treated. It acted as the principal agent of colonisation in the Kwilu basin, a role also played by private companies under the Free State. Even HCB's utopian guise rehashed old Leopoldian tropes. In its time, the Free State had also been originally presented as a humanitarian endeavour, before its brutal guise became the object of a large-scale scandal.[71]

---

71 Donovan, "Congo Utopia," 66.

In the field, the multifaceted nature of the concession would turn into an endless source of conflicts. Far from being inseparable, the moral and economic goals of HCB turned out to be widely incompatible. Professions of faith in the bright future of virtuous colonialism were hardly translatable in practice, and Leverville's incoherent objectives spawned further forms of violence and constraint. As shall be illustrated, the impossibility to act on these imperial fantasies of morality were the main thrust of colonial impotence in the concession and its hinterland.

Chapter 2: Impotent agents

No palavers, no troubles, lack of enthusiasm, lack of prestige,... They all contribute to diminish the professional conscience of our public servants. Their relations with the natives progressively take the form of a politic of interests: living cheaply, even making some profits; to sum up, fulfil their mission without troubles and saving as much money as possible.[1]

General Commissioner Wauters, October 1931.

Introduction

In late 1931, the aftermaths of the *Tupelepele* revolt led to a flurry of soul-searching within the colony's administrative circles (see introduction). The millenarian movement's perceived virulence, and the difficulties encountered by the authorities to suppress it, highlighted the many shortcomings of Belgian colonialism in the Kwango district in three intertwined ways. First, field public servants failed to contain the *Tupelepele*'s rapid spread among local communities in the month of May 1931. Second, *Tupelepele* followers murdered and dismembered a territorial agent in the village of Kilamba on 8 June, which testified to the Belgian officials' vulnerability outside of secured colonial outposts. Third, the *Force Publique* only managed to repress the insurrection after long weeks of violent military campaigns, which shed light on the administration's limited control over the Southwest marshes of the Congo basin. These issues were later addressed in different reports penned either by administrative insiders such as general commissioner Wauters, the right-hand of the Congo-Kasaï's provincial governor,[2] or outsiders such as Eugene Jungers,[3] the president of Léopoldville's court of appeal at the time.

These documents offer precious bottom-up insights on colonialism. They could bluntly address uncomfortable issues, such as the disregard of functionaries for the very rules they were tasked to enforce, or the existence of structural practices of corruption between functionaries and concessionary companies. For instance, the abovementioned quote from Wauters crudely depicts the Kwango district's public servants. They are supposedly unmotivated; they do not uphold to the prestige vested in their function; and they appear to pursue petty objectives – i.e., amassing money – under the guise of their official duties. Wauters'

---

[1] AAB, AIMO 1820, Notes pour M. le Gouverneur de la Province, undated (1931).
[2] AAB, AIMO 1820, Notes pour M. le Gouverneur de la Province, undated (1931).
[3] AAB, AE 3268, Rapport d'enquête sur la révolte du Kwango, 29 November 1931.

description alludes to the existence of a significant contradiction between the virtue that Belgian rule in Congo was supposed to embody (see chapter 1), and the triviality of colonialism as it was effectively enforced on the Southwest marshes of the Congo basin. This very triviality could furthermore be conceptualized as a form of colonial *impotence*.

Impotence as understood here does not equate to powerlessness, for field public servants and HCB employees in the Kwango district did enjoy a limited scope of action. Colonial impotence rather refers to the contradiction at play between how these agents could effectively act and what was expected from them. As detailed in the previous chapter, a set of directives enacted in Europe was expected to ensure the exercise of "virtuous" governance and resource extraction in Belgian Congo. These rules were rooted in fantasies of exotic otherness more than in any pre-existing knowledge of the regions to be subjugated. In reality, in the field, state and company agents did not abide to the model behaviours decreed in Brussels or Port Sunlight. They acted, but not how they should have. If impotent men did not comply with cultural standards of normal masculinity, "impotent" colonial agents similarly failed to act according to what was expected of them. They disregarded the "prestige" associated with their function; they overlooked the rules they were supposed to both follow and enforce; and they ensured that their personal interests prevailed over the needs of the state.[4]

Studying the effective conducts of these agents calls for a nuanced review of recent studies on the multifaceted limitations faced by colonial actors. Maurus Reinkowski and Gregor Thum, for instance, suggested that imperial agents could be confronted to manifold forms of "helplessness." Isolated functionaries could potentially be overpowered by local communities, or lacked the means to maintain the racial barriers which supported their dominant status. Their structural weaknesses therefore hampered the overall success of colonial ventures.[5] Marie Muschalek highlighted the importance for Europeans in the colonies to uphold their prestige and to preserve their honour. Reputation, either individual or collective, was crucial to sustain the colonial hierarchy in a context where a small group of Europeans and their local underlings had to assert their authority

---

[4] On similar discrepancies between principles and practices in colonial settings, see: Romain Tiquet, "Rendre Compte pour ne pas Avoir à Rendre des Comptes: Réflexion sur l'Écrit Administratif en Situation Coloniale (Sénégal, Années 1920–1950), *Cahiers d'Histoire* 137 (2017): 123–140.

[5] Maurus Reinkowski, Gregor Thum, "Helpless Imperialists: Introduction," in *Helpless Imperialists: Imperial Failure, Fear and Radicalization*, edited by Maurus Reinkowski, and Gregor Thum (Göttingen: Vandenhoeck & Ruprecht, 2013), 7–20.

on potentially restive local communities.⁶ Furthermore, Eva Bisschof showed that a vast array of 19th and 20th century scientific and literary productions tackled the psychological pressure experienced by colonialists. Feelings of alienation and powerlessness could lead them to experience a form of "tropical neurasthenia," which would manifest itself by a "dramatic loss of self-control, most particularly of the sexual drive and of violent impulses."⁷

These studies made relevant points on the effective limitedness of colonial hegemonic longings, the importance of statuses in the maintenance of imperial hierarchies, and the brutality exercised by mentally embattled colonialists. However, colonial actors confronted to manifold "failures" could also adopt diverging attitudes and behaviours. First, the limited authority of public servants or company employees in the Kwango district did not make them helpless, but rather expressed itself through the mobilisation of their power in ways that were frowned upon in Europe. Second, the maintenance of prestige and honour appeared to have been more crucial for the higher echelons of the colonial hierarchy than for lower-ranking subordinates in direct contact with the indigenous population. Third, emotions akin to "tropical neurasthenia" did not necessarily lead European men to let loose on their violent impulses. Although violence was ever present in the Leverville concession and its hinterland (see chapter 4), demotivated and isolated public servants also processed their shortcomings in other ways. They could superficially fulfil their duties; use their authority to amass a small private capital; or unlawfully join forces with HCB recruiters, partly to alleviate their loneliness. In short, public servants could prove to be more "petty" than "helpless." Their impotence became manifest in the discrepancy between the aforementioned behaviours and those expected from them.

In this chapter, I will therefore attempt to shed light on manifestations of impotence within the Leverville concession and its hinterland. To do so, I first delve into the structure of public power in the interwar Kwango district. I then tackle the limitations encountered by the state in its attempt to control this area. Finally, I analyse three cases to illustrate the forms that "colonial impotence" could take in the field: 1) tax collection; 2) the practice of the so-called "prix-Etat"; and 3) the tours of inspection functionaries illegally performed with HCB agents.

I will focus predominantly on the lot of public servants, which might seem only loosely related to the Leverville experience. If the scarcity of archival traces left by HCB staff encouraged me to pay more attention to the better documented

---
6 Marie Muschalek, *Violence as Usual: Policing and the Colonial State in German Southwest Africa* (Ithaca: Cornell University Press: 2019), 14–43.
7 Eva Bisschof, "Tropenkoller: Male Self-Control and the Loss of Colonial Rule," in *Helpless Imperialists*, 118.

experiences of functionaries, doing so also allowed for placing the concession in its broader social and political context. As an enclave, Leverville remained inseparable from the administrative units in which it was enmeshed; namely, the territories of Kikwit, Bulungu and Niadi, all part of the Kwango district, itself integrated into the Congo-Kasaï province. The daily governance of Leverville required the company to actively collaborate with functionaries attached to these different structures. Furthermore, the Kwango also constituted HCB's recruitment pool in Southwest Congo, a region toured by its recruiters attempting to round up fruit cutters. This meant that the *Huileries*' agents were not only active within the boundaries of the Leverville circle, but also exerted their duties in its surroundings. The social, administrative and economic porosity that existed between the concession and its hinterland called for me to pay special attention to their manifold interactions.

Agents of empire

A certain discrepancy existed between the official structure of the Belgian colonial state and the effective distribution of power within its neatly outlined hierarchy. Lawmakers in Brussels set up an administrative device constraining the autonomy of field public servants, in order to avoid a repetition of the Free State's unchecked brutality (see chapter 1). However, field realities provided low-ranking functionaries in direct contact with indigenous communities with more leverage than expected.

On paper, the administrative power dynamics was centripetal; the Ministry of Colonies in Brussels officially acted as the source of all power.[8] The closest a public servant was to the minister in the official organogram, the more influence and institutional prominence he could theoretically enjoy. The centripetal nature of Belgian colonial power did not only instate the primacy of metropolitan authorities over their counterparts in Congo; it also asserted the prominence of its administrative capital in the colony's daily governance. Sitting in Boma until 1923 and then in Léopoldville, the General Governor (GG) was at the helm of the executive branch of the colonial state. Officially charged with enforcing the instructions given by the Minister, GGs enjoyed only a limited autonomy in the pursuit of their duties.[9] Legally speaking, they could only promulgate or-

---

[8] Ndaywel, *Nouvelle Histoire*, 354.
[9] André Durieux, *Institutions Politiques, Administratives et Judiciaires du Congo Belge et du Ruanda-Urundi* (Brussels: ed. Bieleveld, 1955), 35.

dinances which specified the terms of application of the laws enacted in Brussels.[10] Further down the ladder stood the province governors, who acted as surrogates of the GGs in their respective regions. They enjoyed an even more limited executive power, embodied in the possible promulgation of decrees, which were subordinated to the GGs' ordinances. One step below the governors were district commissioners, who were in charge of "controlling and supervising the territories"[11] comprised in the district.

Territories were managed at the local level by a territorial administrator, who was assisted by territorial agents.[12] The former was expected to overlook the building of infrastructures, tax collection, the realisation of censuses and the maintenance of public order. Furthermore, they also operated as police judges for minor offences, which effectively blurred the distinction between executive and judiciary power.[13] Territorial agents were the linchpin of Belgian colonialism and acted as "the direct and active agents of colonisation,"[14] according to Minister of Colonies Louis Franck in 1925. They were expected to maintain "constant contact with native chiefs, uphold or enhance their prestige, preserve and advance native institutions, do everything in [their] power to ease relations between Europeans and natives, the penetration of civilisation and trade and the progressive *mise en valeur* of [their] territory."[15] They enabled Belgian colonial dominance by enforcing laws, ordinances and decrees, thereby ensuring the collaboration of indigenous authority figures and overseeing tax collection and public works.[16]

The Belgian colonial organogram suggested that functionaries in the field lacked leverage and autonomy in the pursuit of their duties. They were constrained in theory by the supervision of their chain of command and by their lack of legislative autonomy. In practice, however, ruling Belgian Congo in the interwar turned out to be the affair of largely autonomous agents. Laws, decrees and ordinances were often renegotiated, adapted or simply ignored by governors, commissioners and administrators. They could regard the instructions they received

---

10 Vanthemsche, *La Belgique*, 46.
11 Durieux, *Institutions Politiques*, 45.
12 Vanthemsche, *La Belgique*, 46.
13 Dembour, "La Chicote," 206.
14 *Recueil à l'Usage des Fonctionnaires et des Agents du Service Territorial au Congo* Belge (Brussels: Weissenbruch, 1925), 38.
15 Durieux, *Institutions Politiques*, 46.
16 Samia El Mechat, "Introduction," in *Les Administrations Coloniales, XIXe-XXe Siècles: Esquisse d'une Histoire Comparée*, edited by Samia El Mechat (Rennes: Presses Universitaires de Rennes, 2009), 13.

as either maladjusted to Congolese realities, or as impossible to enforce given the lack of infrastructure and manpower at their disposal.

The multiple fracture lines running through the Belgian administration were already apparent in 1916. In a despatch to Lord Leverhulme, HCB manager Moseley mentioned a "serious matter" to which the company was confronted; namely, "the state of affairs which appears to exist between the colonial office and the GG."[17] "Boma ignores the wishes and instructions sent out from Europe if they are not in accordance to their own views,"[18] wrote Moseley. This hierarchical disregard did not stop at the metropolitan/colonial divide. In districts and territories, commissioners, administrators and agents could benefit from a significant autonomy in the exercise of their prerogatives. The Leverville concession's hinterland was remote from Boma and Léopoldville, scarcely manned and poorly organised. It was challenging for the higher echelons of the colonial administration to control its field agents. This lack of supervision took on two specific guises.

First, territorial public servants who lived and worked in the field could build a social network, binding them to local power brokers outside of the state structure. Through personal contact, they could foster bonds of affection, solidarity or mutual assistance with missionaries, private company agents or indigenous leaders. These networks could provide low-ranking functionaries with a strategic advantage in the pursuit of their goals, whether it was the functionaries themselves who set these goals or they were imposed by their superiors.[19] Second, the management of remote outposts located far from the eyes of their hierarchy gave administrators and agents a significant leverage in how they chose to report on their daily activities. In the interwar Kwango district, field public servants could conceal from their superiors what they did not wish to share, or embellish the facts to their advantage.[20] In June 1932 for instance, the governor of the Congo-Kasaï province mentioned the case of a territorial administrator who, "in order to provide [...] a table reflecting an extraordinary activity, stopped returning to his outpost and instead settled in a lodge in the immediate vicinity of his chief-place."[21] This misrepresentation made it possible for

---

17 UA, LBC/215, Moseley to Leverhulme, 4 March 1916.
18 UA, LBC/215, Moseley to Leverhulme, 4 March 1916.
19 Julia Adams, "Principals and Agents, Colonialists and Company Men: The Decay of Colonial Control in the Dutch East Indies," *American Sociological Review*, 61:1 (1996): 15.
20 See as well: Bruce Berman, John Lonsdale, *Unhappy Valley: Conflict in Kenya & Africa. Book One: State & Class* (London: James Currey, 1990), 157; Tiquet, "Rendre Compte," 130.
21 AAB, AIMO 1855, Lettre du gouverneur du Congo-Kasaï au commissaire de district du Kwango, 9 June 1932.

the administrator to provide the appearance of tirelessly roaming the roads of his territory, while in reality he remained mostly sedentary and inactive.

The effective autonomy of territorial public servants contradicted their subordinate position in the colonial organogram. Assets such a limited hierarchical control; networks of allies and clients; or the possibility to mobilise the state's claim on "legitimate violence" to pursue individual goals go against the idea that field functionaries endured a form of colonial "helplessness." However, their political leeway was also impeded by the administration's uncertain footing in the Kwango district. The limitations they encountered could have led these public servants towards demotivation and privileging personal gains over their official responsibilities.

The shortcomings of power

The disillusioned quote of general commissioner Wauters in the chapter's opening sheds light on the limits of colonial rule in the Kwango district. For instance, Wauters regretted that public servants seemed increasingly driven by the pursuit of their own interest in their "relations with the natives," "relations" which in turn were crucial in the exercise of rule. Enacting colonialism required the maintenance of formalised, almost ritualised, relationships between state representatives and local communities. According to Achille Mbembe, colonizing demanded "a physical contact" between the ruler and the ruled to keep the latter in "a bond of subjection."[22] During these contacts, the state's assertion of sovereignty could take the form of elaborate displays of prestige and might, designed to "impress" its indigenous subjects.[23] Regular visits of state agents to villages for censuses, tax collection or conflict resolution both materialised the state's existence and asserted its hegemonic claims. The fact that agents used these encounters for personal gains therefore hampered their ability to maintain the legitimacy of the colonial order, as expected by their superiors.

Furthermore, Wauters delved into the emotional dispositions of field agents, noting their lack of "enthusiasm"[24] as one of the causes of the *Tupelepele* rebellion. It suggested that in an isolated area such as the Kwango, the state of mind of public servants could have a dramatic impact on the public order. The relational nature of colonial rule, and the importance of the mental and physical

---

22 Mbembe, *The Postcolony*, 175.
23 Helen Callaway, *Gender, Culture, and Empire. European Women in Colonial Nigeria* (London: Palgrave-MacMillan, 1987), 55–57.
24 AAB, AIMO 1820, Notes pour M. le Gouverneur de la Province, undated (1931).

state of field agents in its daily exercise shed light on the structural weaknesses of Belgian presence in and around the Leverville concession.

Throughout the interwar period, the public powers' limited financial means led to a shortage of territorial public servants throughout Equatorial Africa.[25] This situation effectively limited the ability of agents and administrators to set up and maintain relationships with local communities. In March 1913, for instance, the Kikwit territorial administrator mentioned how "relations with chiefs, sub-chiefs and natives" were "very rare [...] because of the lack of sufficient White personnel."[26] The deficit of state representatives in the field was particularly acute in the Kwango district, which remained of secondary importance during the consolidation of Belgian presence in the Congo basin. In November 1925, the Congo-Kasaï governor wrote, "the efficiency of our intervention, our action, [...] depends on our occupation [...] Very important in well-occupied territories, by the administration as well as by private individuals, as in the Bas-Congo, it remains weak in poorly occupied areas in the South of the Kwango, where the public servant is isolated."[27]

Between 1919 and 1931, each of the district's territories were indeed supervised by a maximum of one administrator and three agents. They were expected to work together to oversee hundreds of square kilometres of poorly charted land, which proved to be largely impossible.[28] General commissioner Wauters also invoked the lack of agents to justify administrative deficiencies which contributed to the *Tupelepele*'s emergence: "The lessening of authority has been accentuated by [...] the reduction to a skeletal state of the detachments stationed in the territories. [...] in regions where the native mentality has not yet evolved, and where it is required to act constantly on the clan or the community, these means are insufficient."[29]

The shortage of field agents in the Kwango therefore hampered the possibility for the state to affirm its legitimacy; "relations" established between functionaries and local communities were sporadic at best, if not inexistent. Further-

---

25 See: Ralph Austen, Rita Headrick, "Equatorial Africa Under Colonial Rule," in: *History of Central Africa*, vol. 2, edited by David Birmingham and Phyllis Martin (New York: Longman, 1983), 27–94.
26 AAB, RA/AIMO 190, Rapport trimestriel de l'administrateur territorial de Kikwit, first trimester 1913.
27 AAB, AIMO 1644, Lettre du Gouverneur de la Province du Congo-Kasaï au Gouverneur Général du Congo belge, 14 November 1925.
28 AAB, AIMO 1624, Présence moyenne de personnel des Territoires dans le District du Kwango. AAB, AE 3268, Rapport d'enquête sur la révolte du Kwango, 29 November 1931.
29 AAB, AIMO 1820, Commissaire General Wauters, Notes pr M. le Gouverneur de la Province, undated (1931).

more, the emotional and physical dispositions of territorial administrators and agents could also profoundly influence the state's anchoring in a given region. The scarcity of functionaries implied that indigenous communities would come to associate the colony's might and legitimacy with its individual representatives. In remote areas, agents and administrators literally *embodied* public power. Therefore, the stature, behaviours, traits of character, vigour and abilities they displayed during their rare encounters with indigenous interlocutors were crucial in determining how the Congolese would position themselves with regards to the administration's claims and demands.

The uncertain boundary separating the state and its representatives was symbolised in the expression *Bula Matari*. Meaning "the Breaker of Rocks" in Lingala, *Bula Matari* was allegedly the nickname given to Henry Morton Stanley by his porters. It would later be mobilised by Belgian functionaries to indifferently designate both the overall public power and its individual agents, highlighting how the latter personified the former.[30] Furthermore, the individualized nature of colonial rule could also be observed in the vast variety of naming patterns used by the Congolese to designate either functionaries, missionaries or European employees of private companies. Based on their recipients' appearance, behaviours and attitudes, these names "differentiated situations of oppression and exploitation each European created from those created by his predecessors, contemporaries, and successors,"[31] according to Osumaka Likaka. If territorial public servants embodied the state for the Congolese who encountered them, their varied features also determined the perception of public power.

Throughout the interwar period, the character of public servants played a key role in securing the state's footing in the Kwango district. For instance, in 1915 a new territorial administrator sent to Kikwit to replace his deceased predecessor testified to the difficulties he encountered in asserting his authority.

> Relations with chiefs and natives are far from cordial. It comes from the death of my late predecessor and of my recent arrival in the territory, during my first trip in the area [...] the village of Kumbi completely fled in the bush (village which previously provided porters to the Kikwit collectors) [...] Natives constantly answered that *Malembe* (the late Mr Simon) being dead, there was no more *Bula Matari* in Kikwit and that they no longer want one.[32]

---

30 Bogumil Jewsiewicki, "Political Consciousness among African Peasants in the Belgian Congo," *Review of African Political Economy*, 19 (1980): 25.
31 Osumaka Likaka, *Naming Colonialism: History and Collective Memory in the Congo* (Madison: University of Wisconsin Press, 2009): 60
32 AAB, RA/AIMO 190, Rapport trimestriel de l'administrateur territorial de Kikwit, 1st trimester 1916.

His recollection pointed toward both the polysemy of *Bula Matari* and the importance of individual personalities in anchoring the state in a given region. First, the passing of agent Simon appeared to have coincided with the "death" of the state as a legitimate interlocutor for Kumbi's inhabitants. Second, Simon's legitimacy as an embodiment of colonial power was directly related to his character. He was given the name *Malembe,* which could be roughly translated as "slowly" or "gently." This moniker appeared to suggest that Simon maintained relatively benevolent relations with the local communities, which in turn allowed him to build trust with them. Simon's disappearance seemed to have undercut any form of allegiance which could have linked the state to its colonial subjects.

Sixteen years later, another report underlined how the loss of an agent could hamper the overall state authority. "Territorial agent Gaspard, who benefitted of a strong influence in his territory, died six or seven months ago and territorial administrator Verbist, of fragile health, could not pursue the regular contact established with the populations,"[33] wrote the Kwango's deputy district commissioner. The existence of informal networks of trust and mutual assistance that individual public servants could build during their tenure could not be systematically reclaimed by their successors, which highlighted the personalised nature of colonial rule in the Kwango district.

Furthermore, the relational and affective guise of colonial power in the field went against the idea that functionaries had to imbue their dealings with the Congolese with a uniform sense of prestige and honour. If individual bonds of trust potentially strengthened the state's anchoring in a remote area, "inappropriate" displays of emotions could hamper the administration's claims for dominance. In early July 1931, for instance, in the midst of the *Tupelepele* uprising, territorial agent Cotton decided to leave his chief-post against the will of his superior to bring his wife "to safety" in a nearby Protestant mission. The Kwenge's territorial administrator fumed against his insubordination: "acting as such, [Cotton] provided the Blacks with another proof that the he has no interests in the state's prestige. Their return here became the object of joyful comments [...] He cannot be employed anymore in the Kwenge region."[34] General Commissioner Wauters was similarly critical: "The allegations purported on this agent shed doubt on his professional qualities and his strength of character. [...] You should not lose sight of the necessity to remove without delay the mediocre ad-

---

[33] AAB, AIMO 1820, Rapport du commissaire de district adjoint Dewilliamort, 24 June 1931.
[34] AAB, AIMO 1820, Lettre de l'administrateur territorial de Kwenge à l'administrateur territorial de Kikwit, 7 July 1931.

ministrators and agents of the colony's personnel."[35] By putting his needs before those of the state, Cotton hampered the prestige – and therefore the lasting viability – of the administration. By demonstrating that even he could not rely on the protective power of the very institution he was supposed to embody, the territorial agent bared the state's uncertain footing in the Kwango.

Isolation, vulnerability and the relational nature of colonial rule hindered territorial public servants in the pursuit of their duties. These issues could mentally burden them, which could lead functionaries to lose their composure, and endanger the supposedly firm behavioural boundary setting colonizers and colonized apart. If such breakdowns could lead to violent behaviours (see chapter 4), they could also manifest themselves in a form of apathy.[36] In 1931, General Commissioner Wauters described the general state of demotivation prevailing among the Kwango district's the territorial administration: "too many of our territorial agents perform their duties without enthusiasm. [...] The administrator gets used to limit his relations with the natives to the strict boundaries of his professional duties: tax collection, judiciary enquiries, review of the palavers brought up to him – when he has the time."[37]

The apathy of lower-ranking functionaries further impeded the already fragile grip of the administration on the Kwango district. Unsupervised and unmotivated public servants could for instance avoid to leave their chief-posts, limiting even more their contacts with both their underlings and local communities. Judge Eugene Jungers noted in his 1931 report on the *Tupelepele* uprising, "since 1925, none of the district commissioners have inspected the territories of Kikwit and Kandale. [...] This grave deficiency in the Kwango's administration must be rectified. [...] These inspections should not be limited to motorized displacements from one territory to another and to practically useless inspections of posts."[38]

The loose attitudes of public servants also led them to neglect their outer appearance, a carelessness perceived by colonial insiders as degrading the state's paramount position within the colonial hierarchy. General Commissioner Wauters noted the following in response to his observations:

---

35 AAB, AIMO 1820, Lettre du commissaire general Wauters au commissaire de district du Kwango, 21 August 1931.
36 Sandra Maß, "Welcome to the Jungle: Imperial Men, 'Inner Africa,' and Mental Disorder in Colonial Discourse," in *Helpless Imperialists*, 95.
37 AAB, AIMO 1820, Notes pour M. le Gouverneur de la Province, undated (1931).
38 AAB, AE 3268, Rapport d'enquête sur la révolte du Kwango, 29 November 1931.

> Previously, territorial chiefs presented themselves with a certain decorum; the hierarchy was well-marked, even in the eyes of the natives, made visible by the uniform. Today, what distinguishes, in the eyes of the natives, the administrator from a travelling salesman, the chief from his deputy? [...] The obligation of wearing a uniform would efficiently oppose the tendency to do "shirt-sleeves politics," [...] detrimental to our prestige.[39]

Upholding and displaying prestige through the wearing of uniforms and the strict adoption of racialized codes of conduct was one of the strategies mobilised by colonial actors to assert their claims for dominance in contexts where they found themselves vulnerable.[40] However, in the interwar Kwango-Kwilu, demotivated public servants appeared to have ignored their superiors' admonitions to display colonial prestige at all times. Not tending to themselves, remaining in the relative comfort of their chief-posts or displaying an absence of zeal in the exercise of their duties could therefore be perceived as different manifestations of colonial impotence.

These displays of impotence bridged the gap between principles and practices of colonial rule. The racial hierarchy, which acted as the organising principle of colonial societies, rested on the claim that (male) European imperialist were "capable of rational behaviour and self-control,"[41] to the contrary of colonized populations. The inability of some imperialists to rein in on their impulses therefore threatened the colonial order of things. Vulnerable agents of empire were a liability because they were incapable of behaving appropriately.[42] Impotence shed light on how some Europeans compensated for inabilities to conform to the male imperial ethos. This occurrence suggested that isolation and anxiety did not only resulted in the exercise of violence as a compensation mechanism. "Impotent" public servants kept on performing their duties, yet they acted in ways that were considered unacceptable by their superiors. This chapter's final sections delve into three examples, which illustrate such displays of impotence: fiscal practices, the so-called "prix-état" and the joined tours illegally performed by public servants and HCB recruiters.

---

39 AAB, AIMO 1820, Commissaire general Wauters, Notes pr M. le G de la Province, undated (1931).
40 Muschalek, *Violence as Usual*, 35.
41 Maß, "Welcome," 107.
42 Bisschof, "Tropenkoller," 123.

Fiscal impotence

In the field, the effective behaviours adopted by territorial agents and administrators could significantly divert from the rules and instructions supposed to guide their conduct. This discrepancy was acutely visible in three sets of practices. First, tax collection in the Kwango district remained sparse and occasional, although it embodied the state's sovereignty claims. Second, the rare encounters between functionaries and local communities did not only serve to assert the administration's might and authority. To the contrary, these encounters provided territorial agents with opportunities for prevarication, which were in direct contradiction with the "prestigious" ethos they were supposed to embody. Finally, field public servants sometimes cheated their solitude by joining forces with HCB recruiters during their tours of inspection, a practice thoroughly prohibited by their superiors.

To begin this investigation, I will first focus on taxation. On paper, territorial agents were expected to collect taxes once a year during extensive visits of the region put under their supervision. These fiscal encounters were crucial in exercising the "relational" guise of colonial power. This guise provided field functionaries with the opportunity to practice a series of other administrative acts, which both asserted the state's claims of sovereignty and furthered the administration's knowledge of local communities. Territorial agents were expected to seize these opportunities to draft censuses, update identification booklets, or deliver passports and licenses.[43] These chores amounted to almost ritualised performances of legal-rationalism, during which the state displayed both its ability and right to levy and to grant, embodied in a formalised demonstration of sovereignty.

Every year, territorial administrators had to determine tax rates, on the grounds of propositions made by their district commissioner. This exercise was the result of a difficult balancing act. On the one hand, if taxes were too high, they would become hard to collect, for villages could flee before the arrival of the tax collector (see chapter 3). The administration's inability to catch them would therefore undermine the state's "prestige" and authority. On the other, low tax rates on indigenous households implied that the colony should find other fiscal resources, mostly levied through custom tariffs. However, the author-

---

43 AAB, AIMO 1403, Lettre du GG Rutten au ministre des colonies Pécher, 23 November 1926.

ities feared that high tariffs would both boost illicit trade and force companies to relocate to other colonies.[44]

In the Kwango district, the perception of the head tax on indigenous communities was practically nil in the 1910s. This was another proof of the administration's limited hold on the region. A 1913 report on the territory of Kikwit shed a crude light on these shortcomings: "the state's occupation is derisory. [...] What could four state agents do in a region as vast as Belgium and excessively populated? [...] Native tax collection is virtually inexistent."[45] As time went by, the shortage of agents kept on impeding fiscal policies. A June 1922 report on the occupation of the Moyen-Kwango territory noted that taxes of 1921 never were collected.[46] Still, in January 1931 only 33,7% of the taxes were allegedly gathered in the district in the previous year, the lowest amount by far in the entire Congo-Kasaï province.[47] This limitation meant that accessory administrative tasks were also found wanting. During an inspection of the district in January 1931, the colony's future Governor General Pierre Ryckmans noted that the Kwango's censuses were "very incomplete. Every year, people come out of the bush for the medical prospection, who never paid taxes in their entire life."[48]

In spite of the very practical issues hindering tax collection in the district, the higher echelons of the administration expected field agents to not only pursue their duties as foreseen, but even to increase the fiscal pressure in the wake of the Great Depression. From 1929 onwards, Belgian Congo's export-based economy was hit hard by the global economic crisis. The value of its main exports, such as copper, cotton, coffee and palm oil, fell to historical lows, drying up the colony's fiscal revenues.[49] Tax rates were accordingly increased in order to compensate for these structural losses. The crushing fiscal pressure put on the Kwango district's communities would later be pointed out as having fuelled the resentment of its inhabitants against the administration, which eventually

---

44 Bas de Roo, "The Trouble with Tariffs: Custom Policies and the Shaky Balance between Colonial and Private Interests in the Congo (1886–1914)," *Low Countries Journal of Social and Economic History*, 3 (2015): 16–18.
45 AAB, MOI 3607, Enquête sur le territoire de Kikwit, 21 January 1913.
46 AAB, AIMO 1624, Rapport sur l'occupation de la region du Moyen-Kwango, 11 June 1922.
47 83,1% for the Bas-Congo, 74,3% in Léopoldville's urban district, 51,6% in the Kasaï and 52,39% in the Sankuru. AAB, AI 4739, Controverses et polémiques suscitées par les événements du Kwango, January 1931.
48 Diary of Pierre Ryckmans, entry of 10 January 1931, in *Main d'oeuvre, Eglise, Capital et Administration dans le Congo des Années Trente, vol. I*, edited by Jacques Vanderlinden (Brussels: ARSOM, 2011), 130.
49 Leigh Gardner, *Taxing Colonial Africa: The Political Economy of British Imperialism* (Oxford: Oxford University Press, 2012), 6–7.

led to the *Tupelepele* outburst. In an August 1931 report, the Kwango district assistant commissioner already pointed out excruciating taxes as a widespread grievance circulating among indigenous communities: "th[eir] increase was aimed at countering as much as possible the crisis by an increase in production and therefore of resources, for prices were lower. Making the natives understand this is not easy; the white man paying much less and still selling his goods at high price frustrates them."[50]

After the brutal "pacification" of the district by the *Force Publique* and while the excessive fiscal pressure was widely considered as one of the main causes for the uprising, the higher echelons of the administration demonstrated no leniency with regard to tax collection. To the contrary, the Congo-Kasaï's governor required his underlings to pursue their fiscal duties as thoroughly as possible, even if it required taking harsh measures against the Congolese:

> All of the territorial personnel's efforts must aim at reaching every taxpayer, even in the areas suffering the most from the crisis. One must [...] make the natives understand that they better go to work and gather the amount of money necessary to pay their taxes, rather than [...] expose themselves to the hardships of a prison regime and individual sanctions. [...] Natives who do not get used to the new prices, have to be brought to accept them. No matter what, a lack of production cannot have as a consequence to exempt them from paying their taxes.[51]

The complexity of asserting the state's fiscal prerogatives shed light on a first guise of colonial impotence. There was a clear discrepancy between the theoretical practice of tax collection and its effective enforcement, which was impeded by the skeletal nature of the Kwango district's administrative occupation. Furthermore, issues raised by territorial public servants regarding the hostility brewing among indigenous communities against extreme fiscal pressures did not demur higher ranking officials. The possibility of adapting tax rates in accordance to the overall context prevailing in the field was swiftly cast aside by the Congo-Kasaï's governor. This state of affairs pointed towards the inability for lower-ranking functionaries to effectively pursue their duties within the boundaries set by their superiors. Tax collection in the Kwango district therefore testified to the territorial administration's impotence in the sense that it could not and did not act as expected. However, if colonial impotence could take root in the structural weaknesses of the state apparatus, it also manifested itself in the attitudes

---

50 AAB, AI 4739, Relation entre la crise et la révolte, 7 August 1931.
51 AAB, AI 4739, Instructions du gouverneur du Congo-Kasaï aux commissaires de district de la province, 29 January 1932.

and behaviours employed by individual functionaries in their encounters with local communities.

Impotence and prevarication

In the chapter's opening quote, general commissioner Wauters mentions the "politic of interests" seemingly prevailing among the Kwango district's administrative personnel. This euphemism covers, among others, the drive to hoard which seems to have animated the district's functionaries. Beyond the performance of legal-rational "rituals," petty abuses indeed punctuated their encounters with the Congolese. In his November 1931 report on the causes of the *Tupelepele* revolt, judge Eugene Jungers mentioned the role played therein by "the exactions and illegalities perpetrated by some agents of the colony. Their violent methods."[52] Although strict directives commanded state agents to refrain from abusing their authority, several reports and despatches relayed how they regularly took advantage of their power to further their personal gains.

Spoliations of indigenous communities by functionaries were sufficiently widespread to alarm the colony's central authorities. In November 1926, General Governor Tilkens mentioned in a letter to the Minister of Colonies that he was "forced to acknowledge" the existence of uses of "prevarication"[53] practiced by European public servants. Among these abusive practices, the so-called *prix-état* generated a stringent series of condemnations. *Prix-état* referred to the field administrators' habit of pressuring Congolese into selling them goods or cattle at lower-than-average prices, "sometimes half of their accepted value,"[54] while presenting these forced rebates as a privilege bestowed upon public servants. This practice apparently allowed some administrators to amass significant gains. In August 1932, Tilkens wrote the following:

> The demands of some agents have sometimes overpassed their personal needs and became a truly lucrative operation. Haven't we witnessed, indeed, administrators and territorial agents constituting for themselves with the *prix-état*, herds of big and small cattle, to be resold dearly to traders and private individuals and repeat several times this operation during each of their terms?[55]

---

52 AAB, AE 3268, Rapport d'enquête sur la révolte du Kwango, 29 November 1931.
53 AAB, AIMO 1403, Lettre du GG Tilkens au ministre des colonies Pécher, 23 November 1926.
54 AAB, AI 4739, Lettre du GG Tilkens au ministre des colonies Tschoffen, 13 July 1932.
55 AAB, AI 4739, Lettre du GG Tilkens au gouverneur du Congo-Kasaï, 30 August 1932.

If "prix-état" participated to the display of might performed by functionaries in their encounters with the Congolese, they were the object of contentious interpretations. Some territorial public servants appeared to justify this practice by framing it as a mere form of gift-giving, which testified of their prominence as state representatives. This justification was swiftly cast aside by General Governor Tilkens:

> It cannot be pretended [...] that when a governmental agent arrives in a chieftaincy, the local chief comes forward, already bearing all the foodstuffs needed by the European, and that it would be insulting to refuse "his present." Everybody knows indeed that when a Black man, even a chief or an elder, brings a gift to a White man, it is to receive at least its value in exchange.[56]

Judge Eugene Jungers further argued that the Congolese only accepted the *prix-état* under pressure or menace. "It would be naïve to believe that the natives do not feel robbed by this practice. [...] they only reduce the prices under constraint."[57] Along with excessively high taxation rates, *prix-état* were believed to have contributed to the collective anger of indigenous communities in the build-up to the *Tupelepele* uprising. In June 1932, the Congo-Kasaï governor penned a long letter to the Kwango district commissioner, reiterating the need for his personnel to remain within the boundaries of legality in order to avoid a resurgence of the revolt:

> Illegalities, unfortunately performed too often [...] favour the outbreaks of resistance. [...] The European demands wood, palm wine, eggs, hens. [...] Natives have to cede their huts to new occupiers, who sometimes outnumber them. [...] Women must fetch water and prepare *chikwangues*, while they had to leave their pots and mortars and everything they usually need. [...] It is not surprising that some agents find deserted villages upon their arrival.[58]

In the eyes of governors and magistrates, *prix-état* consisted of a clear abuse of power performed by field functionaries. They were "an exploitation of the prestige of state representatives,"[59] according to Tilkens. However, their widespread condemnation did not seem to lead to their disappearance. *Prix-état* therefore pointed towards another guise of colonial impotence: misconduct. The discrepancy between principle and practices in the exercise of imperial domination was

---

56 AAB, AI 4739, Lettre du GG Tilkens au gouverneur du Congo-Kasaï, 30 August 1932.
57 AAB, AE 3268, Rapport d'enquête sur la révolte du Kwango, 29 November 1931.
58 AAB, AIMO 1855, Lettre du gouverneur du Congo-Kasaï au commissaire de district du Kwango, 9 June 1932.
59 AAB, AI 4739, Lettre du GG Tilkens au ministre des colonies Tschoffen, 13 July 1932.

not only rooted in the structural weakness of the state apparatus. It could also stem from field public servant's conscious disregard for the rules they were expected to follow. Demanding these illegal rebates allowed them to affirm their social prominence while improving their economic standing. Along with territorial functionaries' neglected outfits and the superficial way they performed their duties, *prix-état* testify of the disregard of field agents for their superiors' understanding of colonial prestige.

Impotence on tour

The neglect for rules and directives was further visible in the collaboration of territorial functionaries with HCB recruiters. Given the concurrent economic and administrative occupation of the Kwango district (see chapter 1), public servants and employees of the *Huileries* developed a habit of touring the region together from the early days of the Leverville concession, joining forces in their respective tasks: rounding up fruit cutters and collecting taxes.[60] In his 1931 report, Eugene Jungers mentioned, "territorial agent Gaspard and HCB recruiter Thys" travelled so frequently with one another that "the natives thought that the former was the assistant of the latter."[61]

Legally speaking, these practices were strictly and repeatedly forbidden. A 1916 *circulaire* prohibited territorial administrators and agents of the Kwango to be accompanied by "traders" in their tours of villages.[62] In 1924, General Governor Rutten stipulated again that it was "out of the question" that the administration would provide help to HCB by either "forcing the natives to engage or charging our agents to recruit on their behalf."[63] In a mirroring declaration, Lord Leverhulme also stipulated to Elso Dusseljé that he should not expect any kind of special treatment from the administration: "we have no right to and cannot expect the government officials to insist on the natives working for us rather than in their own villages or for other employers. It is up to us to make service so attractive that they prefer to work for us."[64]

---

60 Nicolaï, *Le Kwilu*, 319.
61 AAB, AE 3268, Rapport d'enquête sur la révolte du Kwango, 29 November 1931.
62 AAB, AIMO 1654, Rappel du commissaire de district du Kwango aux administrateurs territoriaux au sujet du recrutement HCB, 27 October 1923.
63 AAB, AIMO 1654, Lettre du GG Rutten au gouverneur du Congo-Kasaï, 5 January 1924.
64 AAB, MOI 3602, Instructions from Lord Leverhulme to Elso Dusseljé, 8 December 1923.

In the field, however, the territorial administration was regularly involved in workforce recruitment for private companies throughout the interwar era.[65] In spite of regional differences in terms of the extent to which public servants lent a helping hand to the deployment of colonial capitalism, state representatives frequently resorted to coercive and deceptive means to increase the ranks of Congolese wage labourers. Functionaries could reward chiefs who forcibly rounded up a contingent of workers, and they could endorse the signing of labour contracts with recruits who were kept in the dark regarding their rights and duties.[66] In the 1920s, territorial agents actively recruited thousands of workers for the UMHK in the Lomami region, and oversaw the drafting of their contracts in their own offices.[67] In the Province Orientale, from 1921 onwards the administration set up cotton concessions, which encapsulated both a plot of land and the villages on which they were settled. Their inhabitants were barred from offering their labour force to competitors, negotiating buying prices or cultivating other cash crops.[68] Such forms of cooperation were so frequent that they led to a formal complaint from the colony's Catholic vicars, published in the newspaper *L'Essor du Congo* in January 1929: "frequently, the intervention of the colony's agents is necessary to round up a [...] number of Blacks, brought, often against their will, to camps and factories."[69]

Public and private collaborations in workforce mobilisation demonstrated that the close collaboration between HCB and the field administration was neither unique nor exceptional. However, joint tours of tax collection and coerced recruitment were a specific iteration of this general trend, emerging at the crossroads of the concession's needs and of the existence of short-distance recruitment pools. This specific situation led to a relative tolerance from the Kwango district's authorities even after the *Tupelepele* uprising. In February 1932, the district commissioner authorised the joint performance of recruitment and tax collection in cases of force majeure: "[territorial administrators] should abstain from making their agents accompany recruiters. If they deem it absolutely nec-

---

65 David Northrup, *Beyond the Bend in the River: African Labor in Eastern Zaïre, 1865–1940* (Athens: Ohio University Press 1988), 97–100.
66 Seibert, "More Continuity," 382.
67 John Higginson, *A Working Class in the Making, Belgian Colonial Labor Policy and the African Mineworker, 1907–1951* (Madison: University of Wisconsin Press, 1989), 103–108.
68 Osumaka Likaka, *Rural Society and Cotton in Colonial Zaïre* (Madison: University of Wisconsin Press, 1997), 18–20.
69 AAB, AIMO 1644, "Une Protestation des Chefs des Missions Catholiques au sujet du Recrutement de la Main d'Oeuvre Indigène," *L'Essor du Congo*, 24 January 1929.

essary, they should establish a comprehensive and justified report, that should be transferred to me."⁷⁰

The closer we get to the field, the more apparent the disregard for the illegal nature of these collaborations becomes. This state of things can be better understood once considered in the practical context in which the act of colonising effectively took place. Several aforementioned reports and despatches allude to the isolation of public servants, particularly in relatively peripheral areas, such as the Kwango district. Colonial solitude was furthermore widely believed to hamper the mental health of public servants. "Tropical neurasthenia," its cohort of violent and "inappropriate" behaviours, were detrimental to the colonial hegemony at large, especially in regions where the state presence was still skeletal. Allowing the limited European contingents present in a region to join forces could therefore be considered a lesser evil by district commissioners keen on securing the colony's grip on hardly reachable indigenous communities. For territorial agents and HCB recruiters alike, touring villages together was a way to alleviate their solitude and offset their vulnerability outside of the relative security of their chief-posts.

These joint tours not only shed light on the room for manoeuvre that district and territorial functionaries effectively enjoyed. They also offer a window into the corruption of public servants by HCB. Several field functionaries reportedly recruited fruit cutters during their tours of inspection on behalf of the *Huileries*, even when they were not accompanied by a company employee. For instance, the Idiofa territorial administrator complained in November 1923 that "four contingents of workers"⁷¹ were sent to Leverville by his predecessor and handed to the *Huileries'* recruiter, who did not even leave his chief-post. According to Eugene Jungers' November 1931 report, such practices could be directly linked to the existence of a well-oiled, corrupt system through which HCB representatives secured the collaboration of field administrators. "At least half of the government's agents in relation with HCB are absolutely devoted to it, because of the significant advantages they receive from this powerful company, often via a special accountancy, the 'General Expenses' which purpose is to maintain a special and confidential account of these 'operations.'"⁷² Similar accusations can also be found in an internal dispatch sent by the Leverville area district manager to Lever Brothers' headquarters in August 1930, where he mentioned his predeces-

---

70 AAB AIMO 1624, commissaire général Maron au nom du gouverneur de la province de Léopoldville, au commissaire de district du Kwango, February 1932.
71 AAB, AIMO 1654, Lettre de l'administrateur du territoire d'Idiofa au commissaire de district du Kwango, 22 November 1923.
72 AAB, AE 3268, Rapport d'enquête sur la révolte du Kwango, 29 November 1931.

sor's habit of granting "gratuitous advantages"⁷³ to state officials. If bonds of informal solidarity were maintained by public and private low-ranking officials, the probable existence of a sustained system of corruption binding state and company together further highlighted the structural discrepancy between the official virtuous guise of colonial efforts in and around Leverville and their unlawful, and at times violent, enforcement.

Indeed, the recruiting of fruit cutters was not the only illegal act that could be jointly performed by HCB recruiters and territorial agents. Far from prying eyes, bolstered by the presence of their armed suite of Congolese auxiliaries and possibly inebriated, the Kwango's Europeans potentially asserted their might through the arbitrary exercise of manifold brutalities. One specific case has been particularly well documented. This case followed the visit of an HCB employee and a field public servant to the village of Kilamba on 13 May 1931. Less than a month later, territorial agent Maximilien Balot was murdered and dismembered by *Tupelepele* adepts in this very place.

According to several accounts,⁷⁴ territorial agent Burnotte and HCB recruiter Van Hombeek visited Kilamba to jointly pursue their respective duties. As it often occurred, adult male inhabitants of the village had already fled prior to their arrival in order to escape both taxation and recruitment. Van Hombeek and Burnotte therefore resorted to their usual method of retaliation, hoping this would lead to the men's return. They set up camp in the village and ordered their armed underlings to seize and detain the remaining women and to confiscate the villagers' cattle. For four days, Burnotte and Van Hombeek remained in Kilamba, living off the inhabitants' resources. They were joined every night by the manager of a nearby post of the *Compagnie du Kasaï*, Collignon. At the end of heavy drinking sessions, the men indulged themselves in the company of local women. Collignon then raped two villagers, Kizela and Kafutshi, the wives of a man named Matemo.

On 16 May 1931, Burnotte, Van Hombeek and Collignon eventually left Kilamba, freed the captured women and took ten cutters along. On 2 June 1931, Matemo went to the factory where Collignon worked to confront him with regard to

---

73 Lettre de C. Dupont à Elso Dusseljé, 21 August 1930, in Vanderlinden, *Main d'Oeuvre* (2014), 24.
74 A witness called Giawunga, interviewed by Gize Sikitele on 18 September 1970, and the results of interrogatories made by Judge Jungers during his investigation on the revolt in October-December 1931. See Gize Sikitele, "Histoire de la révolte des Pende de 1931" (PhD Diss. University of Lubumbashi, 1986), 121–126. AAB, AE 3268, Rapport d'enquête sur la révolte du Kwango, 29 November 1931.

the rape of the two women, Kizela and Kafutshi.⁷⁵ The two men engaged in a heated argument during which Collignon hit Matemo. Collignon filed a complaint against Matemo on the very same day and was quickly informed that territorial agent Maximilien Balot, on duty in the area, would soon pass by Kilamba to start an investigation.

The joint tours performed by HCB employees and territorial agents shed light on a third guise of colonial impotence: abuse. These frowned-upon collaborations stand at the meeting point of the structural weakness of the state's presence in the Kwango district and of the effective autonomy that territorial functionaries demonstrated in the exercise of their duties. They remained relatively tolerated in light of field realities, yet they provided both public and private agents with the opportunity to resolutely overpass the boundaries of their functions. Against all rules and directives, HCB employees and territorial agents could exert a regime of terror in the villages they toured. Furthermore, in direct violation of the ethical contract binding state and company together, low-ranking actors appeared to have been bound by practices of concussion. Far from demonstrating a form of "helplessness," the discrepancy between the goals and the means of colonial domination manifested itself in the resort to illegal and "dishonourable" displays of imperial might.⁷⁶

Conclusion

When the dust settled on the "pacified" Kwango district in late 1931, administrative reports on the possible causes of the *Tupelepele* revolt began to emerge. Both insiders and outsiders painted a bleak portrait of the region's state of affairs. The administration was weak, and many functionaries were deemed unmotivated, predatory, violent or downright corrupt. Private humiliations, collective spoliations, punitive tax rates and coerced recruitments fuelled the widespread resent-

---

75 For both Vanderstraeten and Jungers, the cause of Matemo's ire resided less in the rape of his wives than in Collignon's subsequent negligence to materially compensate him for indulging with them, as "Pende customs" allegedly required. However, given the overall violent context of the trio's sojourn in Kilamba, there was plausibly little consent in the sexual relations that could occur between Collignon, Kizela and Kafutshi. Explaining Matemo's behaviour towards Collignon as mainly resulting from the latter's disregard for customs overlooks the power dynamics in which in which these events took place. See Vanderstraeten, *La Révolte*, 23; Amandine Lauro, *Coloniaux, Ménagères et Prostituées au Congo belge (1885–1930)* (Brussels: Labor, 2005), 40–43.
76 Maurus Reinkowski, Gregor Thum, "Helpless Imperialists: Introduction," in *Helpless Imperialists*, 8.

ment of local populations against both public servants and concessionary companies.

These multifaceted shortcomings pointed toward a crucial aspect in the exercise of colonial rule: its relational guise. Colonizing required bringing colonizers and colonized together to assert the power of the former through elaborate displays of dignity and might.

In principle, encounters between state representatives and African "subjects" were designed to affirm the public power's primacy and singularity among the local European contingent. Functionaries were distinguishable from company employees or missionaries both by their appearance and the ritualised actions they performed. They wore uniforms embodying their prestige and manifesting their rank, and they carried out regal prerogatives such as collecting taxes, establishing censuses or delivering identity booklets. The state's claim for supremacy among colonial institutions was also materialised in its alleged monopoly on legitimate violence. Functionaries were imbued with the power to punish and repress, which was in principle strictly constricted by sets of rules and regulations.

Colonisation thus required physical contact. For Achille Mbembe, it even necessitated a "phallic" form of contact, akin it to a "coitus" granted with "the characteristic feature of making horror and pleasure coincide"[77] (see introduction). Building on Mbembe's metaphor, the phallic guise of colonialism, made visible in the physical encounters between the state and its subjects, offered a window into forms of colonial impotence. Like colonialism, impotence is inherently relational; it manifested itself through an "improper" performance during intercourse. When actors of colonialism failed to conform to expected rules, guidelines and attitudes, they displayed metaphorical forms of impotence.

Colonial impotence not only covers their inability to act, embodied in the manifold limitations that actors of imperialism encountered. It also encompasses the diverse ways Europeans made use of their leeway and autonomy to consciously disregard laws and instruction. Failing to uphold to their "prestige" by neglecting their attire or by extorting "prix-état" countered as much the virtuous guise of colonial endeavours than structurally failing to collect taxes or being too ill to perform specific duties. Conceptually speaking, impotence therefore offers a way to consider the multifaceted discrepancies between colonial principles and practices beyond the restrictive framework of "failure" and "weakness," which can only partially explain the divergences between colonialism imagined and enforced.

---

[77] Mbembe, *The Postcolony*, 175.

Furthermore, these manifestations of "colonial impotence" occurred across the Kwango, a district where the administration was unevenly distributed, as in the rest of the colony. Strategic nodes such as Leverville existed alongside villages where taxes had sometimes never been collected. Frederick Cooper has rightly pointed out that colonial power in Africa was "arterial." According to Cooper, colonial power was "concentrated spatially and socially, not very nourishing beyond such domains."[78] Administrative duties could therefore not be performed in the same way in a well-controlled enclave such as an HCB concession as in a village like Kilamba. However, public agents appeared to have held the same disregard for top-down rules and instructions in both contexts. Colonial impotence could therefore be considered as a red thread, bringing together colonial governance both within and outside of these "arteries," which are sometimes regarded as markedly different.

Impotence not only refers to a person's inability to perform their duties for a lack of means of knowledge. This idea also encompasses the person's ability to coerce and constrain outside of the framework in which those powers were bestowed. Colonial impotence encompasses the manifold ways in which empire building deviated from its expected goals, whether from powerlessness or through disobedient agency.

If impotence alludes to the limits faced by colonial actors in the pursuit of their agendas, the present chapter has only glossed over the main impediment they faced in enforcing their hegemonic longings, namely the agency of indigenous communities. The next chapter turns to the multifaceted ways the Kwango district's inhabitants avoided, made sense of and countered colonial efforts in the region.

---

[78] Frederick Cooper, "Conflict and Connection: Rethinking Colonial African History," *The American Historical Review* 99:5 (1994): 1533.

Chapter 3: Ordering and evading

Introduction

The present chapter focuses on how the autonomous actions of Congolese communities effectively hindered both HCB and the administration's ambitions, and therefore played a key part in making their respective agents "impotent" (see introduction and chapter 2). I share three case studies, which shed light on the agency deployed by indigenous HCB employees and their families to both counter and make sense of colonial demands. I first document the unsupervised mobility of fruit cutters and their families in and out of the Leverville concession. I then explore how elders attempted to deceive field public servants during official enquiries. Finally, I delve into the ways villages that provided workers to HCB harboured and propagated a forbidden animist cult. Taken together, these phenomena shed light on how inhabitants of the Kwango district both attempted to evade the grip of the *Huileries* and the state and endeavoured to bring back a form of order to social dynamics, which were profoundly disrupted by colonial demands.

In the spring of 1933, squads of colonial functionaries roamed through the villages of the Kamtsha-Lubue territory. They were on the lookout for any information related to *Lukusu*, a secretive and rapidly disseminating anti-witchcraft practice. For about twenty years, *Lukusu* spread along the waterways of the Congo basin before reaching Kamtsha-Lubue, a recruitment pool of the Leverville concession, in late 1932. For Belgian functionaries, *Lukusu* was difficult to grasp. Its goals, devices and performances seemed to be constantly morphing. *Lukusu* remained shrouded in mystery; most Congolese were reluctant to disclose any specifics about *Lukusu*'s inner workings or about the communities which had already adopted it.

Less than two years had passed since the brutal repression of the Kwango uprising when *Lukusu* was first spotted in villages which previously embraced the *Tupelepele* (see introduction and chapter 2). Public servants feared that *Lukusu* would also turn into a new millenarian revolt, which would be even more difficult to suppress than the last. In December 1932, the Congo-Kasai Governor had already stated that local communities were "only waiting for a signal, in this case the passage of large herds of wild animals or flocks of birds, to begin a bloody but victorious insurrection."[1] Therefore, for Kamtsha-Lubue's functionar-

---

[1] AAB, AIMO 1625, Lettre du gouverneur du Congo-Kasaï au commissaire de district du Kwango, 8 December 1932.

ies, locating and understanding *Lukusu* became a top priority. It required them to interrogate elders, chiefs and clan heads, their key informants for all things "traditional," which mostly remained beyond the functionaries' reach. Such investigations, however, often turned out to be fruitless. For instance, on 11 May 1933 territorial administrator Weekx questioned a "clan chief" named Manisa. Weekx asked him why his "village danced in honour of the ancestors" several nights earlier. To this query, Manisa simply replied, "we are not dancing at the moment."[2]

All across colonial empires, individuals and communities mobilised countless strategies to counter, soften or evade the grip of colonial actors. Manisa's sibylline answer could be seen as one of the many ways for those living under colonial rule to "[work] the system [...] to their minimal disadvantage,"[3] to quote Eric Hobsbawm. Avoiding directly replying to a question meant refusing to disclose information, which in turn hindered the administration's ability to survey and control indigenous communities.

This chapter focuses on three practices of indigenous communities in and around the Leverville concession to elude the demands of both HCB and the Belgian administration. First, fruit cutters and their families could settle within the concession's premises but outside of the administration grasp. By doing so, they took advantage of the diverging goals of company and state to carve up a space of relative autonomy for themselves. Second, elders, chiefs and clan heads consciously provided false information to field public servants performing ethnographic enquiries. This action allowed them to avoid the coerced displacement of their communities by the administration. Third, protean healing techniques such as *Lukusu* could be mobilised to restore a form of balance to a social order profoundly disrupted by colonialism. Far from European prying eyes, *Lukusu* also provided an opportunity for elders to partially reclaim their former paramount position.

For more than six decades, historians have endeavoured to study the ways colonized peoples attempted to counter and respond to the hegemonic longings of colonial institutions.[4] Research on what has broadly been coined as "resistance" against colonialism has, however, encountered several impediments. Frederick Cooper noted that such "resistances" have often been romanticized and idealised by scholars, which has led them to overlook their complexity, lim-

---

[2] AAB, AIMO 1625, Procès-verbal d'interrogatoire du prévenu Manisa, 11 May 1933.
[3] Eric Hobsbawm, "Peasants and Politics," *The Journal of Peasants Studies*, 1:1 (1973): 13.
[4] Klaas van Walraven, John Abbink, "Rethinking Resistance in African History: an Introduction," in *Rethinking Resistance: Revolt and Violence in African History*, edited by Jon Abbink, Mirjam de Bruijn, Klaas van Walraven (Leiden: Brill, 2003), 1.

itations and inner tensions.⁵ For Eric Allina-Pisano, resorting to the framework of "resistance" could turn the multifaceted and sometimes contradictory goals of its actors into a historically inaccurate Manichean narrative, pitting the "good" colonized peoples against the "evil" colonizers.⁶ For instance, *Lukusu* was not only a secretive way to mend the harm brought upon communities by colonialism; it was also a manner for elders to reinstate their fledging authority. Conflating all *Lukusu* adepts as uniformly engaged in a struggle against a monolithic colonial oppressor would disregard the plurality of motives and strategies pursued by different segments of local communities.

Historians' enthusiasm for "resistance" mostly led to two shortcomings. Early studies were strongly influenced by Marxism and anticolonial nationalism. These frameworks often led to simplified readings of the past, which overstated the importance and ideological coherence of violent uprisings.⁷ They also neglected the existence of more low-key and small-scale forms of opposition to colonialism, such as Manisa's uncooperative behaviour during his interrogation. From the early 1990s onwards, this strand of research was supplanted by the study of "everyday" forms of resistance, which brought to the fore how practices such as foot dragging, flight or false compliance could constitute less spectacular yet highly effective forms of struggle.⁸ In turn, the enthusiasm for the "everyday resistance" framework was not without flaws. It led to some overbearing readings, where almost any action purported by colonized individuals or communities could come to be read as a form of "resistance," neglecting again the complex and sometimes contradictory motives of the "colonized" engaging in specific behaviours.⁹

In order to avoid the pitfalls of "resistance" as a concept, some historians have resorted to "agency" to approach the scope of actions taken by individuals and communities in the wake of colonisation. Agency could be broadly defined as "the interactive response brought by different actors to the problems posed by changing historical situations".¹⁰ This angle fostered enticing research. For instance, David Gordon has shed light on forms of "spiritual agency" in Central

---

5 Cooper, "Conflict and Connection," 1552.
6 Eric Allina-Pisano, "Resistance and the Social History of Africa", *Journal of Social History* 37:1 (2003): 190.
7 Van Walraven, Abbink, "Rethinking," 32.
8 Allina-Pisano, "Resistance," 190. For example, see: James C. Scott, *Weapons of the Weak: Everyday Forms of Peasant Resistance* (Bloomsbury: Yale University Press, 1985).
9 Van Walraven, Abbink, "Rethinking," 5.
10 Mustafa Emirbayer, Ann Mische, "What is Agency?," *American Journal of Sociology* 103:4 (1998): 970.

Africa by studying how the cult of ancestors' spirits brought cohesion to different anti-colonial movements. Gordon did not consider such beliefs in the invisible world as "a remnant of tradition," but rather as "an outcome of and engagement with a particular form of modernity."[11] The ever-morphing nature of *Lukusu*, endlessly adapting to answer the needs of the communities who adopted it, could be read as form of spiritual agency, stemming from the brutal confrontation of the Congolese with colonial modernising agendas.

Hence, scholars have long demonstrated that people were never passively "colonized," but rather deployed their agency in countless ways to limit and oppose imperial attempts at domination. I do not intend to rehash these already proven points; instead, I use displays of indigenous agency as a way to study the inner functioning of colonialism in the interwar Kwango district. The previous chapter approached colonial impotence as the discrepancy between the behaviours expected from and performed by Europeans in the field. This chapter sheds light on how the actions of the Congolese "made" colonial actors impotent.

Studying the ways indigenous communities attempted and managed to avoid colonial hegemonic goals also allows me to make two further points. First, it contributes to reveal different fracture lines running through the Kwango district. Rather than suggesting that socially homogeneous groups of "colonizers" and "colonized" opposed each other, these case studies shed light on the inner tensions perceptible across these broad categories. On the one hand, the unsupervised settlement of fruit cutters and their families within the Leverville concession but outside of their designated chieftaincies served the HCB's interests against those of the state, leading in turn to tensions between both institutions. On the other hand, the secrets of *Lukusu* were shared within circles of elderly initiates who did not hesitate to monetize their knowledge. Monetizing rituals allowed them to improve their social and economic standing at the expense of their own communities.

When these three case studies are read alongside the previous chapter, similarities appear in the strategies put in place by both Europeans and Congolese to find their footing in the colonial order of things. Elders, fruit cutters, HCB recruiters and territorial agents alike seemed to have devised makeshift strategies to secure their position in an environment they perceived as hostile and uncertain. Initiates who mastered *Lukusu*'s secrets rituals managed to amass money by diffusing the practice, while some territorial agents built small fortunes through the

---

[11] David Gordon, *Invisible Agents: Spirits in a Central African History* (Athens: Ohio University Press, 2012), 3.

practice of *prix-état*. In a similar fashion as territorial agents embellishing their reports in order to preserve their own freedom, elders refused to provide information that the administration could use to curtail their autonomy. These observations echo Florence Bernault's study of the "transactional" nature of colonialism in Gabon. According to Berhault, "proximate, conversant and compatible imaginaries" existed across the racial divide, alongside countless forms of (im)material exchanges tying up both groups together.[12] The present study suggests that not only imaginaries but also practices could echo one another. Far from the orderly private utopia engineered by Lord Leverhulme (see chapter 1), the interwar Leverville concession and its hinterland thus appear as marred by uncertainty and competition.

Eluding control: the *villages doublures*

This section sheds light on how the Leverville concession's business model unexpectedly led to the emergence of informal settlements called *villages doublures* and to unsupervised migrations of fruit cutters and their families.[13] These were specifically consequences of palm oil production and hampered the strict control that the administration endeavoured to hold over both villages and the movements of the Congolese. In the meantime, these arrangements were beneficial for HCB, for they ensured the presence of workers close to its palm groves without costing much to the company. The emergence of *villages doublures* testified to the fruit cutters' ability to use the contradictory goals of public and private actors in order to improve their social and economic standing.

Contractually speaking, the Leverville concession's palm oil workers were divided into two categories: fruit furnishers and fruit cutters. Fruit furnishers originated from the concession area. They were not formally employed by HCB and were free to pluck oil palms on their own lands and to sell palm fruits either to oil companies or to private individuals in local markets.[14] However, this workforce was far from sufficient to sustain HCB's raw material needs. The *Huileries* therefore had to rely on an influx of contractual workers recruited in neighbouring territories.[15] Officially designated as fruit cutters, they were hired to provide

---
12 Bernault, Colonial Transactions, 5–7.
13 This section is based on Benoît Henriet, "'Elusive natives'": Escaping Colonial Control in the Leverville Oil Palm Concession, Belgian Congo, 1923–1941," *Canadian Journal of African Studies*, 49:2 (2015), 339–361.
14 AAB, AIMO 1855, Note sur les fournisseurs de fruits au Kwango, 25 November 1941.
15 Nicolaï, *Le Kwilu*, 338–339.

HCB with 200 crates of palm fruit, each weighing around 35 kg, for their contracts to be fulfilled. Cutters came predominantly from the Gungu territory, which was located South of Leverville. This area was more populated, had fewer palm trees than the lands allotted to HCB. Fruit cutters' engagement brought them far from home, for they had to cover a distance ranging from 50 to 150 kilometres to reach the palm groves they had to harvest. At the end of each month, these workers were paid in accordance to their productivity. The company was obligated to take their housing, feeding and medical care in charge, as well as providing them with a machete and blankets for the time of their employment (see chapter 5).[16]

Fruit cutters usually settled for a limited time inside the groves, living in makeshift villages which they built without giving any notice to the territorial administration. Fruit cutters' temporary relocation in the concession was also not covered by the mandatory "mutation passport," which all Congolese were obligated to fill out should they have to reside outside of their designated chieftaincies for more than a month.[17] Furthermore, cutters often did not travel alone; relatives usually accompanied them to the Leverville concession to work as aides or cooks (see chapter 6). New recruits settled in the same spots as the cutters who had fulfilled their contracts and were thus being replaced.[18] As these temporary villages became permanent places of residence, their inhabitants began to grow food crops and to raise cattle.[19] Administrators had to coin a new term to designate these hamlets born out of the labour needs of the Leverville concession; they became known as *villages doublures*. This neologism alluded to the fact that they represented a "doubling" of the workers' home villages nested in the concession.

It is not possible to assess with complete accuracy the number of people who temporarily resided in *villages doublures*, for statistical evidences are both patchy and often unreliable. According to 1934 statistics, approximately 11000 fruit cutters were hired every four months to work in Leverville. Given that most of them were accompanied by at least one aide, this meant that in 1934 up to 66000 individuals moved between the concession and their homes, spend-

---

[16] AAB, AIMO 1855, Contrat d'engagement coupeur de fruits HCB, September 1923.
[17] *Recueil à l'Usage des Fonctionnaires et des Agents du Service Territorial au Congo Belge* (Brussels: Weissenbruch, 1930), 232–233.
[18] AAB, AIMO 1855, Lettre de l'Assistant-Administrateur Moulin, 25 July 1934.
[19] AAB, AIMO 1856, Lettre du Gouverneur Général au Chef de la Province du Congo-Kasaï, 20 April 1938.

ing a few weeks or months in the *villages doublures*.[20] Although these figures might be exaggerated, it is certain that thousands of men, women and children travelled in and out of the concession without any form of administrative supervision during the interwar.

Villages doublures became a major object of concern for colonial authorities, for two predominant reasons: 1) they were located outside their inhabitant's chieftaincies; and 2) they were populated by families of varied origins. On paper, each indigenous community of rural Belgian Congo belonged to a chieftaincy, a territorial unit placed under the guardianship of a *chef médaillé*. These authority figures were designated by the territorial administration, and were appointed in principle on the grounds of "local customs."[21] Their key position as representative of the state and depository of "traditional" authority was symbolised by the awarding of a medal, from which they took their name. *Chefs médaillés* were expected to relay and enforce the administration's demands; for instance, they might facilitate tax collection, guaranteeing the public order and providing workers for compulsory labour.[22]

If the effective power of territorial agents greatly fluctuated according to their health, character and embeddedness in local networks (see chapter 2), the authority and legitimacy of *chefs médaillés* likewise depended on the circumstances. The duties purported upon them by the administration had little to do with the roles that "Big Men" played in Central Africa prior to colonization.[23] Whereas villages heads were expected to be concerned with their community's prosperity, colonial chieftainship was mostly responsible for extracting wealth and precious labour force from the community at the benefit of an outer power. If some *chefs médaillés* managed to answer the administration's demands, often through the mobilisation of coercion, others were frequently punished by territorial administrators for failing to fulfil their obligations.[24]

However, by temporarily settling outside of their chieftaincies, fruit cutters and their aides effectively avoided the grasp of their *chefs médaillés*. Given that the obligations binding chiefs and their "subjects" supposedly rested on the precedents of tradition, they did not fall under authority of the local desig-

---

20 AAB, AIMO 1855, Lettre du commissaire de la province de Léopoldville A. de Beauffort au commissaire de district du Kwango, 5 April 1934.
21 "Décret sur les chefferies et sous-chefferies indigènes," *Congo Belge: Bulletin Officiel 1910*, (Brussels, Hayez, 1910), 460–461.
22 Léon Strouvens, Pierre Piron (ed.), *Codes et Lois du Congo Belge* (Brussels: Larcier, 1958), 769.
23 See: Vansina, *Paths*, 73–81.
24 Robert Eugene Smith, "Les Kwilois Parlent de l'Epoque Coloniale," *Annales Aequatoria*, 26 (2005), 168–175.

nated chief when they resided in the concession.²⁵ They were thus able to avoid their fiscal and labour duties and were also out of reach for screening and vaccination campaigns (see chapter 5).

Movements between the cutters' homes and *villages doublures* were not high in number or regularly occurring, but rather spontaneous and happening on an individual basis. Some people settled in the groves for a few days, while others lived there permanently. These villages sheltered its inhabitants from the grip of the state, which seemed to have played a major part in their attractiveness. In June 1937, the Kwango District Commissioner estimated that at least half of the men living there did not work for HCB.²⁶ Furthermore, administrative supervision seemed to have been unwelcomed by their inhabitants. A report from the same year mentioned that when territorial agents attempted to visit some *villages doublures*, most inhabitants had already fled prior to their arrival.²⁷ In September 1939, it was reported that some cutters would even deliberately slow down their work pace in order to "postpone, as long as possible, the moment when they would have to reintegrate their territory."²⁸

In the eyes of the administration, *villages doublures* also led to a worrisome increase of the Leverville concession's "ethnic" diversity. The dangers arising from perceived intermingling of workers of diverse origins in enclaves of strategic importance was a common concern for Belgian Congo's employers. In the 1920s, the *Union Minière* for instance struggled to respond to the emergence of "voluntary associations" among its cosmopolitan workforce. These informal support groups gathered workers of the same origin and merged class- and identity-based solidarities, which potentially threatened the company's hegemonic designs.²⁹

The administration initiated several strategies to defuse such dangers. Chieftaincies and mutation passports were partly aimed at clearly separating so-called "ethnic groups" and limiting their contacts with one another. Dividing communities on the grounds of what state actors believed to be clearly defined and separated "ethnic identities" was also aimed at preventing the "traditional order" from crumbling under the weight of colonial transformations. For in-

---

25 AAB, AIMO 1856, Rapport sur la question des villages doublures dans les cercles des HCB, 13 April 1937.
26 AAB, AIMO 1856, Lettre du Commissaire de District H. Vandevenne au Chef de Province de Léopoldville, 9 June 1937.
27 AAB, AIMO 1856, Rapport du FOREAMI sur les villages-doublures du Kwango, 1937.
28 AAB, AIMO 1855, Lettre du Commissaire de District assistant F. Peigneux au Chef de Province de Léopoldville, 7 September 1939.
29 Higginson, *A Working Class*, 79–85.

stance, some customs were deemed to be necessary to uphold a form of morality in rural areas, including regulating marriage, kinship and sexual behaviours.[30] Public servants feared that once fruit cutters were isolated from their home community, they would be keener to engage in "inter-ethnic" relationships. Authorities feared that these relationships would foster a general state of "debauchery" in the palm groves, encouraging polygamy and unplanned pregnancies. By way of example of this phenomenon, a 1923 letter from the colony's Governor General mentioned the risk that *villages doublures* would shelter "stray wives," who had fled their homes in neighbouring chieftaincies.[31]

Unlike the administration, HCB representatives were satisfied with the emergence of *villages doublures*. "They provide a […] fortunate solution to the issue of fruit cutters' housing. […] Their atmosphere is more favourable to the Black than the atmosphere of an artificial camp, even one equipped with all sanitary facilities. There, the native keeps his crops, his usual diet and the majority of his traditions,"[32] wrote the company's General-Administrator in 1937. Technically speaking, these spontaneous settlements were not officially considered as workers' camps. Therefore, the company did not have to provide costly medical and social care to their inhabitants (see chapters 1 and 5).

Villages doublures were a prime example of an unexpected symbiosis between the interests of actors who would, at first sight, appear to be contradictory. Territorial agents complained that fruit cutters escaped the administration's supervision thanks to the company's complacency, as HCB managers did practically nothing to report the illegal settlements mushrooming in their concession.[33] A March 1937 letter, written by a medical officer to the colony's General Governor, suggested that the "greatest freedom" fruit cutters allegedly enjoyed in *villages doublures* was the company's "best propaganda" to attract potential workers.[34] By effectively sheltering fruit cutters and their aides from the administration's demands, Leverville's management seized the opportunity offered by local com-

---

30 Amandine Lauro, "'Une Oeuvre d'Étaiement et de Reconstruction'. Notes sur la Fabrique du Droit Coutumier, le Pouvoir Colonial et l'Ordre du Mariage dans Le Congo Belge de l'Entre-Deux-Guerres." In *Droit et Justice en Afrique Coloniale: Traditions, Productions et Réformes*, edited by Bérengère Piret (Brussels : Presse de l'Université Saint-Louis, 2013), 180.
31 AAB, AIMO 1856, Lettre du gouverneur général du Congo belge M. Rutten au gouverneur de la province du Congo-Kasaï, 11 octobre 1923.
32 AAB, AIMO 1856, Lettre de l'administrateur-général des HCB E. Dusseljé au gouverneur général, 1 February 1937.
33 AAB, AIMO 1856, Lettre du chef de province A. De Beauffort au commissaire de district du Kwango, 30 July 1936.
34 AAB, AIMO 1856, Lettre du médecin-directeur du FOREAMI au gouverneur général, 18 March 1937.

munities' mobility and desire to escape the state's grip to improve the concession's fledgling productivity.

Villages doublures shed light on an interesting paradox resulting from the commodification of "unscalable," naturally-growing products by colonial capitalism. The administration's efforts to "stabilize" African workers and their families came to grips with the need for some companies to rely on the very mobility of their workforce to reach and harvest primary resources. Tensions arising between HCB and public authorities were not unique. For instance, logging companies in interwar French Equatorial Africa also needed to secure a steady flow of transient workers between rainforest camps and villages. It came to grips with official policies endeavouring to "stabilize" workers in a fixed place, where they could be optimally supervised.[35]

Furthermore, the existence of such makeshift arrangements testified to the limited viability of the plans devised in Brussels and Port Sunlight to "virtuously" manage the concession (see chapter 1). Leverville's power of attraction resided more in the relative shelter it provided from the state than in its ambitious paternalism. Field circumstances and indigenous agency shaped the course of the concession's history, perhaps even more than Lord Leverhulme's dreams of building a tropical utopia on the shores of the Kwilu River (see chapter 1).

Deceiving public servants

The spontaneous and unsupervised circulation of fruit cutters in and out of *villages doublures* was not the only form of migration related to the foundation of the Leverville concession. The Kwango district's administration and HCB's management also envisioned displacing entire communities closer to the *Huileries*' palm groves in order to answer the company's ever-pressing need for workers.[36] On paper, it was strictly forbidden to forcibly remove Congolese from their home territories to accommodate the economic demands of private actors.[37] Public servants nonetheless saw how such plans could also serve the state's interests. They thought that clustering communities together close to economic centres such as Leverville and based on the grounds of their shared "ethnicity" would simultaneously make them easier to supervise and improve the district's eco-

---

[35] Clotaire Messi Me Nang, *Les Chantiers Forestiers au Gabon. Une Histoire Sociale des Ouvriers Africains* (Paris: L'Harmattan, 2014), 220–223.
[36] This section is based on Benoît Henriet, "Des Ethnographes Anxieux: Pratiques Quotidiennes du Pouvoir au Congo Belge, 1930–1940," *Vingtième Siècle*, 140:4 (2018): 41–54.
[37] *Recueil à l'Usage des Fonctionnaires et des Agents du Service Territorial*, 1925, 66–67.

nomic output. However, these schemes relied on the collaboration of elders. They were deemed to be the only ones who knew enough of the history of their community to provide the administration with the necessary information for regrouping clans who were thought to originally belong together. Elders, in turn, took advantage from their pivotal position to deceit state investigators in order to prevent the inception of these forced migrations.

In the interwar, colonial powers all over sub-Saharan Africa commissioned numerous studies on the cultures and histories of the communities they sought to rule. They were mostly carried out by civil servants with no prior background in ethnography.[38] One of the main objectives underlying the collection and "rational" classification of this data was to adapt general laws and directives to local contexts.[39] Belgian Congo encompassed a vast array of pre-existing polities, each characterized by different organizing principles, forms of power and logics of legitimacy. Better understanding the "customs" which presided over their organisation was crucial to ensure their incorporation in the colonial order.

This official ethnography also sought to alleviate the administrations' anxiety. Many state actors feared that a brutal dismantling of "traditional" institutions would foster political instability and be detrimental to colonial authority.[40] From the early 1920s onwards, functionaries from the Kwango district observed harbingers of this menace in the alleged intermingling of diverse "ethnicities" in the field. A territorial administrator almost poetically described the district's social organisation, which he compared to "a conglomerate of heterogeneous fragments, hybridized by contacts and infiltration, [...] like the detached leaves of a felled tree, scattered by the winds in all directions."[41]

This metaphor evoked a widely-held belief in Belgian Congo's administrative circles. Many functionaries envisioned pre-colonial Africa as having been divided between large and "ethnically homogeneous" polities, which held almost no relation to each another. It was believed that these communities came to be fragmented with time, leading to the stratification of Central Africa into smaller and increasingly interwoven groups. In the eyes of the administration, customary leaders therefore lacked authority and legitimacy, which hampered their crucial role as potential *chefs médaillés*. Such readings of the continent's past were er-

---

38 Marc Poncelet, *L'Invention des Sciences Coloniales Belges* (Paris: Karthala, 2009), 95–97.
39 Poncelet, *L'Invention*, 584.
40 Nancy Rose Hunt, "Colonial Medical Anthropology and the Making of the Central African Infertility Belt," in *Ordering Africa: Anthropology, European Imperialism and the Politics of Knowledge*, edited by Helen Tilley and Robert Gordon (Manchester: Manchester University Press, 2007), 252–255.
41 AAB, AIMO 1599, "Les Bambala, Bangongo, Bahungana," undated.

roneous. To quote Sara Berry, African societies were "changing and dynamic," and have always been characterized by "fluid and ambiguous"[42] differentiations, far from the rigid identities imagined by colonial public servants. However, to answer this alleged issue, Minister of Colonies Louis Franck encouraged from 1921 onwards the creation of "great chieftaincies," where one paramount chief invested by the administration would rule over a large community built out of scattered groups deemed to share the same "ethnicity."[43]

In June 1932, more than ten years after the inception of the "great chieftaincies" scheme, the Congo-Kasai governor ordered a string of surveys aiming to "better understand the origins, traditions, customs, tribal organization and kinship ties uniting neighbouring groups, the founders of clans and tribes, and the succession of chiefs."[44] Territorial public servants were ordered to be on the lookout for linguistic, cultural, organizational or "racial" similarities between the communities they visited. They were instructed to interview elders, chiefs and clan heads to sketch out collective genealogies and trace back the "origins" of these "fragmented" communities. When the "original" identity of a group was "scientifically" established, the administration could plan its regrouping with its long-lost "ethnic" fellows under the allegedly legitimate authority of a paramount chief.[45]

Once regrouped, these great chieftaincies could also be settled in strategic areas, such as the Leverville concession and its immediate hinterland, in order to optimize their economic output. Many administrators believed that each "ethnic group" possessed specific aptitudes and talents, which could be potentially put at the service of the colonial economy. A March 1932 report, for example, stated that "the Bahungana are blacksmiths," while "the Batsamba [are] specialized in the extraction of iron ore and its smelting."[46] While some communities had indeed developed sophisticated metallurgy techniques, such generalizations reflected a lack of understanding of the complexity of their social structures. Smelters were, for instance, an elite group of initiates who did not share the se-

---

[42] Sara Berry, "Hegemony on a Shoestring: Indirect Rule and Access to Agricultural Land," *Africa*, 62 (3), 1992, 330–331.
[43] Loffman, *Church, State*, 119–124.
[44] AAB, AIMO 1855, lettre du gouverneur du Congo-Kasaï au commissaire du Kwango, 9 June 1932.
[45] AAB, AIMO 1855, lettre du gouverneur du Congo-Kasaï au commissaire du Kwango, 9 June 1932.
[46] AAB, AIMO 1856, Problèmes de glissement de populations vers les palmeraies Kwenge du Kwilu, 29 March 1932.

crets of their craft with the rest of their community.⁴⁷ However, essentialist beliefs in the conflation of aptitudes and "ethnicity" partially determined where regrouped "great chieftaincies" would be settled. In the Kwango district, HCB and the territorial administration tried for instance to move Bapende communities from their home territory of Gungu towards the Leverville concession, for they were considered to be specifically gifted at cutting palm fruits.⁴⁸ In these enclaves of concentrated European presence, they would also remain within the administration's reach, which would ease their taxation, medical supervision and mobilisation for compulsory labour (see chapter 2).

Figure 5 illustrates these initiatives and shed light on their scope. It is a reproduction of a sketch from a 1932 aborted project, which sought to displace several villages inside of the Leverville concession. The arrows mark the migration routes that neighbouring communities would have taken towards the areas delimited by numbered rectangles, located either in the heart of the concession's palm groves or close to HCB outposts such as Leverville and Kwenge.

Before organising the displacement of villages, public servants were required to retrace the origins of the targeted communities, in order to bring an "ethnic" coherence to these schemes. Their enquiries focused especially on the genealogy of their ruling dynasties and the recouping of their migratory movements. Territorial agents sometimes alluded in their report to the existence of legendary long-lost kingdoms to which the Kwango's inhabitants would have originally belonged. An undated report on the "origins of the Bambala and Bangongo" mentioned "a powerful kingdom on the west coast, which must have occupied vast areas, from which most of the clans that invaded [...] the entire Kwango district seem to have originated."⁴⁹ According to its author, the origin of these scattered communities could be traced back to the "*Masanji* kingdom*," thought to have crumbled under the pressure of slave raids, invasions, exodus, "usurpation of authority" and "interbreeding with refugee groups."⁵⁰

The vague output of these ethnographic enquiries reflected the difficulty of collecting reliable data in the field. Elders, chiefs and clan heads were indeed reluctant to act as the administration's informants. The territorial administrator of Bas-Kwilu noted in 1935 that "the natives are so afraid of being regrouped together [...] that they do everything they can to make their stories differ from one

---

47 See Zoé Strother, "Eastern Pende Construction of Secrecy," in *Secrecy: African Arts that Conceals and Reveals*, edited by Mary Nooter (New York: Center for African Art, 1993), 156–178.
48 See Henriet, "'Elusive Natives'", 350–355.
49 AAB, AIMO 1599, "Les Bambala, Bangongo, Bahungana," undated.
50 AAB, AIMO 1599, "Les Bambala, Bangongo, Bahungana," undated.

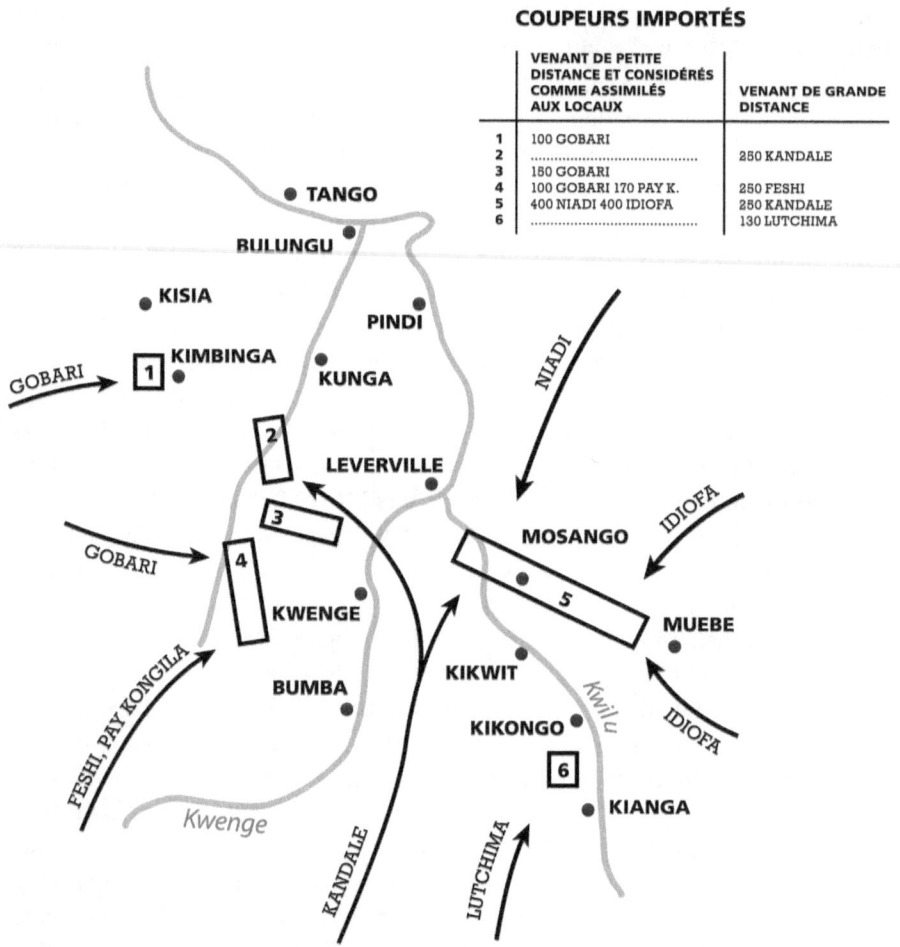

Figure 5: Annotated map envisioning village displacements, AAB, AIMO 1856, map by Iris Vandevelde 1932

another."⁵¹ Similar practices regularly occurred when indigenous authority figures faced colonial administrators' need for data. For Sara Berry, African informants of colonial public servants often "[took] advantage of the interest of officials in traditions by providing information that is favourable to them."⁵²

---

51 Archives of the Bandundu Province, Bandundu (APB), M. Wilsens, "La peuplade des Bayenzi," Territoire du Bas-Kwilu, rapport d'enquête, 1935, cited in Smith, "Les Kwilois", 168–169.
52 Berry, "Hegemony," 334.

Ultimately, the administration's ethnographic surveys did not lead to large-scale, organised migrations. The government's inability to collect valuable data on indigenous histories, customs and traditions shed light on the manifold limits of imperial ambitions. Congolese communities retained a significant advantage when functionaries inquired into their social and political organisations. Omitting or concealing information was a powerful tool to concretely counter the hegemonic aspirations of colonial authorities.

The aborted creation of "great chieftaincies" offers crucial information on the power dynamics at play in the interwar Leverville concession and its hinterland. First, it testifies to the widely-held belief by European actors, public and private alike, that their endeavour was to bring order where chaos used to prevail. The Leverville concession was envisioned as a way to introduce an efficient and paternalist form of capitalism on the shores of the Kwilu river, bent on both righting the wrongs of the Free State, and on rationally exploiting the region's profuse palm groves (see chapters 1 and 6). Similarly, failed attempts at building great chieftaincies endeavored to reinstate long-lost "customary" polities while optimally inserting them in the colony's economic and administrative order. The ultimate inability of both actors to fulfil these goals once again sheds light on the multifaceted limitations of colonial ambitions.

Second, the collaborations at play in this population regrouping scheme were markedly different than those emerging in the wake of *villages doublures*. The former relied on the existence of shared interests between HCB and the administration, while the latter brought to the fore how the *Huileries* could come to shelter its workers from the state's grip. The existence of simultaneous and yet contradictory migration strategies supported by HCB demonstrated how the supposed "order" that colonialism would bring to the Kwango district effectively materialised in a series of makeshift plans. One of the few common features shared by *villages doublures* and population regrouping were their illegal nature. It was forbidden for the Congolese to settle outside of their chieftaincies without the administration's assent, as much as it was forbidden to forcibly displace villages to accommodate the needs of private companies. However, such schemes either took place or were thoroughly considered. Rules and laws could be side-lined in the effective deployment of colonial order in the interwar Kwango district.

Third, the conspicuous choice of indigenous informants to deceive public servants illustrated their pivotal role as potential enablers of colonialism. The administration's effective weakness in the Kwango district implied that territorial functionaries could hardly resort to force or constraint to pursue sovereign prerogatives such as collecting taxes or upholding the public order (see chapter 2). *Chefs médaillés* were envisioned as a network of trusted relays within local communities who could enforce the state's decision while ensuring their legitimacy thanks to the aura of "customary" authority they supposedly held. However, guaranteeing the articulation of rural communities to the colonial order of things necessitated a thorough knowledge of their inner workings. In the case of forced collective migrations, elders used their position as information brokers to prevent villages from being forcibly displaced. If they occasionally acted as a protecting force, they could also take advantage of their privileged status to reinstate their authority.

Lukusu and sense-making

The emergence of *Lukusu* in the Kamtsha-Lubue territory brought field functionaries to interrogate the elders again in order to understand and suppress what appeared to be a potentially seditious movement.[53] As in the case of village displacements, most of these reluctant informants consciously attempted to cloud the issue rather than to enlighten administrators. Maintaining the secrecy surrounding *Lukusu* was necessary to ensure its potency and its ability to regenerate a social order brought upside-down by colonialism. However, this action also allowed the elders, economically and politically marginalised in the colonial hierarchy, to secure or improve their social standing.

The anti-witchcraft and healing practice of *Lukusu* was first mentioned by colonial observers in and around Kamtsha-Lubue in 1932 after spreading along Central African routes for over two decades.[54] *Lukusu* constantly morphed along its journey, gaining new attributes, rites or qualities as it passed from one community to the next. The diffusion of *Lukusu* in the Kwango district, for instance, coincided with the inclusion of a basket containing one or several snakes to its rituals. The snakes were thought to be the mouths through which ancestors' spirits would speak to their descendants.[55]

The sustained diffusion of *Lukusu* over large stretches of Central Africa testified to the infinite plasticity of "traditions" in the region, highly adaptable and translatable in rapidly changing settings.[56] This very plasticity made such heal-

---

[53] This section is based on Henriet, "Facing," 219–241.
[54] Jan Vansina, "Les mouvements Religieux Kuba (Kasaï) à l'Époque Coloniale," *Etudes d'Histoire Africaine* 11 (1971), 162.
[55] Jan Vansina, "Lukoshi/Lupambula: Histoire d'un Culte Religieux dans les Régions du Kasaï et du Kwango (1920–1970)", *Études d'Histoire Africaine*, 5 (1971), 63–64.
[56] Terence Ranger, "The Invention of Tradition in Colonial Africa," in *The Invention of Tradition*, edited by Eric Hobsbawm and Terence Ranger (Cambridge: Cambridge University Press, 1983), 247.

ing movements a potential counter-force against colonialism. Their constantly changing nature made them difficult to locate, describe and contain by European forces, marking the limits of the state's effective power.

Lukusu would become widely adopted because of the existence of a shared repertoire of cultural practices among the societies of the Congo basin. Communities believed in the restorative power of *bwanga* such as *Lukusu*. *Bwanga* were "spiritual medications," which required absorbing certain combinations of substances and strictly avoiding a series of taboos. Made from mineral, vegetal, and animal ingredients, a *bwanga* materialized the influence of spirits in the visible world. According to Wyatt McGaffey, its efficacy did not rely on the medical properties of its components, but rather on "material metaphors," whereas each ingredient was culturally linked to the powers attributed to the spirit it represented.[57] Taboos mirrored the metaphoric elements of the charm. By avoiding specific foods and behaviours, the follower put themselves into a relation of similarity with the spirit active in the *bwanga*.[58] Along the trade routes and waterways of Central Africa, *bwanga* circulated and morphed among populations with similar or connected cosmogonies.[59] Villages and clans were pervaded by the same anxieties—fear of sickness and barrenness, of curses and witches—and were receptive to the same answers to their woes. Within and across cultural clusters, variants appeared in the narrative of a new *bwanga*, allowing it to be widely adopted. The protean nature of *bwanga* eased its adaptation by communities who could invest different meanings in the same symbols.[60]

Spirits have long played an active part in the historical dynamics Central Africa. They could both either guarantee the stability of the social and political order, or they could disrupt it, mostly by enabling the evil doings of *ndoki* (witches).[61] *Lukusu*, and the promises it carried of answering the personal and collective woes of indigenous communities through the benevolent intervention of ancestors' spirits, could be seen as a way for Congolese men and women to explain and to solve the dramatic changes they witnessed in their everyday lives.

Asking for the intervention of ancestors' spirits allowed Congolese communities to both make sense of and attempt to counter their encroachment by colonial forces. Spiritual revivalism under colonialism could take a violent guise,

---

57 Wyatt MacGaffey, *Kongo Political Culture: The Conceptual Challenge of the Particular* (Bloomington: Indiana University Press, 2000), 84.
58 Wyatt MacGaffey, "Fetishism Revisited: Kongo "Nkisi" in Sociological Perspective," *Africa* 47, 2 (1977), 174.
59 MacGaffey, *Kongo Political Culture*, 74.
60 Vansina, "Lukoshi/Lumpambula," 89.
61 Gordon, *Invisible Agents*, 10.

such as during the *Tupelepele* revolt of 1931 (see introduction and chapter 2). However, in many cases, engagements with the invisible world attempted to restore a form of balance to a social order profoundly disrupted by the demands of colonial public servants, companies and missionaries. These dynamics could be observed all over colonial Africa, where the collapse of precolonial social order was "filled by an upsurge of crisis cults based on spirit possessions, as if to reconstitute a nostalgic past,"[62] according to Klaas van Walraven and John Abbink.

At its very core, *Lukusu* remained an anti-witchcraft practice, a way to detect those using "the power of words and thoughts" to hurt others.[63] It had to be adopted by entire villages, children included, to ensure that hidden sorcerers exerting the dark arts on their peers would not escape detection.[64] All of the cultural clusters in which the *bwanga* spread shared a collective anxiety about the existence of *ndoki*, hexing their relatives out of jealousy for their prosperity or fertility.[65] *Lukusu* provided a cure for communities marred by "spiritual insecurity," where nightmares, sickness, unexpected deaths and barrenness were read as the visible results of dark magic.[66] A 1933 enquiry on *Lukusu* alluded to ad hominem accusations of witchcraft that could only be dismissed by the ritual absorption of the *bwanga*. Interrogated on 26 May 1933, "clan chief" Bongo-Betshy was required to justify his rationale for adopting *Lukusu:*

> Q: Why did people take the *bwanga* [...] in your village?
>
> A: It's Koie, Kimpata's village chief, who wanted us to take the *Lukusu*.
>
> Q: What were his motives?
>
> A: Koie accused us of killing people with spells, to seize their belongings. It is because we killed people he said, that we have a lot of money. If you don't drink the *Lukusu,* I will consider you to be witches.[67]

---

62 Van Walraven, Abbink, "Rethinking," 37.
63 John Janzen, "Ideologies and Institutions in Precolonial Western Equatorial African Therapeutics," in *The Social Basis of Health and Healing in Africa*, edited by John Janzen and Steve Feierman (Berkeley: University of California Press, 1992), 196.
64 Vansina, "Mouvements Religieux Kuba," 156.
65 Peter Geschiere, Cyprian Fisiy, "Domesticating Personal Violence: Witchcraft, Courts and Confessions in Cameroon," *Africa* 64, 3 (1994), 324–24.
66 Filip de Boeck, "Être un Danger, Être en Danger: Exclusion et Solidarité dans un Monde d'Insécurité Spirituelle," in *Sorcellerie et Violence en Afrique*, edited by Bruno Martinelli, Jack Bouju (Paris: Karthala, 2012), 85–88.
67 AAB, AIMO 1625, P.V. d'interrogatoire du prévenu Bongo-Betshy, 26 May 1933.

The same day, another man, Katshinga, provided similar answer to the investigator:

> A: We took *Lukusu* because we were accused of being sorcerers [...]
>
> Q: You knew very well that the State was opposed to *Lukusu*, why did you break the rules?
>
> A: We were accused of sorcery. What else could I do?[68]

Bwanga such as *Lukusu* were first and foremost designed to regenerate the social body by cleansing families and clans of witchcraft from "the frightening notion that there is hidden aggression and violence where there should be only trust and solidarity."[69] In the cases of both Bongo-Betshy and Katshinga's, the taking of *Lukusu* appeared to be immediately linked to accusations of participation to occult practices. For the former, the charge was somehow substantiated by his relative wealth, thought to have been extracted at the expense of his "victims."

If *Lukusu* was a collective endeavour, passing from one village to another, elders played a central role in its diffusion. A community desiring to adopt the *bwanga* had to send a delegation of elders to a neighbouring agglomeration that had already accepted it. An initiate – *capita bakumu* – would then visit the village of the demanding party and provide *Lukusu* to a group of elders, teaching them how it should be prepared.[70] Only then could *Lukusu* begin its proper adoption by the whole community, as related in a confidential note from October 1932:

> The candidate steps over the bell which is placed on the ground; he then sits on his ankles and turns his back on the bell, which is placed underneath him. Then, the *capita bakumu* approaches the back of the candidate, armed with a double-edged knife and mimics twice to strike him on the top of his head; then, he comes in front of the candidate and makes him swallow a pinch of the *bwanga*, before the candidate rises up and steps over the bell backwards.[71]

According to Mulende, a witness interrogated on 26 May 1933, *Lukusu* was accompanied by the following taboos:

> Those who took *Lukusu* are forbidden to eat bananas or any other fruit, or the *ngai-ngai* vegetable (guinea sorrel), should kill and eat white hens and goats, [...] one should not have sexual relations with his wife during the day. When it rains, the wife must leave

---

68 AAB, AIMO 1625, P.V. d'interrogatoire du prévenu Katshinga, 26 May 1933.
69 Geschiere, Fisiy, "Domesticating Personal," 324.
70 Vansina, "Mouvements religieux Kuba," 167.
71 AAB, AIMO 1625, Note sur le Nkisi Lukoi ou le serpent qui parle, 22 October 1932.

the bed and squat down next to it while the husband remains in bed; women are not allowed to cook in the village; it is forbidden for men to look at women as they cook, if a woman is cooking and it starts to rain, she must stop immediately and throw everything on the ground, [...] those who took *Lukusu* must not wear anything of white colour. Finally, when everyone has taken *Lukusu*, we can eat again all the forbidden meals.[72]

The efficiency of a *bwanga* was thought to depend on the strict following of taboos, for they established a direct relation between the charm and those who benefitted from it. The types of requests detailed above were consistent with the behaviours known to have been attached to other *bwanga*. Indeed, they often prescribed different rules for men and women, commanded sexual abstinence and enumerated dietary restrictions. By sharpening gender differences and ordering the followers to adopt behaviours markedly dissimilar from their daily conduct, taboos fostered an auspicious social dynamic in which magic could occur. Initiate's attitudes regarding consumption and relations highlighted and enhanced their difference with non-initiates, thereby strengthening their relationship with the *bwanga*.[73]

As early as January 1933, territorial officials of the Kwango received the first information on the diffusion of a *bwanga* whose characteristics echoed those of *Tupelepele*. Its rapid expansion and enigmatic nature would encourage officials on the ground to redouble their efforts to identify and arrest its propagators, thus containing the threat of a new rebellion. Between April and June 1933, an official investigation conducted by the administration targeted the elders in particular, perceived as both prime informants and potentially the secret leaders of *Lukusu*.

However, these enquiries ended in failure. On 1 May 1933, territorial agent Mons wrote to his superior: "No one around me wants to inform me [...] I have made many arrests [...] nobody says a word."[74] The provincial attorney general complained the same month about the inability for officials to gather information: "Interrogation transcripts often mention the things that were said, what the elders said that they wanted, without making a sufficient effort to investigate beyond the vagueness of such declarations. These 'elders' need to be named. We can act against individuals, but not against abstractions."[75]

---

[72] AAB, AIMO 1625, P.V. d'interrogatoire du témoin Mulende, 26 May 1933..
[73] Wyatt MacGaffey, "African Objects and the Idea of Fetish," *RES: Anthropology and Aesthetics* 25 (1994): 128–29.
[74] AAB, AIMO 1625, Lettre de l'agent territorial Mons à l'administrateur territorial de la Kamtsha-Lubue, 1 May 1933.
[75] AAB, AIMO 1625, Lettre du procureur général au commissaire de district du Kwango, May 1933.

As observed in the case of ethnographic data collection, elders managed to counter public servants' thirst for information. Some attempted to conceal their reluctance to cooperate, such as "Chief Gamineye," "showing excessive subservience, which does not prevent him from providing us with false information," according to a May 1933 report.[76] Others simply denied any involvement in *Lukusu*, as illustrated by this exchange between territorial administrator Gustave Weekx and "group leader Okubongo": "You claim not to know the reason for the introduction of *Lukusu*? – I assure you that I do not know."[77] Ultimately, interrogations and monitoring of cultural practices provided little comfort to the administrators. "We live in uncertainty," wrote the Kwango District Commissioner in May 1933 mentioning the "complete silence"[78] of their informants on *Lukusu*.

If the intenion of *Lukusu* was to regenerate social bodies by expelling the malevolent forces acting from within, it also allowed senior initiates to enhance both their social and economic status. The sharing of healing rituals among older, high-ranking men was not uncommon in Central Africa. John Janzen showed how *Lemba*, corporate groups of prominent *nganga* (healers) present for centuries in Lower Congo, was only accessible to the wealthier elements of their community, who were paid for their services.[79] Similarly, all of those who took *Lukusu* had to pay beforehand, possibly half a franc for a child and two francs for an adult.[80] In October 1932, a territorial administrator even claimed to have seized the impressive amount of "1300 francs" gathered during initiation rituals.[81] Incidentally, elder initiates who financially benefited from *Lukusu*'s diffusion were among those marginalized inside the colonial economic and political rationales for two main reasons.

The first reason was that the state made wages in cash mandatory in 1910 to ensure that the Congo could generate its own fiscal revenues (see chapter 2).[82] This system excluded the elders in principle from the monetized economy, for they were physically unable to make a living using their labour force. Second,

---

[76] AAB, AIMO 1625, Rapport hebdomadaire sur la marche de la promenade militaire effectuée dans la région "Kamtsha," 11 May 1933.
[77] AAB, AIMO 1625, Procès-verbal d'interrogatoire du prévenu Okubongo, 20 May 1933.
[78] AAB, AIMO 1625, Lettre du commissaire de district du Kwango au gouverneur du Congo-Kasaï, 29 May 1933.
[79] Janzen, "Ideologies and Institutions," 204–10.
[80] AAB, AIMO 1625, Note sur le Nkisi Lukoi ou le serpent qui parle, 22 October 1932
[81] AAB, AIMO 1625, Contribution à l'enquête sur la secte secrete Lukoshi, par l'administrateur territorial Jalhay, 16 October 1932.
[82] "Rapport du Conseil Colonial sur le projet de décret réglant le louage de services et le recrutement de travailleurs," in *Congo Belge: Bulletin Officiel 1910* (Brussels: Hayez, 1911), 680.

elders also lost political prominence in the colonial hierarchy. In precolonial Central Africa, villages tended to be comprised of a council of clan heads who played a significant role in communal decision making.[83] To the contrary, colonial chieftainship only recognized individual "chiefs" as legitimate interlocutors, thereby side-lining these pre-existing collective institutions. In *Lukusu*, however, only high ranking elders could become *capita bakumu*, which enhanced both their prestige and economic standing.[84] The prominence of the older generations in *Lukusu* did not escape the notice of the Belgian administration, as the struggle to contain and erase it essentially took the form of a repressive campaign targeting the local elite.[85]

The diffusion of *Lukusu* sheds light on the multifaceted nature of indigenous reactions to colonialism. "Resisting" did not only mean countering or escaping the most pressing demands of European forces, but also attempting to respond to the havoc from colonialism in Central Africa. Political hierarchies were redesigned by the creation of chieftaincies, economic structures by the introduction of wages and taxes, societies by the mores and values that the state, companies and missions sought to promote. As with other healing movements, *Lukusu* attempted to bring a form of clarity and metaphysical soothing to distressed communities by easing the benevolent agency of their ancestors' spirits. Its power of attraction resided in its healing promises, rather than in any rallying potential against colonial power.

To conclude, state agents' attempts to contain and suppress *Lukusu* illustrates once again the crucial role played by elders in the colonial order. They were both key informants and potential adversaries for the administration. Furthermore, their pivotal position somehow mirrored the ambiguous role played by the Leverville concession's management, simultaneously acting as enablers and inhibitors of the public power, according to their own strategic interests. *Lukusu* demonstrated once more the multiple social fracture line traversing the Kwango district in the interwar.

Conclusion

Although disparate at first sight, *villages doublures*, failed planned migrations and *Lukusu* appeared to share two overarching, common characteristics. First,

---

[83] Vansina, *Paths*, 78.
[84] Vansina, "Mouvements Religieux," 167.
[85] For more information on the targeting of elders during the repression of Lukusu, see: Henriet, "Facing," 230–234.

they all alluded to forms of evasion from the grips of the colonial administration. Second, they testified to the attempts pursued by different social categories to bring order to a hostile and uncertain environment.

Villages doublures were a way for fruit cutters and their relatives to evade state control by temporarily settling in the Leverville concession. The elders' ability to withhold information when interrogated both contributed to the derailment of the displacement of villages and shielded *Lukusu* from the prying eyes of public servants. These forms of evasion were neither simultaneous nor coordinated. They did not form a consciously planned strategy to counter colonial longings for hegemony. However, once considered together, they testified to the ability of local communities to set up a variety of obstacles, which, once aggregated, significantly hindered the anchoring of the colonial state in the Kwango district. James C. Scott resorted to the metaphor of a "coral reef" to qualify how the multiplication of "everyday" forms of resistance could organically coalesce and, in time, significantly impede colonial power.[86] In and around Leverville, flight, deceit and secrecy significantly contributed to building such a "coral reef," partially sheltering indigenous communities from colonial encroachment.

To another extent, the displacement of villages and *Lukusu* served to bring order and security to communities marred by a feeling of vulnerability and uncertainty. From the beginning, the Leverville concession was fantasized as the utopian rational ordering of allegedly chaotic "tropics" (see chapter 1). Planned migrations materialised this will to "order" the shores of the Kwilu River. They were seen as a way to both reinstate long-lost "legitimate" authorities under administrative oversight and to improve the concession's economic turnout. At the same time, *Lukusu* was also a way for indigenous communities reluctantly implicated in the making of the "virtuous" concession to find a form of stability. It allowed invisible forces to play a more active and benevolent part in everyday life and helped to reinstate former elites in their paramount positions. Florence Bernault mentioned the existence of a "conversant imaginary" shared by European and indigenous communities in colonial Gabon. In and around the Leverville concession, plans and practices alluded to a diagnosis shared by Europeans and Congolese alike of a chaotic world in dire need of being mended and organised, a social field where solidarities were fluctuating. Key informants were potential foes, and allies could very well pursue diverging goals.

Those individuals pursuing order and certainty in an attempt to secure their social standing mostly relied on makeshift strategies, such as illegal planned mi-

---

86 James C. Scott, "Everyday Forms of Resistance," *The Copenhagen Journal of Asian Studies*, 1:4 (1989): 49.

grations, informal settlements, or infusing specific meanings into a protean healing practice. However, better understanding these displays of agency requires paying attention to the broader, violent context in which these practices of flight and ordering took place. The Leverville concession and its hinterland were characterized by a multifaceted brutality. This history will be presented in the next chapter.

Chapter 4: An indescribable ugliness

The general aspect of Leverville is one of indescribable ugliness. [...] Leverville is not an attractive place to be in. It is 600 miles from a telegraph office, on a small river with no passing traffic except HCB; but it happens to be one of the wealthiest areas of Elais palm trees in the world. The life of a white man in one of these places must be terrible beyond words.

Diary of T.M. Knox, 23 November 1924.[1]

Introduction

In late 1924, Lord Leverhulme paid one final visit to "his" HCB concessions. He was accompanied by his personal secretary, T.M. Knox, who noted his own impressions of Congo in a private diary. The entry of 23 November – cited above – contained a dreadful depiction of Leverville. Under Knox's pen, the *Huileries*' crown jewel became a remote and alienating eyesore, where the "social life [...] must at any rate become dangerously similar to that at the school of Mr Perrin and Mr Traill,"[2] a reference to a 1911 novel about bitter rivalries between teachers in an isolated Cornish public school. Knox was not the only person to experience Leverhulme's tropical utopia as a claustrophobic enclave. In November 1931, for instance, judge Eugene Jungers urged the colony's authorities to "investigate what happens behind the philanthropic façade showed to distinguished guests, the two splendid hospitals of Tango and Leverville and the magnificent brick-walled camps, exposed to the river banks."[3] For Jungers, the concession's hidden, "ugly" side was made visible in a "village of imported workers [..] so miserable, so disgusting that I can say that I have never seen anything similar in the twenty years I spent in the Congo. [...] The Blacks occupying these huts are living like animals."[4]

Both Knox and Jungers described the concession as a toxic environment, fostering tensions or dissimulating its dark inner workings under a thin layer of virtuous paternalism. Knox's allusion to the "ugliness" of Leverville referred to its unpleasant appearance and forsaken location, yet it also provided a relevant entry point to approach its *metaphoric* ugliness; the endemic brutality that Jungers more openly mentions. The dire living conditions of fruit cutters indeed tes-

---

1 UA, UAC 2/34/4/1/1, Diary of T.M Knox, 23 November 1924.
2 UA, UAC 2/34/4/1/1, Diary of T.M Knox, 23 November 1924.
3 AAB, AE 3268, Rapport d'enquête sur la révolte du Kwango, 29 November 1931.
4 AAB, AE 3268, Rapport d'enquête sur la révolte du Kwango, 29 November 1931.

tified to the structural violence of Leverville, which relegated a segment of its reluctant workers in disparaged hamlets. It could also be manifest in the company's brutal recruitment campaigns, when fruit cutters were forcibly rounded. Furthermore, HCB's business model was also inherently violent. Although Leverville's paternalism was designed to attract voluntary workers, the company resorted to coercing male recruits and illegally relied upon women and children for heavy manual labour. The commodification of palm fruits was also supervised by a chain of intermediaries, who often took advantage of their privileged position to extort goods, money and (sexual) services from HCB workers.

In this study of the multifaceted violence of Leverville, I focus on forced recruitment, hidden labour and abuses of power. Taken together, they testify to the brutality implemented to bring the "utopian" vision of the concession to life (see chapter 1). Furthermore, these three case studies highlight the continuities between violent practices in the Congo Free State and in Leverville. Even if HCB was destined to pioneer benevolent ways of extracting Congolese natural resources, it still made use of the Free State's brutal exploitation models, such as coerced recruitment and reliance upon a network of abusive intermediaries to oversee the fruit cutters' daily activities.

This chapter approaches violence from both bottom-up and top-down perspectives. On the one hand, there is a focus on a series of Congolese actors, such as sentries, messengers and *capitas*, who were in charge of ensuring the daily functioning of palm oil production. These agents infused the concession's inner workings with violence, both to increase the company's productivity and to their own benefit. On the other hand, the chapter sheds light on the ever-present, structural character of Leverville's violence, which is visible in the concession's resorting to exploiting women and children for burdensome tasks, such as porterage, from which they were legally exempted.

The many faces of colonial violence

In recent years, scholars of colonialism have paid more attention to daily guises of colonial constraint. Historians have argued that the inherent brutality of colonialism could take many forms, and be as much present in corporeal punishment as in the strategies put in place to coerce indigenous communities to work, pay their taxes or be vaccinated (see chapters 2 and 5).[5] The concurrent

---

5 See for instance the special issue of *Vingtième Siècle* on everyday colonial policing in Africa, edited by Romain Tiquet: *Vingtième Siècle*, 140:4 (2018).

existence of individual and collective forms of constraint, simultaneously occurring at both macro and micro levels, testify to the structural violence of modern imperialism.⁶

Studying forced recruitment, female and child labour and individual maltreatments not only contributes to making sense of the Leverville experience; it is also crucial to reframe the concession's brutal idiosyncrasies in their broader historical continuum. For Raphaëlle Branche, violence occupies a crucial place in the history of colonialism. According to Branche, violence is a constant feature of mankind's history, but it espouses specific forms, motives, justifications, targets and objectives in different settings. Paying attention to the particular forms taken by given expressions of violence, studying their fluctuations in space and time provide precious information on the unique fields of tensions at play in a given historical object.⁷ In the context of interwar Central Africa for instance, traumas fostered by the brutality of colonial conquests pervaded the further stages of imperial histories, morphing along with time and circumstances.⁸ If one considers colonial violence in the broader spectrum suggested by Branche, it becomes easier to understand how exactions similar to those perpetrated in the Congo Free State could still occur within the "virtuous" structure of Leverville (see introduction and chapter 1). Similarly, Nancy Rose Hunt also evoked how the traumas inherited from the Free State kept on pervading the daily life in former rubber concessions of the Equateur province. According to Hunt, the private colony's violence still "bled into post-Leopoldian [milieus], through imagination, ongoing traffic, and the reproduction of capital and extraction."⁹

As I previously illustrated, concessions such as Leverville constitute nodes of strategic importance in the colonial canvas (see introduction and chapter 2). Such enclaves were characterised by a greater concentration of institutions, infrastructures and European agents than other parts of Belgian Congo. For Jean-François Bayart, these very nodes, which can include mines, missionary outposts, plantations and hospitals, constitute privileged observation spots of the mundane guise of colonial violence.¹⁰ Studying protean displays of brutality and constraint in Leverville can therefore serve three intertwined purposes. First, as underlined by Branche, it offers precious information on the specific power dynamics at play at a micro-historical level. Second, it connects these unique

---

6 Samuel Kalman, "Introduction: Colonial Violence," *Historical Reflections*, 36:2 (2010): 1.
7 Raphaëlle Branche, "La Violence Coloniale: Enjeux d'une Description et Choix d'Écriture," *Tracés* 19 (2010), 31.
8 Branche, "La Violence," 35.
9 Hunt, *Nervous State*, 31.
10 Bayart, "Hégémonie et Coercition," 127.

forms of brutality to the structural nature of colonial violence. In the present case, it lays bare the continued existence of Leopoldian exacting practices in the interwar. Third, it contributes to a clearer understanding of how colonial power was enforced in its strategic enclaves.

To close this lengthy introduction, I invite the reader to consider whether the metaphor of "ugliness" is the most appropriate way to characterize Leverville's protean brutality. I am not the first to propose correlating these terms in the context of Central African history. Pedro Monaville has described the reminiscences of colonial violence in Congo as a "distinctive ugliness," one that continues to fester in Belgian collective memories.[11] In the case of Leverville, "ugliness" seems particularly relevant to speak of the grimness of the concession, as well as to shed light on how this violent guise was intrinsically conjoined to its seemingly virtuous ambitions (see chapter 1).

The epigraph from T.M. Knox at the start of the chapter also alluded to the "indescribable" nature of Leverville's "ugliness." Knox was referring to the impossibility of conveying with words the hopelessness oozing out of this assemblage of corroded industrial plants and ramshackle accommodations. However, pursuing the metaphoric reading of his diary entry, "indescribable" could also speak of the difficulty of documenting and accurately depicting Leverville's violence. Public and private archives related to the concession are often silent on coercive practices. When they mention forms of brutality, they often remain shrouded under a veil of vagueness. For instance, strategies of forced recruitment become "the method of authority"[12] under the pen of interwar public servants. Furthermore, oral enquiries I performed in the former Leverville concession mostly brought to mind distant memories of violence, distorted by time, nostalgia and the passing of direct witnesses. My oldest interlocutors were young children in the interwar, who possessed only vague reminiscences of Leverville's inner workings, mostly passed on by now deceased relatives. Many of the individuals invoked *chicottes*, prison cells and constraint when they spoke of HCB. However, even these recollections did not stop them to recall the concession's heydays as a bygone era of prosperity. "Labour was forced to some extent, it wasn't good, but it was for our own sake,"[13] Pemba Dimamaso shared with me. He then was the director of what remained of Leverville's palm oil mills in 2015.

---

11 Pedro Monaville, "A Distinctive Ugliness: Colonial Memory in Belgium," in *Memories of Post-Imperial Nations: The Aftermath of Decolonization, 1945–2013*, edited by Dietmar Rothermund (Cambridge: Cambridge University Press, 2015), 58–75.
12 AAB, AIMO 1652, Situation de la main d'oeuvre dans le cercle de Lusanga des HCB, 1931.
13 Pemba Dimamaso (b. 1961), 4 August 2015, Lusanga.

The profound intertwining of violence and "virtue" in collective memories of Leverville was perhaps best embodied in the following painting (figure 6). Since 1989, it has adorned the walls of the *Cercle Elaeïs*, the now-derelict private club of senior Unilever workers in Lusanga, the former Leverville. This composite work illustrated various aspects and actors involved in the mobilization of HCB workers. On the left stand an administrator and a messenger, coercing a worker to climb a tree by lighting a fire at its roots. In the background, a policeman and another messenger are trying to catch a runaway worker. On the right, a company agent—distinguishable from the administrator by his white garment—distributes rations of *makayabu* (salted fish). He is probably accompanied by a *Coastman*, a West African clerk, who is recognizable by his striped loincloth and black blazer.

Figure 6: Mural by Sissi Kalo, Cercle Elaïs, Lusanga, 1989. Picture taken by the author.

The artist was called – or more likely nicknamed – Sissi Kalo, and was commissioned to decorate the company's offices with a series of paintings. This strikingly brutal reminiscence of the past was chosen to brighten up a room dedicated to after work socialization and pleasant activities for the labour elite of the *Plantations Lever au Zaïre* (PLZ), the name taken by HCB between 1971 and 1997.

This image shares many common motifs with other depictions of colonial times in Congolese "popular painting." From the 1970s onwards, naïve portraits as well as historical scenes painted by artists with no formal training became a regular fixture in the living rooms of the Zairian middle-class.[14] Representations of the colonial past were in high demand in the pictorial repertoire of popular painters. These paintings mostly shared a series tropes and archetypes – a juxtaposition of disjointed events in a single frame – with a main scene consisting of the public flogging of a man by an African soldier under the supervision of a European official. Used and re-used by many urban artists, the visual recollection of colonial times tended to take the shape of public torture and humiliation.[15]

Some of these common elements are present in Sissi Kalo's mural; the flogging with the administrator smoking a pipe, which can be read as a manifestation of detachment;[16] and the enacting of violence by an African intermediary. However, the main contrast between this oeuvre and the colonial archetype of popular paintings is the representation in the very same scene of HCB's paternalism, symbolized by the distribution of rations (see chapter 5). Decades after the *Huileries*' colonial business schemes were abandoned, Leverville remained alive in local memories as a place where violence and "benevolence" were concurrent and coexistent. Let us now turn to the first guise of the concession's "ugliness": its coercive recruitment practices.

Violent recruitment

This section sheds light on the effective strategies put in place by HCB and state agents to overcome the reluctance of Congolese men to work as fruit cutters. Forced recruitment was officially outlawed in Belgian Congo, and ran contrary to the virtuous objectives of Leverville. However, the concession faced a structural shortage of voluntary recruits, which hindered its profitability. A series of ad-hoc arrangements emerged to coercively round up HCB workers. This trend arose from the discrepancy between Leverville's moral and economic objectives. However, most archives tend to euphemise the effective forms of unfree labour existing in Leverville. This strategy, which created a discursive gap between the exercise of violence and its paper trails, could be conceptualised as a form of lexical

---

[14] Bogumil Jewsiewicki, "A Century of Painting in the Congo: Image, Memory, Experience and Knowledge," in *A Companion to Modern African Art*, edited by Gitti Salami, Monica Blackmun Visonà (New York: John Willey and Sons, 2013), 338.
[15] Tom Turner, "Images of Power, Images of Humiliation: Congolese "Colonial" Sculpture for Sale in Rwanda," *African Arts*, 38:1 (2005): 70.
[16] Turner, "Images of Power," 61.

distancing.¹⁷ It allowed both field agents and their superiors to appear to respect legal boundaries, while they effectively engaged or condoned illegal forms of recruitment.

It remains difficult for today's observers to accurately describe the forms of coercion exerted on potential HCB recruits in Leverville. Instructions given to company representatives in the field were often contradictory. Vague words such as "propaganda," "(moral) constraint," "intervention," and "method/policy of authority" regularly appear in administrative despatches touching on the recruitment of Leverville workers. Authors of administrative reports and despatches penned vague instructions and accounts of their activities, allowing sufficient space for interpretation by their recipients as to avoid explicitly condoning or instigating illegal practices. These strategies were by no means limited to the interwar Kwango-Kwilu. To the contrary, they belonged to the coercive arsenal of colonial actors throughout Africa. For instance, Frederick Cooper noted how "the carefully chosen words" of field administrators in late 1930s Ivory Coast failed to paint an accurate picture of the practices of constraint effectively used to mobilize workers.¹⁸

In Leverville, such lexical distancing was found in both top-down instructions and bottom-up reports. First, superiors of field agents could lecture their underlings on the importance of respecting legality when enlisting workers, employing vague and sometimes contradictory turns of phrases. This strategy gave much leeway to HCB recruiters or field public servants when they had to enforce their superiors' instructions. For instance, this manifest ambiguity was present in an April 1928 letter from Minister of Colonies Jaspar to Governor General Tilkens, in which Jaspar relayed to Tilkens Leverville's chronic shortage of fruit cutters:

> The report of the consultative committee underlines [...] that recruitment of workers can only be performed in a context of freedom; it admits, on the other hand, the necessity of administrative propaganda to bring the natives to collaborate to the country's *mise en valeur*.
>
> This intervention will never take the form of constraint, even moral, and will remain therefore in the domain of a general propaganda in favour of wage labour and its advantages for the natives. Nonetheless, it does not exclude indications, and even advises, in favour of private companies [...].

---

17 Emmanuel Blanchard, Joël Glasman (2012), "Le Maintien de l'Ordre dans l'Empire Français : une Historiographie Emergente", in *Maintenir l'Ordre Colonial. Afrique et Madagascar (XIXe-XXe siècles)*, edited by Jean-Pierre Bat, Nicolas Courtin (Rennes: Presses Universitaires de Rennes, 2012), 30. Branche, "La Violence", 38–40.
18 Frederick Cooper, *Decolonization and African Society. The Labor Question in French and British Africa* (Cambridge: Cambridge Univeristy Press, 1996), 81.

> This propaganda in favour of labour should be considered as a social and moral duty, and is for the administration and especially for the territorial service, an essential and permanent obligation. [...]
>
> A period of transition is necessary during which the intervention of the territorial service, at least of its subaltern agents, can be exerted in a more direct manner, in favour of recruitments which, by their ends and methods, justify the government's benevolence.[19]

While asserting the necessity of freedom in recruitment, the minister left the door open for the effective constraint of workers. He did so by first neglecting to specify the precise meaning "propaganda" and, more critically, by envisioning a "period of transition," where "persuading" recruits could go beyond merely advertising for private employers. Furthermore, the minister suggested that African intermediaries ("subaltern agents") such as *chefs médaillés*, soldiers, and messengers could take the burden of such "persuasion" on their shoulders, as they did in Sissi Kalo's painting.

Other despatches also floated the idea that a "transition period" was necessary to familiarize the Kwango communities with wage labour. In a December 1931 letter to the *Huileries'* Director-General, the Commissioner-General of Congo-Kasai – the right-hand of the provincial governor – evoked the future "suppression of the *policy of authority* that your company had to follow until recently" (my emphasis).[20] A similar euphemism appeared in the same year under the pen of senior public servant and future General Governor of Belgium, Pierre Ryckmans, in a report on labour conditions in Leverville: "during the successive openings of its sectors in the Kwilu, HCB applied the *method of authority* for the recruitment of their personnel, the only possible one with the extremely primitive races populating their concession."[21] These documents condoned forced recruitment as transitory and unavoidable, yet they did not remark upon how or why it was practiced.

Second, bottom-up reports of field agents to their hierarchy also contained vague admissions of participation to coercive recruitments. In a report to the Kwango district commissioner in August 1923, for instance, the territorial administrator of Feshi – one of the company's recruitment pools – wrote that the "natives of the territory have never been constraint to go to the HCB" while nevertheless mentioning a few lines later that "there has certainly been a bit of

---

[19] AAB, AIMO 1644, Lettre du ministre Jaspar au GG Tilkens, 30 April 1928.
[20] AAB, AIMO 1856, Lettre du commissaire général Wauters au directeur général des HCB, 31 December 1931.
[21] AAB, AIMO 1652, Situation de la main d'oeuvre dans le cercle de Lusanga des HCB, 1931.

moral constraint: gifts to chiefs, description of the advantages of workings for HCB..."[22]

If reports and dispatches remain astoundingly silent on the precise nature of "propaganda," "authority" or "constraint," other documents were more explicit. Destined for a private audience, or written by individuals unrelated to either the administration or the company, they could shed a much-needed light on what recruitment effectively meant for those who had to perform them, and they mostly painted an unflattering picture of the involvement of territorial public servants. In the letters that Ryckmans wrote to his wife Madeleine during his 1931 visit to Leverville, he mentioned the confessions of a missionary that he chose to leave out of his final report: "he declares that people only engage because the territorial agent accompanies the recruiter. [...] that the territorial personnel is, if not bought, at least intimidated; convinced that anyone who does not go along with HCB will be displaced – conviction, one again, based on experience" (on the participation of territorial public servants to HCB recruitment, see chapter 2).[23]

Furthermore, the report penned by judge Eugene Jungers after the *Tupelepele* revolt (discussed in chapter 2) explicitly mentioned "the resort to violence of colony agents and chiefs acting on behalf of the recruiters." According to the magistrate:

> Recruitment, after fifteen years of existence of HCB, only occurred in the Kandale territory through the direct constraint by state agents, administrators, or chiefs acting on the recruiters' behalf in exchange for gifts [...] The territorial administrator was required to provide the amount of men requested by the district commissioner, who determined the quota – it is the word he used – to be provided by each territory.[24]

Paul Raingeard de la Bletière, a French doctor in charge of vaccination campaigns by the colonial administration, also published a vitriolic attack in 1932 against the labour practices of palm oil companies in the Kwango district.[25] Some of his more stringent criticism concerned the role of territorial agents: "recruitment and compliance to the employment contract are ensured by prison

---

22 AAB, MOI 3602, Lettre de l'agent territorial de Feshi au commissaire de district du Kwango, 9 August 1923.
23 Lettre de Pierre Ryckmans à Madeleine Ryckmans, 15 January 1931, in Vanderlinden (ed.), *Main d'Ouvre*, 142.
24 AAB, AE 3268, Rapport d'enquête sur la révolte du Kwango, 29 November 1931.
25 Paul Raingeard de la Bletière, "La Main d'Oeuvre au Kwango," *Revue de Médecine et d'Hygiène Tropicale* 24 (1932): 21–48.

and chicotte, generously distributed by state agents, who lowered themselves at the role of […] of the companies' own tormentors."[26]

Furthermore, I could also find memories of coercive labour practices in interviews I conducted in the summer of 2015 in the former Leverville concession. Christophe Mwazita, a retired cutter whose father worked for the company at the end of the interwar, recalled, "the white man needed a lot of people, boys and cutters, you were not asked to work, you had to go. The first thing that happened to you when you arrived at Leverville was the *chicotte*, to discipline you. […] the white man did not administer it himself, it was the role of the policemen, the white man only gave the instructions".[27] For Gaston Willia Fetsi, an elderly cutter, "recruiters got in touch with the village chief, who selected the teams that had to go. He sent away the stubborn, and the state 'took care' of them: they received the chicotte, were thrown in a cell, had to pay a fine and then had to go work for the company."[28] For Fabien Kalaki, who was born in the early 1930s, "at the beginning, the men refused recruitment and fled into the forest. […] The chief was involved; he pursued the fugitives in the forest to catch them. [He] was sometimes invited to Leverville to be paid according to the number of recruits he sent there."[29] Jean Ndeke Lutanda shared, "when labour was forced, workers were chosen by the village chief, who designated those who already knew how to cut."[30]

These memories mostly highlight the crucial role played by indigenous leaders in the recruitment process. European actors – be they HCB employees or public servants – only appear as undifferentiated entities such as "the state" or "the white man." The distortion of time, and the fact that all of these testimonies were either second hand or childhood memories, partially explained why chiefs, as the everyday personification of authority, left a more profound imprint on my interlocutors than territorial agents and recruiters, who only occasionally visited their communities. The *chicotte* was a key element in recollections of colonialism. Whipping was one of the most common sanctions exerted in Belgian Congo, which explains its central role in visual depictions of the colonial past.[31] State agents were uncertain that other forms of punishment, such as incarceration, were efficient and effectively understood as such by the Congolese.[32]

---

26 Raingeard de la Bletière, "La Main d'Oeuvre," 38.
27 Christophe Mwazita (born 1946), camp Kalamba, Lusanga, 4 August 2015.
28 Gaston Willia Fetsi (born 1923), camp Avion, Pindi, 6 August 2015.
29 Fabien Kalaki (born 1933), Ifwani – Kakobola, 10 August 2015.
30 Jean Ndeke Lutanda (born c. 1940–1945), Ifwani – Kakobola, 10 August 2015.
31 Bayart, "Hégémonie et Coercition," 141–143.
32 On the resort to the *chicotte* by administrators, see Dembour "La Chicote," 205–225.

Discourses on the inevitability of coercion to stimulate recruitment are profoundly entrenched in another key element of the colonial rhetoric: the supposed lazy atavism of African men.[33] "No one will question that the native prefers to happily vegetate in his village, making his wife or wives do the work, rather than accepting, in exchange for a salary, a difficult work in mines, oil mills, factories or plantations,"[34] stated the explanatory note appended to a revision of the colony's labour legislation. The alleged unwillingness of the Congolese to engage in wage labour was perceived as a sufficiently serious threat to Congo's economic health to be countered by harsh measures, even if it became necessary to circumvent colonial ethics. "Freedom to be lazy is not considered everywhere as absolute and by wanting to allow it as such, no matter the contingencies, we risk undermining the country's position in the global economic struggle, which becomes fiercer every day,"[35] wrote General Governor Rutten to Minister of Colonies Houtart in 1926. Five years later, while visiting Leverville, Ryckmans also expressed that "the adoption of a regime of true liberty would imply the immediate closing of the factories."[36]

Private and public authorities were ambivalent about coercion in the recruitment of HCB fruit cutters. Its existence was known, considered to be problematic; partially forbidden but still practiced, and more or less tolerated. This was justified on different grounds: the need of a transition period to introduce the Kwango inhabitants to wage labour, the inherent "laziness" of African men, and the certainty that indigenous workers, even when coerced, would be better off than left out of the monetised economy.

Lexical distancing, characterising official narratives of coercion, went further in my opinion than an ad hoc dissimulation of abuses and illegalities. It was a practical tool of governance, which allowed colonial actors to fill the gap between the virtuous and violent guises of their enterprise. In Leverville, it was a way to euphemise the concession's ugliness by cloaking it under a veil of vagueness.

Lexical distancing constituted a form of colonial coded language, allowing messages to flow between subordinates and their superiors and to be understood by all parties without explicitly violating the colony's laws. It was not a coinci-

---

[33] Seibert, "More Continuity," 343; Northrup, *Beyond the Bend*, 100; Tiquet, *Travail Forcé*, 153–161.
[34] AAB, AIMO 1415, Modifications aux décrets des 16–3–22 et 16–6–21. Contrat et hygiène des travailleurs. Exposé des motifs, undated.
[35] AAB, AIMO 1598, Lettre du GG Rutten au ministre Houtart, 3 August 1926.
[36] Pierre Ryckmans to Madeleine Ryckmans, 18 January 1931, in Vanderlinden (ed.) *Main d'Oeuvre*, 146.

dence that more precise descriptions of effective coercion appeared in private correspondence but not in administrative despatches or official reports. The only official actor who openly denounced abusive recruitment practices was Eugene Jungers, a magistrate who asserted his independence by openly challenging what was carefully hidden by agents with vested interests in HCB's recruitment practices.

Lexical distancing was another corollary of colonial impotence. The inability of HCB to mobilise voluntary workers demonstrated the discrepancy between its goals and its practices and implied that Leverville field employees and their allies within the administration (see chapter 2) could not act as expected. Their careful, almost coded, discursive practices were one of the strategies they could mobilise to effectively deal with this inadequacy.

Abuses of power

Violence was illegally employed to round up recruits. It was also pervasively present in encounters between the concession's workers and the Congolese intermediaries in charge of overseeing them. Sentries, messengers and *capitas*, who were deemed as indispensable linchpins in Leverville's extractive schemes, often brutalised fruit cutters and their families for the sake of either the state, the company, or themselves. Although such abuses were regularly denounced and were deemed to be counterproductive, they were mostly tolerated both by the company and by public servants. The inability of HCB or the administration to rein in their underlings constituted a further testimony of colonial impotence.

Cutting palm fruits was much more similar to the tapping of wild rubber than to agricultural activities. Along with their aides, cutters roamed through the concession's palm groves, looking for fruit clusters to cut and bring to the company's buying posts. They extracted resources in extensive, poorly charted lands, widely dissimilar to the standardized rows of crops found in plantations. Contrary to the working areas of farms, mines and industrial plants, the groves areas were not strictly delimited, and could not be easily supervised by foremen. It was therefore quite challenging for the company to monitor its employees. HCB nevertheless resorted to "fruit sentries," indigenous agents charged with ensuring the steady output of fruit cutters. These intermediaries were vested with loosely defined tasks, which all relied on their ability to exert constraint. According to Mr. Moorat, the vice-director of Leverville in 1930, sentries "do not have predefined tasks, they are "jack of all trades" who give a hand where it is necessary."[37] For Charles Dupont, general director of the concession in 1930, sentries were "a kind of police force charged to bring back to work recalcitrant cutters or deserters, or to push the men whose output is not sufficient."[38] A territorial administrator denounced sentries' supervision of cutters as a form of "disguised constraint."[39]

The resort to sentries, effectively acting as the *Huileries*' mercenaries, constituted a form of continuity with Free State practices. In rubber concessions, private militias employed by companies such as the ABIR and the *Anversoise*[40] were authorised to both exert police prerogatives in the name of the state and supervise the labour of rubber tappers. They often resorted to violence to stimulate productivity.[41] In August 1930, Charles Dupont recognized that "the employment of sentries [is], in a modified form, the old system of sentries of the ABIR."[42]

Within the supposedly "virtuous" enclave of Leverville, the resort to Free State extraction models led to comparable results. Recruiting workers under duress to harvest naturally growing products implied resorting to violent intermediaries for their supervision. These similarities highlighted how the legacy of Leopoldian colonialism still pervaded Belgian imperialism long after the private colony's official dismantling. The transition from the Congo Free State to a Belgian possession was intended to instigate a more humane and legalist form of governance, habits, and structures. However, decision-makers could not be changed from one day to the next. Many Free State administrators remained in place in the early structures of Belgian Congo, and the confusion between public and private interests that infamously characterized the previous era continued to dictate the colony's economic activities well after 1908.[43]

Public servants' opinions diverged regarding the role played by fruit sentries. After witnessing their doings in 1931, Ryckmans was sceptical, to say the least: "although closely monitored, they constitute a nuisance. For few benefits, they cause significant troubles. They act like true gadflies, whose idiotic zeal mostly

---

[37] Entretien avec Pierre Ryckmans, in Vanderlinden (ed.) *Main d'Oeuvre*, 301.
[38] Dupont to Dusseljé, 21 August 1930, in Vanderlinden (ed.) *Main d'Oeuvre*, 24.
[39] AAB, AI 4739, Note sur la situation économique des territoires de Kandale, Kikwit, Bulungu et Niadi, 6 January 1932.
[40] Anglo-Belgian India Rubber Company and *Société Anversoise du Commerce au Congo*.
[41] Lancelot Arzel, "Des Chasseurs en Guerre : Imaginaires et Pratiques Cynégétiques dans les Pacifications de l'Etat Indépendant du Congo 1885–1908," in El Mechat (ed.), *Coloniser, Pacifier*, 155.
[42] Dupont to Dusseljé, 21 August 1930, in Vanderlinden (ed.) *Main d'Oeuvre*, 18.
[43] Vellut, "Hégémonies en Construction," 326; Seibert, "More Continuity," 375.

takes the form of screams, insults, petty hassles, a constant pursuit; they molest, obsess and exasperate cutters without much improving their outputs."[44]

Ryckmans also consigned in his personal diary, "sentries are scoundrels. State agents are somehow powerless in the matter."[45] However, other functionaries were less critical. Kwango district commissioner, Albert Van de Casteele, wrote a lengthy letter in October 1930 to Elso Dusseljé – the then HCB delegate administrator – where he emphasised the necessity for fruit sentries in spite of their unreliability:

> Sentries [were] keeping you *au courant* of the work of the natives, telling you whether they were collecting your products to sell them to the Portuguese traders [...] to call a chief or to transmit a message [...] to correspond rapidly with the administrative staff or the territories. These sentries have certainly been used to bring back to work unwilling or run-away natives, and to control the natives whose output was insufficient. This is logical. You had the responsibility of your direction, your agents, of their *secteur* and their post. You had to take action against workers who had freely contracted, and for a futile reason abandoned, reduced or ceased their work. As these men were often far away from the nearest European post, and as the European in charge could not be everywhere at the same time, you had to employ Black intermediaries or sentries.[46]

Resorting to fruit sentries in the Leverville concession highlighted the continuities between Leopoldian and Belgian exploitation practices. This action also illustrated the ambiguous role that local intermediaries could play when enforcing the demands of colonial institutions. Sentries had loosely defined duties and effectively acted both as foremen and as policemen. Furthermore, another form of ambiguity also characterised the work of Congolese messengers in Leverville, who were simultaneously at the service of HCB and of the administration. Officially, messengers were in charge of carrying letters on behalf of public servants. In practice, they also participated to the supervision of fruit cutters, like sentries did. Both the daily duties of messengers and their source of their income testify of the multifaceted collusion existing between the administration and the *Huileries* in the Kwango district. According to Ryckmans' 1931 report,

> The administration made the great mistake of hiring for a long time certain messengers funded by the company. This practice was theoretically justified by the fact that the administration lacked the necessary funds to hire more messengers. HCB's industrial occupation rendered more intensive relations with villages necessary. To avoid being constantly told

---

44 AAB, AIMO 1652, Situation de la main d'oeuvre dans le cercle de Lusanga des HCB, 1931.
45 Notes prises par Pierre Ryckmans au cours d'entretiens, in Vanderlinden (ed.), *Main d'Oeuvre*, 297.
46 Van de Casteele to Dusseljé, 7 October 1930, in Vanderlinden (ed.), *Main d'Oeuvre*, 65.

that messengers were lacking, HCB offered to pay the salaries of the surplus personnel. It was normal in the society's behalf, but the state should never have accepted this expedient. [...] It should not place administrators in an equivocal posture. [...] We consider that the resort to state messengers should be condemned in general. They have no competence to evaluate the situations, to possibly judge the validity of excuses of cutters accused of laziness. They only understand one thing: that they are in charge of putting people to work; a task they fulfil without measure in their choice of means, being more or less persuaded of their impunity for the natives rarely dare to complaint of their abuses.[47]

The company thus bankrolled intermediaries working for the colonial state and used them to round up and supervise fruit cutters. Although this practice ran against the orderly and virtuous principles of Leverville, Elso Dusseljé advocated for the resort to messengers to the HCB's board of trustees in September 1930.

An administrator who has an immense territory to manage has at his disposition only a few messengers who are continually *en route* on his behalf. Thus, when we ask for the help of the administrator in the form of a messenger to accompany one of our recruiters [...] or for the purpose of letting a native chief know that we want to see him; or again, when the production of a village dropped too abruptly, the administrator cannot always help us, and without this form of assistance our difficulties are greatly increased. [...] I would be very surprised if the engagement of these messengers by the administrators, with the consent of the district commissioner really is illegal, given that nobody has attempted to conceal this procedure.[48]

Whether illegal or not, Dusseljé's justification highlighted the loose attitude of both public and private actors regarding the separation of their prerogatives. It seemed logical for the *Huileries*' area manager to ask messengers working for the administration to round up cutters or to summon indigenous chiefs to Leverville. In return, the district commissioner seemed to accept that messengers working for HCB and the administration at the same time to remain on the company's payroll. Although Ryckmans regretted this ambiguous state of affairs, he nevertheless stopped short of condemning it. Similarly, Dusseljé did not hesitate to assert the righteousness of the messengers' role in labour recruitment and supervision to the company's board even when it seemed to openly contradict the *Huileries*' moral agenda.

As illustrated in Sissi Kalo's painting, local intermediaries thus exerted a vast array of violent practices on behalf of a colonial ensemble, consisting of lower-ranking public servants of the Kwango district and Leverville's management. These intermediaries participated in the forced recruitment of fruit cutters;

---

47 AAB, AIMO 1652, Situation de la main d'oeuvre dans le cercle de Lusanga des HCB, 1931.
48 Dusseljé to the HCB board, 30 September 1930, in Vanderlinden (ed.), *Main d'Oeuvre*, 39.

hassled them in the groves; and transmitted orders, directives and summons in the name of both the *Huileries* and the state. Furthermore, they also used their privileged position as holders of an informal "right" to be violent for their own benefit. Both written archives and oral testimonies point towards the prevarication performed by both messengers and *pointeurs* or *capita-ngashi*, who were in charge of collecting fruit clusters and paying the cutters at the company's buying stations. According to Ryckmans,

> *Capita-ngashi* sometimes are dreadful tyrants, as only the Blacks who hold power over other Blacks can be. They demand *matabiches* (briberies); a hen, a calabash of palm wine, a pineapple... sometimes the favours of a beautiful woman. What if they refuse? They are denied their pay. [Some cutters] are smarter: they have an agreement with the *capita*, in return for gifts, he note crates under their name that they have never delivered.[49]

Former HCB workers also reported abuses perpetrated by company workers they called *pointeurs*. Two interlocutors I met during my fieldwork mentioned that *pointeurs* took advantage of the cutters' illiteracy. Instead of marking the adequate number of crates provided by fruit cutters in their registers, *pointeurs* purposely wrote down a lower number and kept the difference for themselves.[50] However, *capitas* and *pointeurs* were not the only intermediaries who took advantage of their position. Jungers also reported similar abuses perpetrated by messengers, who compensated their limited or inexistent wages by seizing the resources of the communities they "visited."

> When they "worked" outside of their villages, they had to feed themselves off the backs of others, for they were not paid. [...] They perpetrated countless abuses: extortion of foodstuffs, arbitrary arrests and incarcerations, assaults to obtain women and palm wine,... [...] I had the opportunity [...] to caught two messengers red-handed [...] one laying in a hut with a women he reclaimed, the other busy stuffing a hen in a basket, which he extorted from an old man under the menace of having sex with his wife.[51]

The Congo-Kasaï governor relayed similar observations in the aftermath of the Kwango revolt. "Exactions perpetrated by the insufficiently supervised auxiliary personnel form the basis of all movement of insubordination. They are mostly

---

49 Journal de Pierre Ryckmans, 19 janvier 1931, in Vanderlinden (ed.), *Main d'Oeuvre*, 147.
50 Georges Zolochi (b.c. 1925–1930), Ifwani-Kakobola, 10 August 2015. Lumène Wenge (b. 1931), Nzaji, 11 August 2015.
51 AAB, AE 3268, Rapport d'enquête sur la révolte du Kwango, 29 novembre 1931.

the doings of messengers: [...] confiscation of hens, women, of diverse gifts, of porters. Menaces, arbitrary arrests."[52]

When considered together with reports of exactions perpetrated by Belgian field public servants and HCB recruiters (see chapter 2), these abuses demonstrated that encounters between agents of colonialism and indigenous communities in and around Leverville were, more often than not, marred by violence. Furthermore, such episodes did not systematically serve the objectives of the company or the administration. Recruiters, territorial agents, sentries, *capitas* and messengers could also use their parcel of power to their own benefit.

Unlike the "method of authority" used to forcibly recruit fruit cutters or to "stimulate" their productivity, the prevarication of the Kwango district's inhabitants did not help consolidate the power of colonial institutions. Abuses performed for the sake of individual agents' personal enrichment or pleasure ran against the interests of the state and the company, impeding the "prestige" of its representatives and fuelling the resentment of indigenous communities against colonialism. Although such predations were regularly documented, it seemed that few disciplinary measures were taken against their perpetrators. The impunity of the violent agents who embodied colonialism in the field both testified to the weakness of colonial mechanisms of control, and demonstrated how the Free State's violent guises still "bled into post-Leopoldian milieus,"[53] as Nancy Rose Hunt has suggested.

The concession's violence was linked to its agents' impotence, a necessity to bridge the gap between its virtuous objectives and the impossibility to effectively enforce them. Practices of forced recruitment for Leverville were deemed as an "inevitable" and "transitory" phase of the colonization process. Similarly, the presence of violent intermediaries vested with ambiguous duties also appeared, under the pen of both public servants and company managers, as a sometimes regrettable yet unavoidable outcome of concessionary dynamics. Leverville's "ugliness" was not always concealed; its brutal guise was sometimes hiding in plain sight. However, the contradiction between this multifaceted violence and the company's virtuous ethos did not challenge the utopian narrative championed by its founders (see chapter 1). Paper trails of brutalities occurring in and around the concession were justified by the alleged backwardness and atavistic laziness of the Congolese, and not by the inadequacy of Leverville's paternalism to its field of action.

---

52 AAB, AIMO 1855, Lettre du gouverneur du Congo-Kasaï au commissaire de district du Kwango, 9 juin 1932.
53 Hunt, *Nervous State*, 31.

Translucent workers

The discrepancy between Lord Leverhulme's virtuous plans and the concession's "ugliness" was not only manifested in forced recruitment and individual brutalities. It was also visible in the company's resort to the illegal use of female and underage workers. Although they were not officially employed by HCB, the *Huileries* could not have functioned without their contribution. Female and underaged workers cooked the cutters' meals, brought fruit clusters to the company's buying stations, and participated to the processing of palm oil. When Leverville's managers were criticised for relying on these illegal workers, they invoked unchangeable local "traditions" to deflect these accusations.

Colonial archives related to women and children are notoriously scarce.[54] Under the pen of colonial actors, women and children mostly appear as targets of social engineering, bounded to ambitions of regulating African matrimonies, sexualities, familial arrangements and education.[55] Therefore, investigating the labour practices of women and children is a complex endeavour. "Working" in interwar sub-Saharan colonies was narrowly defined as male wage labour. Activities performed outside of the monetized economy, especially by individuals categorized as non-adult males, were mostly overlooked by colonial observers.[56] Even more so than women, pre-pubescent children taking part in colonial workforces were left out of despatches and reports.[57] European observers often considered that African cultures oppressed women by putting them in charge of arduous tasks such as cropping, while men remained "indolent." Regulations and policies were subsequently tailored to relegate the women into households, confident that such rules would "free" them of the excessive burden from "traditions."[58]

In spite of these difficulties, however, it is still possible to delve into the complexities of the Leverville concession. Studying Leverville requires investigating female and pre-pubescent labour. The concession's extractive practices necessi-

---

[54] Catherine Coquery-Vidrovitch, *Les Africaines. Histoire des Femmes d'Afrique Noire du XIXe au XXe Siècle* (Paris: Desjonquères, 1994), 109.
[55] Marie Rodet, "C'est le Regard qui Fait l'Histoire. Comment Utiliser des Archives Coloniales qui nous Renseignent malgré elles sur l'Histoire des Femmes Africaines," *Terrains & Travaux*, 10 (2006), 18–9.
[56] Rodet, "C'est le Regard," 19.
[57] Beverly Grier, "Invisible Hands: the Political Economy of Child Labour in Colonial Zimbabwe, 1890–1930," *Journal of Southern African Studies*, 20:1 (1994), 28.
[58] Emily Lynn Osborn, *Our New Husbands are Here. Households, Gender, and Politics in a West African State from the Slave Trade to Colonial Rule* (Athens: Ohio University Press, 2011), 149–150.

tated the resort to numerous aides and porters, roles which were often occupied, however informally, by fruit cutters' female and underage relatives. The scarcity of "able-bodied men" willing or coerced to work for the HCB also meant that children and teenagers toiled in the company's oil mills and ships.

In spite of a paucity of data, female and underage HCB workers were not entirely absent of colonial archives. They are not invisible, relegated far from the gaze. They are rather *translucent*, hardly perceptible in colonial paper trails. There are no reports on their recruitments, their exact number, no official census integrating cutters' relatives in the company's workforce. However, Leverville's women and children are occasional topics of correspondence, or they occupy a few paragraphs in official reports and accounts of visits of the concession. Retracing their history requires patching up together the scattered archival fragments of their existence.[59]

In January 1931 for instance, Pierre Ryckmans described in a private letter to his wife Madeleine the heavy labour that women had to perform on the *Huileries*' behalf:

> We attended a fruit buying, [...] there are, so to speak, only women, their basket exactly fills a standard 25 kg fruit crate. [...] On our way back, we are passing by posts where fruits are still being bought. Women, always. Three carry, in addition to their heavy basket, a small child.... One is pregnant.... [...] It happens that women that left home before dawn, come back exhausted at one in the afternoon, only to go back to work again, and start all over again the next day, and the day after...[60]

The mobilisation of able-bodied men for fruit cutting meant that other social categories would have to assume accessory tasks, such as bringing fruit clusters to the company's outposts. Throughout the 1920s and 1930s, the *Huileries*' impact on indigenous women – their daily life, their "morality" or the formation of conjugal bounds – became a regular point of discussion and contention among colonial actors. They were mostly articulated around the tensions between moral discourses on the "preservation" of Congolese females and households and the imperatives of *mise en valeur*.

One of the major issues regarding female labour discussed by company representatives and administrators was whether fruit cutters' wives should carry

---

[59] Gyanendra Pandey, "Voices from the Edge: The Struggle to Write Subaltern Histories," in *Mapping Subaltern Studies and the Postcolonial*, edited by Vinayak Chaturvedi (London: Verso, 2012 (2000), 282–4.
[60] Pierre Ryckmans à Madeleine Ryckmans, 19 January 1931, in Vanderlinden (ed.), *Main d'Oeuvre*, 147.

palm fruits between the palm groves and HCB's buying stations. In his 1931 report, Pierre Ryckmans summed up the discomfort of some European observers:

> As in all of Africa, porterage, in the Kwilu, is the women's task. [...] It is a truly regrettable situation. [...] Regarding native mentality, it seems impossible to prevent that most of the porterage imposed upon the cutter would be delegated to his wife. We cannot ask the company to refuse the fruits that would be brought by a woman. What we can ask is for HCB to bring the buying stations as close as possible from the harvest zones. [Women have] to gather the fruits in the forest, to decorticate them, to bring them in the morning at the reception centre, to wait there sometimes for long before the *pointeur* agrees to begin the operations, then comes home tired...to start the ordinary household tasks. One should not be surprised if the woman, especially the Christian woman, hesitates to bind her life to a cutter husband; it is one of the causes that turn young Christians away from the profession.[61]

On the one hand, Ryckmans invoked what constitutes a central element in the defence of women's participation to palm oil labour: the alleged importance of "customs" and "traditions" in the gendered repartition of tasks, in which the burden of agriculture and porterage supposedly rested on female shoulders. It was also a central topic in a bitter conflict pitting the general director of Leverville Charles Dupont against his predecessor, Elso Dusseljé, in 1930. Dupont invoked women's porterage to substantiate his accusations of mismanagement against Dusseljé:

> Amongst the abuses which I noticed at that time, the porterage completely retained my first attention. I observed that it was, in actual fact, affected almost exclusively by the women folk, sometimes by mothers carrying their nurslings with them, over incomprehensible distances, going up to 36 or 40 km per day, going and returning.[62]

Dusseljé defended himself by describing female porterage as an age-old custom that could hardly be discouraged:

> It is perfectly well known to all who profess any knowledge of the native mentality and customs of primitive races, that the male is assisted in his work (be it fishing, hunting, woodcutting for his own account or work for a third party) by his women folk and that he always leaves the work of porterage to the women. That can never be put a stop to [...] as the products of the forest [...] are always carried by the women from the forest to the village [...] Not in a single instance has a woman been engaged by the Company for work of any description while I was in charge [...]. No-one can, therefore, talk about porterage by women, although, for the reasons already given, there are number of them who do assist their men-folk. [...] As I have witnessed in all the other Areas, it is solely because the women were assisting their

---

61 AAB, AIMO 1652, Situation de la main d'oeuvre dans le cercle de Lusanga des HCB, 1931.
62 Dupont to Dusseljé, 21 August 1930, in Vanderlinden (ed.), *Main d'Oeuvre*, 13.

husbands and—I cannot emphasize it too strongly—because long-established native custom requires them to undertake porterage and similar heavy manual work for their men-folk.[63]

Dusseljé's justification interestingly pointed towards a disengagement of the company's responsibilities in abiding by the colonial moral agenda if its workers simply followed their "traditions." Dusseljé refused to qualify female participation to palm fruit extraction as porterage, but rather as a customary form of conjugal collaboration. The management could not forbid it, for those women were not officially included in the *Huileries*' workforce. Authorities' tolerance of female labour when it was deemed as customary became even more visible regarding the tasks performed by pregnant women. In spite of the colony's demographic crisis in the interwar (see chapter 5) and the apparent discomfort of colonial field actors at the sight of expecting mothers carrying fruit baskets approximately weighing 25 kilos, little was done to discourage it. Dusseljé once again deemed these habits as unchangeable in a 1930 letter to *Huileries*' administrative board:

> I have, personally, time and time again when camping in native villages, seen pregnant women, coming from the forest towards evening, carrying their baskets supplies of food, water, manioc, and even palm-fruits when they were the wives of cutters. The loads were enough to make one shudder, especially having regard to their condition, but when (as I have done on scores of time) I drew the attention of the men on the injustice of this situation, they merely shrugged their shoulders and the women themselves laughed broadly. [...] As natives and especially such natives are incapable of following our reasoning in these and allied matters, these women (whom we had prevented from being employed on carrying fruit) were and always are employed on sundry tasks connected with their daily life – often of a far more strenuous nature – until the day of their confinement.[64]

As Terence Ranger famously suggested, the invention and codification of "customs," "traditions" and "uses" played a significant part in colonial governance. Imperial powers imported and adapted their own social, cultural and political practices in Africa while attempting to refashion those encountered on the spot to ease the subversion of indigenous communities. For instance, chieftaincy was codified and profoundly redesigned to match European interpretation of executive power (see chapter 3). According to Ranger, these "invented traditions," however, "were marked by their inflexibility," which "totally misunderstood the

---

[63] Dusseljé to the HCB's administrative board, 30 September 1930, in Vanderlinden (ed.), *Main d'Oeuvre*, 39–41.
[64] Dusseljé to the HCB's administrative board, 30 September 1930, in Vanderlinden (ed.), *Main d'Oeuvre*, 39–40.

realities of pre-colonial Africa," where "custom was loosely defined and infinitely flexible."⁶⁵

Female porterage in Leverville exemplified the petrification of traditions once they were deemed compatible with colonialism. Women carried heavy loads and participated in various forms of physical labour before the concession's inception. However, colonial cash cropping profoundly transformed the pre-existing gendered distributions of tasks.⁶⁶ Without being formally employed by HCB, fruit cutters' wives and female relatives were also drawn into the monetized economy, actively participating in the *Huileries'* extractive practices. The function they occupied within the concession's economic structure might have been related to their previous duties, yet carrying baskets of fruits from the palm groves to buying stations manned by *capita-ngashi* had little to do with non-capitalist forms of labour prevailing in the region before the colonial conquest, such as artisanal palm oil production for one or several households. Rather, these new forms of labour testified to the plasticity of gender roles, taking on new guises in ever-shifting power dynamics. In return, these new forms of labour, although outlawed, were providentially coined as unmovable traditions when they benefitted colonial agendas.⁶⁷

In the Leverville area, there was another social group, which was sheltered in principle from participating to wage labour but found itself at the heart of tensions between morality and *mise en valeur*. This group was comprised of the prepubescent children in the concession. Two kinds of labour were demanded from children in the concession. First, so-called "boys" – teenagers, some young adults and a few women – assisted cutters in the groves. Second, underage children were hired in the company's industrial posts and on its fluvial fleet. As for female porterage, child labour was not introduced in the Kwango-Kwilu through colonial capitalism. Throughout sub-Saharan Africa, children formed a major component of a household's workforce, and often acquired skills by accompanying and helping older members of their community in their daily tasks.⁶⁸ However, the enrolment of prepubescent or adolescent Congolese in colonial labour rested on different premises than apprenticeship or participation to communal

---

65 Ranger, "The Invention," 247.
66 Jean Allman, Victoria Tashjian, *"I Will Not Eat Stone": A Women's History of Colonial Asante* (Portsmouth: Heinemann, 2000), 5–6.
67 Amandine Lauro, "Une Oeuvre," 165–6.
68 Saheed Aderinto, Paul Osifodunrin, "'500 Children Missing in Lagos': Child Kidnapping and Public Anxiety in Colonial Nigeria," in *Children and Childhood in Colonial Nigerian Histories*, edited by Saheed Aderinto (New-York: Palgrave-Macmillan, 2015), 98.

tasks. It seems instead to have been motivated by the scarcity of available adult male workers, whether coerced or not.

In and around the HCB's oil mills, as well as on the company's boats navigating up and down the Kwilu and its tributaries,[69] children and adolescents were sometimes formally integrated into the company's payroll, although the tasks they had to perform did not always coincide with those for which they were officially recruited. In principle, according to the *Huileries*' rules and the colony's laws:

> It is strictly forbidden [...] to employ small children for ordinary work; no child under 10 years old must be hired, except for the special work of kernels picking and coarsening, and fruit picking in the decorticating shed at the agricultural posts, for which boys of 8 to 10-year old may be engaged and employed, but not younger and only for this work. [...] Those employed solely on kernel picking in the station and fruit picking in the decorticating sheds at the posts, are to be engaged at lower rates.
>
> When small boys are considered to be adults by the State and liable for head tax, their wages must be increased to the minimum amount paid to adult ordinary labourers.[70]

Because child labour was partially legal and markedly cheaper, HCB managers employed underage workers for tasks they could not legally perform yet which did not require the labour force of adult males.[71] For instance, Dr. Raingeard noted,

> Traders requisition children as young as 4 or 5 and send them to the oil mill. If the manager is remotely scrupulous, he uses them for light works, yet, too often, they are entailed to both heavy and light work; which allows the use of all adults for fruit cutting and to keep some pocket money, the child being marked as an adult on the post's register but earning only half of the adult's salary. [...] In principle, according to the companies' rules, the employment of women and children under 12 years old is forbidden, in principle only, for these rules are only made to be shown during inspections, and only verbal instructions matter.[72]

HCB's local staff might have benefitted from the benevolence and the bounds of solidarity that united them to territorial agents and administrators in perpetuat-

---

[69] "HCB boats servicing the Kwilu for the collection of fruits have always been manned by kids (*par des gamins*)." AAB, AIMO 1654, Dr Lejeune: Note pour M. Le gouverneur concernant les protestations des HCB suite à mes inspections à Leverville, au Kwilu et à Basongo, March 1924.
[70] AAB, AIMO 1652, Wages and rations for the Brabanta Area, undated.
[71] Hamilton Sipho Simelane, "Landlords, the State and Child Labor in Colonial Swaziland, 1914–1947," *The International Journal of African Historical Studies*, 31:3 (1998): 572.
[72] Raingeard, "La Main d'Œuvre," 31–2.

ing what was considered as abusive employment of children. In May 1923, Niadi's territorial administrator wrote to the Kwango district commissioner that eight months before he witnessed "at Tango, children work[ing] from 7AM to 10PM without interruption [...] I knew it for I resided in Tango in September, but I did not wish to signal it back then, for it would have constituted from my behalf a breach to the rules of hospitality that had been offered to me."[73]

In 1924, HCB's delegate-administrator justified the resort to children in the company's oil mills by insisting on the lightness of the tasks demanded from them, as well as on the *force majeure* nature of this labour, generated by the lack of available able-bodied adults:

> Pushing Decauville wagons does not require much force. Our young workers treat it as a game. Regarding the loading of steamers by teenagers, we are convinced that [it] was only occasional. We have prescribed [...] to our district chief to make sure that our recruitments target as few as possible the non-adult workforce. [...] Yet it is evident that we could not entirely forbid the employment of non-adults.[74]

Child labour went against both the law and the moral agenda shared by the company and the administration, and levered more criticism outside of the Kwango district than porterage by women. It made HCB's underage workers more translucent than their female counterparts, even less susceptible to have left archival traces. It is, therefore, impossible to retrace the individual trajectories of the children toiling in HCB oil mills and ships, to understand how they ultimately ended up in there. However, in spite of the illegality of using child labor, along with the controversial nature of this trend, the *Huileries* still managed to resort to pre-pubescent workers throughout the interwar. The imperatives of *mise en valeur*, the suspension of the colony's laws and the company's ethos during a nebulous "state of exception," certainly contributed to this apparent tolerance.

Conclusion

Leverville's "virtuous" ambition appeared inextricably bound to the protean exercise of violence. Brutality marred interpersonal contacts, when sentries, *capitas*, messengers, territorial agents or recruiters came into contact with indigenous communities. It was also present in the concession's very structures.

---

[73] AAB, MOI 3602, Lettre de l'administrateur territorial de Niadi au commissaire de district du Kwango, 31 May 1923.
[74] AAB, AIMO 1654, Lettre de l'administrateur-délégué des HCB au gouverneur du Congo-Kasaï, 8 April 1924.

Violence was embedded in HCB's economic model, which could not function without the forced mobilisation of fruit cutters, and of resorting to women and children for tasks they were not supposed to perform.

This chapter tackled the elusive traces in archives and memories left by this ever-present violence. Forced recruitment was euphemised in official despatches, justified as a fleeting necessity and bound to disappear in a more "civilised" future. Although structural, the concession's violence nested in the interstices and blind spots of Leverville's utopianism. It was exerted by intermediaries with loosely defined duties; ordered and reported with a characteristic vagueness; and cloaked under the veil of unshakable "traditions." The concession's violence testified to the makeshift, improvised strategies of control and coercion that colonial institutions put in place to safeguard their interests, even at the disregard of laws, ethics and regulations.[75] Like the practice of *prix-état* outlined in chapter two, abuses performed by intermediaries further highlighted how individuals to whom parcels of "legitimate" power were allotted could use them at their own benefit, even at the behest of their employer.

Leverville's "ugly" violence did not emerge spontaneously, but could be directly linked to the traumatic inception of European rule in the region. The virtuous concession looked somehow similar to the rubber regions of the Congo Free State. As Nancy Rose Hunt suggested, Leopoldian traumas still "bled" into the Belgian Congo, surviving in enclaves which relied on similar practices of extraction, mushrooming at the crossroads of public and private interests.

Violence offered another insight into the multiple incarnations of Leverville. The concession began as a utopian fantasy of tropical paternalism. It materialised as an impotent machine, unable to fulfil the objectives it was assigned to achieve. It was also a conglomerate of violent encounters and structures; maybe not "indescribable," but nevertheless difficult to accurately map. Furthermore, Leverville was also a series of paternalistic interventions. For HCB workers and their families, it existed in the form of food rations; of clothing that could only be worn for specific occasions; and in vaccination campaigns and compulsory screening for tropical diseases. These "moral" guises of the Leverville project and their embodied consequences are the focus of the next chapter.

---

75 Romain Tiquet, "Maintien de l'Ordre Colonial et Administriation du Quotidien En Afrique," *Vingtième Siècle*, 140:4 (2018), 4.

Chapter 5: The concession embodied

Introduction

This chapter delves into the history of Congolese bodies in Leverville as seen through the lens of HCB's civilizational endeavours. Policies of eating, clothing, and healing enforced in the concession shed light on how the company put its workers' bodies front and centre of its paternalist ambitions. A visible improvement of their physical and "moral" standing through the rationalisation of their food intakes, the covering of their skin and the improvement of their health would have testified of HCB's successful civilizational prospects. However, the shortcomings of these policies brought instead the tensions between Leverville's virtuous and violent guises to the fore. Rations were insufficient, garments scarcely distributed, screenings and shots thoroughly avoided. Rather than compensating for coerced recruitment or poor working conditions, these strategies formed an integral part of the continuum of constraint imposed upon the concession's inhabitants.

Eating, clothing and healing constitute many ways to observe how the concession was *embodied*. If bodies are the vessels people use to navigate and act upon the world, *embodiment* refers to how the world, in return, influences and shapes those vessels. For Steven van Wolputte, "embodiment" speaks of "the "lived" experience people have of their bodies."[1] Embodiment determines one's "being-in-the-world," for one's thoughts and actions, as well as one's morals and movements, are inextricably tied to physicality. Human beings cannot experience the world without a body, and no mind can function without one.[2] Furthermore, the "lived experiences" which bodies go through are profoundly influenced by the time and space in which people find themselves. An individual's social status in any given culture shapes her or his embodied experience. Every society has its own rules, which dictate "proper" bodily conducts, movements, or ornaments from undesirable ones.[3] These rules often embody social hierarchies, for some actions, garments, or gestures might be expected from certain groups of people while being restricted for others.

---

[1] Steven van Wolputte, "Hang on to Your Self: of Bodies, Embodiment and Selves," *Annual Review of Anthropology*, 33 (2004): 254.
[2] Malcolm MacLachlan, *Embodiment: Clinical, Critical and Cultural Perspectives on Health and Illness* (Maidenhead: Open University Press, 2004), 2–4.
[3] See for instance the seminal article of Marcel Mauss on "body techniques": Marcel Mauss, "Les Techniques du Corps," *Journal de Psychologie* 32:3–4 (1934).

https://doi.org/10.1515/9783110652734-009

In this chapter, I resort to the conceptual framework of embodiment to demonstrate that the concession did not only exist as physical enclave, but also as a field of social interactions. Being part of Leverville meant undergoing a series of shared corporeal experiences. Eating rations and wearing imported clothes, visiting company hospitals, encountering medical examiners, or actively trying to avoid them were as many embodied ways to live the concession.

Embodying colonialism

In order to understand the corporeal aspects of Leverville, it is necessary to briefly review the ways embodiment has previously been mobilised by scholars of colonialism. The historiography of empires has led to two major strands of research regarding "colonised" bodies. Some historians have investigated the multifaceted processes of disciplining underwent by indigenous populations under colonial regimes. Others studied the ability of imperial subjects to use their bodies against oppressive power structures. Both approaches can be productively combined in order to paint a complex picture of colonialism as an embodied experience.

The historiography of embodiment in the 19th and 20th century world owes a great deal to the trailblazing work of Michel Foucault. According to Foucault, "modern" bodies undergo a multifaceted process of disciplining to ensure their smooth incorporation into economic and political rationalities, a process he calls "anatomo-politics."[4] Institutions such as schools, barracks, prisons or factories produce "docile" bodies which will eventually find a useful and productive purpose.[5] Foucaldian readings of embodiment have long inspired scholars of colonialism, who both echoed and nuanced his observations in a diverse array of settings and chronologies.[6]

---

[4] Michel Foucault, *Histoire de la Sexualité I: La Volonté de Savoir*, (Paris: Gallimard, 1976, 2010), 182–3.
[5] Bryan S. Turner, *The Body & Society* (London: Sage, 2008), 3.
[6] See for instance: James S Duncan, *In the Shadows of the Tropics: Climate, Race and Biopower in Nineteenth Century Ceylon*, (Aldershot: Ashgate 2007); David Scott, "Colonial Governmentality," *Social Text* 43 (1995), 191–220; Steven Pierce, Anumpama Rao (ed.), *Discipline and the Other Body. Correction, Coroporeality, Colonialism* (Durham-London: Duke University Press, 2006); Ann Laura Stoler, *Race and the Education of Desire. Foucault's History of Sexuality and the Colonial Order of Things* (Durham-London: Duke University Press, 1995); Meghan Vaughan, *Curing their Ills: Colonial Power and African Illness* (Stanford: Stanford University Press, 1991).

Drawing on Foucault's study of medical institutions as crucial nodes in the disciplining of bodies, Alexander Butchart retraces for instance the "construction" of African bodies by European gaze and healing techniques. By borrowing Foucaldian readings of the body as a "fabricated entity," he observes how Africans were apprehended as "objects of knowledge and targets for intervention" [7] from the 16th century onwards. They were successively used as subjects to be classified by taxonomy, cured and converted by missionaries, and exploited by colonial capitalism.

However, Foucaldian frameworks leave little place to agency. "Disciplined" bodies are hardly able to escape the entangled straitjacket of power relations which constrain them. A parallel strand of research has attempted to shed light on how individuals could use their bodies to revolt and resist. For Carrie Noland, if culture is embodied, it could also be challenged through corporeal performance.[8] If "modern" bodies are shaped and disciplined to conform socio-cultural expectations, it is through the very performance of what she calls "non-normative gestures" that groups and individuals can confront an oppressive status quo and alter historical trajectories in unexpected ways.[9] In a similar vein, Yolanda Covington-Ward traced back the *longue durée* history of "embodied resistance" in Congo. For her, bodies are "sites of power struggles," which means that "strategic uses of the body" – such as religious performances – could challenge existing power structures. She convincingly retraces how movements like trembling and jumping enacted by early followers of Simon Kimbangu were interpreted as signs of dissent by colonial authorities, and were deemed as sufficient motives for their arrest.[10] The history of eating, clothing, and healing in Leverville demonstrate how both approaches can be simultaneously mobilised to study different forms of embodiment.

Colonies in general, and colonial enclaves such as Leverville in particular, are privileged spots for the observation of collision and coalescence between culturally-determined embodiments. According to Marcel Mauss, societies shape bodies differently, even in their most mundane aspects. Seated positions, for instance, are markedly different from one point of the globe to the other.[11] In that

---

7 Alexander Butchart, *The Anatomy of Power: European Constructions of the African Body* (London-New York: Zed Books, 1998).
8 Carrie Noland, *Agency & Embodiment. Performing Gestures/Producing Cultures* (Cambridge: Harvard University Press, 2009), 2.
9 Noland, *Agency & Embodiment*, 30.
10 Yolanda Covington-Ward, *Gesture and Power: Religion, Nationalism and Everyday Resistance in Congo* (Durham-London: Duke University Press, 2016), 71–106.
11 Mauss, "Les Techniques."

extent, cultural encounters could also induce profound transformations of embodiments. Colonialism did not create entirely new embodiments, but rather stimulated new ways of being-in-the-world which both drew upon and coexisted with previous uses. Furthermore, these embodiments could also be contested or reclaimed by colonial subjects. The study of eating, clothing, and healing in Leverville shows therefore how a seemingly totalizing paternalist project effectively faced different limitations.

This project was first limited by impotence, by the unbridgeable contradiction between the principles and the practices of colonial rule in the concession. The second issue was the agency of the Congolese; how workers and local communities escaped and challenged HCB's social policies. Third, some of HCB policies were strategically scaled down by company agents to ensure the viability of the concession. Taken together, these three focal points and limitations shed light on a single defining feature: the fluidity of embodiments. Disciplined, yet autonomous, moving between villages, palm groves and HCB outposts, alternately clothed and bare skinned, Congolese bodies in Leverville were not transformed once and for all by a colonial machinery. They experienced instead forms of embodiments which fluctuated through time and space.

Contested rations

Food was a crucial topic for the actors involved in managing Leverville. For the company, it was necessary to both guarantee the reproduction of its workers' labour force, albeit at a minimal cost. For the colonial administration, public health imperatives required that Congolese diets should be monitored and "scientifically" quantified. HCB workers, on their end, looked to be sufficiently fed with foodstuffs matching their tastes. The manifold tensions arising from these contradictory agendas shed light on the effective limitation of colonial aspirations to supervise and standardise the food intakes of the concession's workforce.

Since its inception, HCB was contractually obligated to provide a daily ration to its workers, as stipulated in its 1911 founding convention.[12] However, the Kwango-Kwilu's environment and social fabric were detrimental to the implementation of large-scale farming schemes. Small crops were usually laid out

---

12 "Projet de décret approuvant une convention conclue le 21 février 1911 entre le Gouvernement du Congo belge et la Société "Lever Brothers Limited" et ayant pour objet la concession de terres à une société à constituer sous le nom de: "Société Anonyme des Huileries du Congo Belge," in *Annales Parlementaires 1911*, Document parlementaire n°126.

on the outskirts of villages to provide cassava, millet, or amaranth to a community without generating much surplus.¹³ Few inhabitants devoted themselves to cattle breeding. According to a 1931 report, most of the flocks in the Kwango district were goats and hens, the former being widely used to pay taxes, bridewealth or settle palavers.¹⁴ The limited scope of agriculture and animal husbandry both hampered the steady supply of food for the HCB's workforce, and generated occasional famines in the district's savannah areas.¹⁵

The main issue faced by the company's management was the provision of meat for its employees; meat was both scarce and in high demand. HCB staff member C.W.S Sellars recalled in his memoirs a particularly vivid scene taking place at Leverville in the early 1930s. Although enlivened by its author's racist gaze, this vignette alluded nonetheless to a structural meat shortage:

> One day there was no lack of meat. During the afternoon, crowds flocked into Leverville and all the mill boys were excited. The mystery was solved when the S/W Kwango was sighted. She had been designed for salvage work and had a 30 tons sheerlegs between bridge and bows. On this occasion, she was being used for ordinary cargo purposes but to our astonishment, an elephant was suspended from the sheerlegs, well clear of the water. It was a unique sight. It had been picked up several miles away. It must have died, sink in the water and putrefied. Blown up with noxious gas, it rose again, became partially submerged and was spotted by the crew who had no difficulty in persuading the captain to turn the ship and hoist the elephant out of the water. When he berthed at Leverville, the wharf was teeming with excited natives. The Captain offered the carcass, without success, to anyone willing to pay him 2000 francs (about 12 pounds). He borrowed our butcher boy who with two of the boys carved up the beast, on the wharf, under the glare of the lights. It was rotten with worms but who cared? Meat and worms would all be smoked together to provide a feast fit for chiefs. Three men were inside that mountain of flesh, hacking off lumps. Control was impossible and much of it never paid for.¹⁶

Unintendedly, meat shortage created a business opportunity for HCB by way of Lever Brothers' global networks. Between 1919 and 1922, the company had founded three whaling stations – in the Hebrides on the South-East coast of Africa and in the Shetlands – for the production of whale oil.¹⁷ In July 1924, a plan was hatched to use the mammals' flesh to feed HCB workers. A by-product of oil production, whale meat was unmarketable for Western consumers and usually

---

13 Nicolaï, *Le Kwilu*, 227–9.
14 AAB, RA/CB 157, Rapport agricole pour le district du Kwango, 1931.
15 An episode of famine occurred in the territory of Feshi in 1937. AAB, AGRI 360, Lettre du gouverneur général Ryckmans au ministre des colonies Rubens, 9 June 1937. Nicolaï, *Le Kwilu*, 228.
16 UA, UAC 1/11/14/3/12, *Congo Memories*, C.W.S Sellars.
17 Lewis, *So Clean*, 10.

repackaged as animal food.¹⁸ A series of letters exchanged between William Leverhulme Jr. and Max Horn shed light on the management's enthusiasm for this scheme:

> We are endeavouring to prepare whale meat by special pickle so that it will keep good for transportation to the Congo. [...] Our food expert, Sir James Crichton Browne and others inform us that whale meat contains a larger percentage of vitamins and nourishment than any other mammal flesh. [...] I have great hopes that in whale meat we may find the solution of providing meat for the Congo native and, as you know, it is meat that the Congo native desires all the time. [...] We could provide many thousands of tons of whale meat for consumption in the Congo if our experiment proves that it is possible.¹⁹

T.M. Knox, Leverhulme's personal secretary, provided additional details about the new business development: "Whale meat from Harris is to be smoked salted and dried, cut into slabs and baled and sent out here, landed at 2,5 francs per kilo and sold at 4 francs. Only workers from HCB will get it for their rations."²⁰ This plan highlighted how the concession became slowly inscribed in the global networks of the Lever Brothers consortium. In addition to providing raw materials for the mass production of consumer goods, the Leverville area also progressively became a potential market for Lever Brothers (by)products.

This project also illustrated how the company's social policies could be used to increase its own profits. Tons of inconvenient mammal flesh, unpalatable to Western consumers, could be turned into a source of revenue. It seems, however, that the plan did not meet the management's expectations. There are few archival mentions of whale meat consumption in the concession, and none seem to indicate that HCB employees favoured it. This absence of data would suggest that the experiment turned short after a few months or years.

As shown in Leverhulme's letter, pickled whale meat was not only envisioned as a way to commodify by-products, but also as a much-needed source of "vitamins and nourishment" for the Congolese. In the interwar, nutrition came to play an increasingly prominent role in the "civilizing mission".²¹ Africans were deemed incapable of properly feeding themselves, and therefore needed the intervention of colonial actors to improve their physical standings. "Colonial experts" downplayed Congolese eating habits, considered both unbalanced and insuffi-

---

18 On the persistent distaste of Western consumers for whale meat, see: Nancy Shoemaker, "Whale Meat in American History," *Environmental History*, 10:2 (2005), 269–294.
19 UA, LBC/229, William Lever, Jr. to Max Horn, 2 July 1924.
20 UA, UAC/2/34/4/1/1, Diary of T.M. Knox, 18 November 1924.
21 Vaughan, *Curing*, 141.

ciently nutritive. For instance, René Mouchet, the colony's assisting chief doctor, wrote the following excerpt in 1930:

> The Black adopted for unclear reasons a diet where fresh or vitamin-rich foodstuffs are rare. [...] He usually extensively cooks his meals [...]: meat boiled until it becomes fibrous, flour patiently stirred with regular additions of water until obtaining a sticky mash, several types of leaves hacked into spinaches: even bananas are pounded into an endlessly cooked paste.[22]

To ensure both the preservation of the Congolese population and to provide colonial companies with a healthy workforce, the composition of the rations given to their indigenous employees were left to specialized doctors, who were in charge of creating standardized meals that had to be "sufficient, healthy and varied, with foodstuffs that could be found on the spot at reasonable prices. One also has to take into account the individual tastes of some races. [...] The doctor's role is to take care of all matters of cooking, organize and supervise them."[23] It was not only the composition of meals that had to be supervised by doctors, but also the frequency of their distribution:

> Rations should always be given in kind. Ration given in cash is always poorly used. [...] It is best to make daily distributions of rations. Provided on lengthy intervals, it is badly distributed. One gorges oneself on the first day without thinking about tomorrow, sells a part of the ration.... Everything suggested by the most extraordinary short-sightedness will be done by the native.[24]

From 1921 onwards, the colony's provincial governors were in charge of enforcing ordinances regarding the "hygiene and security" of the local workforce, which specified the type of rations they should receive. Their content was elaborated in accordance with the advices of medical teams and local company managers. Legal rations were also composed according to the supposed "physical characteristics" of local populations, the kind of labour they had to perform, and the types of foodstuffs locally available.[25] In Congo-Kasaï, rations had to comprise "for one unit of proteins, 0,8 units of fat and 4,5 units of carbohydrates." [26] Workers were subsequently forbidden to either sell or buy a part of their rations.

---

22 René Mouchet, *Le Problème Médical au Congo* (Liège: H. Vaillant-Carmanne, 1930), 27.
23 Mouchet, *Le problème*, 34–5.
24 Mouchet, *Le problème*, 35.
25 Giovanni Trolli, "L'alimentation Chez les Travailleurs Indigènes dans les Exploitations Commerciales, Agricoles, Industrielles et Minières du Congo," *Africa: Journal of the International African Institute*, 9:2 (1936): 200.
26 Trolli, "L'alimentation," 202.

The basis for calculating the needs of indigenous households was the daily amount of food deemed necessary for an "able-bodied man," the primary target of recruitment. Women's and children's intakes were calculated as a ratio of the men's: "3/4 for a woman, 2/3 for a child of older than 10 and 1/3 for younger children."[27] For the Kwango district in 1934, the rations were estimated as follows:[28]

	Male	Female	Child older than 10	Child younger than 10
Manioc (cassava)	700 gr chikwangue. or 500 gr manioc flour	525 gr chikwangue or 375 gr manioc flour	460 gr chikwangue 333, 33 gr manioc flour	260 gr chikwangue 166,66 gr manioc flour
Corn, rice or millet flour	250 gr	187,5 gr	166,66 gr	83, 33 gr
Groundnuts	50 gr	37,5 gr	33,33 gr	16,66 gr
Beans	50 gr	37,5 gr	33,33 gr	16,66 gr
Palm oil	50 gr	37,5 gr	33,33 gr	16,66 gr
Bananas and other supplies	50 gr	37,5 gr	33,33 gr	16,66 gr
Optimal daily ration	950 gr	712,5 gr	633, 33 gr	316,66 gr

These rules and plans highlight the crucial role played by alimentation in the emergence of colonial embodiments. Rations were broken down into legally determined nutrient intakes and standardised amounts of local foodstuffs. This appears to bepart of a process of Foucaldian "anatomo-politics," a reshaping of African bodies to ensure their productive incorporation in the colonial power structure. Furthermore, forbidding workers to commodify rations also played an important part in creating a moral bond between employers and employee, a way for companies to act as benevolent providers of food. However, this moral and rational agenda faced several obstacles and criticism, even within colonial circles.

During a 1923 tour of inspection in the Leverville concession, Dr. Emile Lejeune, the Congo-Kasaï province's medical supervisor, noted that the four different types of ration provided to HCB workers were all "deficient in albumin, carbohydrates, fat and calories."[29] Palm oil, although produced on the spot, was mostly absent from the rations, and no food was provided to workers on Sundays. According to his report:

---
27 AAB, RA/CB 157, Bilan de l'alimentation végétale indigène du district du Kwango, 1934.
28 AAB, RA/CB 157, Bilan de l'alimentation végétale indigène du district du Kwango, 1934.
29 AAB, AIMO 1654, Hygiène des travailleurs dans les exploitations des HCB de Lusanga, 1923.

> Each team of 20 men is tended to, in principle, by a "kook" (sic) who cooks the daily ration, rice, in a large iron basin. At lunchtime, the rice is distributed on palm leaves, and speedily consumed in the open air with a bit of dried fish that the Blacks eat raw, probably because they lack the pans to cook it. Oil, when there is some, is poured on the rice. The Blacks are only eating once a day. Some keep a part of their meal to eat it cold on the evening. But sometimes there are no cooks. [and] It is usual in Leverville to pretend that the ration is sufficient!![30]

Dr. Emile Lejeune's report was not the first time that a medical official openly criticized HCB's alimentation policy. A year prior, Belgian Congo's medical chief Alphonse Rhodain had already warned the company's management that they were not sufficiently feeding their workers.[31] Both Lejeune and Rodhain petitioned the authorities to see changes in the *Huileries*' practices. "I protested against the insufficiency of the ration. [...] these deficiencies came from the fact that for reasons of expediency, starches are provided in rice. In Basongo, the ration amounted to 1800 calories!," wrote Lejeune to the Congo-Kasaï governor in March 1924.[32] Three months earlier, Rodhain had also harshly criticized HCB: "I could not hide my stupefaction when noting that workers were not rationed on Sunday. It is truly shameful."[33]

Furthermore, foodstuffs provided by the *Huileries* were often unpalatable to workers. The most contentious type of food was rice – the ration's main staple – introduced in the Leverville area by the company. During his 1923 inspection, Dr. Lejeune noted that the company at least tried to provide different type of foods, which might be palatable to the "tastes and habits" of the different populations living in the concession, mostly through the possibility of receiving either manioc, millet or corn flour along dried fish, palm oil and rice. He noted nonetheless, "the idea would be good, but in fact the Blacks do not have a choice; they receive the foodstuffs that are in stock and not always according to the amounts prescribed by the company, which are already insufficient."[34] The same year, Feshi's territorial administrator wrote to Leverville's general director following the death of several workers originating from Moyen-Kwenge. Their passing was attributed by their companions to "the alimentation to which they were not accustomed, rice

---

30 AAB, AIMO 1654, Hygiène des travailleurs dans les exploitations des HCB de Lusanga, 1923.
31 AAB, AIMO 1654, Lettre du médecin provincial Lejeune au gouverneur de la province du Congo-Kasaï, 8 August 1923.
32 AAB, AIMO 1654, Dr. Lejeune, Note pr M. le gouverneur concernant les protestations des HCB à la suite de mes inspections à Leverville, au Kwilu et à Basongo, March 1924.
33 AAB, MOI 3602, Lettre du Dr. Rodhain au gouverneur général Rutten, 25 January 1924.
34 AAB, AIMO 1654, Dr. Lejeune, "Hygiène des Travailleurs dans les exploitations des HCB dans le cercle de Lusanga," 1923.

or smoked fish, while these folks mostly eat manioc and native vegetables, and sometimes meat [...] few deaths occur after each recruitment and these gossips regarding rice are not made to encourage the natives to go and work for your company."[35]

The inadequacy of the company's food to local tastes seemed to have been a central argument of workers when they refused to be recruited. Still in 1923, Idiofa's territorial administrator reported: "chiefs are all telling me that their people refuse to go to Lusanga for the food imposed to them is rice while their alimentation is millet."[36] Five months later, the Governor General wrote to the Minister of Colonies: "natives originating from Katmcha-Lubue area refuse to reengage in the Lusanga circle because they are malnourished – they receive an alimentation to which they are not accustomed."[37]

On the other hand, the company's management tried to convince public servants that they did their best to provide food suiting the tastes of their workforce. In 1924, the HCB's delegate administrator wrote to the Congo-Kasaï governor:

> We endlessly tried to feed the Black with local products. But our attempts at cultivation have been extremely costly and we had to renounce. On the other hand, we tried in vain to buy foodstuffs to the natives [...] but unfortunately they cannot be stored because they cannot be kept. [...] we bought 30 tonnes of millet flour for the natives we intended to recruit in Kamtcha-Lubue. The government just closed this territory for recruitment. Workers originating from other regions [...] refuse to eat millet flour. We are therefore losing these 30 tons [...] in pure waste.[38]

Tensions around rations bring to the fore the role of Congolese bodies as sites of colonial contentions. New, "rational" embodiments by the standardisation of food intakes were doubly contested. They were criticised by workers manifesting their distaste for rice, and by medical officials who downplayed their sufficiency.

If both company managers and colonial doctors agreed on the importance to supervise the eating habits of Congolese workers, practical measures remained a topic of dispute, which showed how their social agendas did not always overlap. HCB management relied on the import of foodstuffs such as rice or whale meat

---

35 AAB, MOI 3602, Lettre de l'administrateur territorial de Feshi au directeur-general du cercle de Leverville, 23 August 1923.
36 AAB, MOI 3602, Lettre de l'administrateur territorial d'Idiofa au directeur-général du cercle de Leverville, 31 May 1923.
37 AAB, MOI 3602, Lettre du GG Rutten au ministre des colonies Franck, 11 October 1923.
38 AAB, AIMO 1654, Lettre de l'administrateur délégué des HCB au gouverneur de la province du Congo-Kasaï, 19 January 1924.

while attempting to generate new profit by reselling their own by-products, or by limiting the rations' size. On the contrary, medical officials insisted on more substantial rations composed of local aliments. Although the overall objective of "improving" workers' bodies by rationalisation was broadly agreed upon, it still led to opposing visions, and sometimes to bitter contentions. Both the insufficient size of the ration and the whale meat scheme illustrated how Leverville managers strategically limited the company's civilizational ambitions to safeguard its own profit margins.

Furthermore, if rations materialized colonial beliefs in civilizational and corporeal improvements through rationalisation, they also had a symbolic meaning. By distributing foodstuffs, companies such as HCB acted as benevolent providers and hoped therefore to foster feelings of loyalty among their workforce. Potentially, such exchanges in kind could indeed resonate with pre-existing forms of power relations and bounds of allegiance. Florence Bernault noted that eating constituted a "rich and multi-layered idiom of empowerment and agency"[39] in late 19th-century Equatorial Africa. It metaphorically recovered the possibility for an authority figure to increase and redistribute wealth at the benefit of his community.[40] Furthermore, according to Michael Schatzberg, ensuring that everyone was properly fed was one of the main tokens that a chief properly fulfilled his duties.[41] In Leverville, however, fruit cutters used their distaste for unknown foodstuffs as a prominent argument for avoiding working for the company. Rejecting company rations therefore played a double role. First, workers actively refused to partake of the new "rationalised" embodiment put forward by the company. Second, in complaining about rations they rebuffed HCB's attempts to position itself as a benevolent provider, thereby undermining its overarching civilizing claim.

Taken together, the rations' inadequacies demonstrated how a seemingly totalizing "anatomo-political" project was effectively constrained by multifaceted limitations. Rations were small and unpalatable, unable to effectively fulfil their purpose. However, attempts to alter Congolese bodies in the concession did not stop at the transformation of diets. This action also comprised the covering of workers' and inhabitants' bodies.

---

[39] Bernault, *Colonial Transactions*, 170.
[40] Bernault, *Colonial Transactions*, 170.
[41] Michael Schatzberg, *Political Legitimacy in Middle Africa. Father, Family, Food*, (Bloomington-Indianapolis: Indiana University Press, 2001), 149–50.

The ambivalence of clothing

"Friends and collaborators." Such was the description written at the back of these two undated pictures (see figures 7 and 8), probably taken in the early 1930s. Behind the imposing figure of Elso Dusseljé and one of his unnamed employees posed a group of Congolese men and women. In the first photograph, most of them are bare-chested, with women kneeled on the foreground. In the second, the same group of Congolese are now fully clothed. The women stand on their feet and wear a colourful variety of *pagnes*, while most men are sporting white shirts. It appears to illustrate the civilizing process at play in Leverville, where half-naked *basenjis*[42] ("savage", i. e.) would turn into fully clothed workers.

Such "before and after" tropes regularly appeared in colonial imageries. Photographs taken in industrial settings were often intended to provide visual proofs of successful civilizational endeavours, easily illustrated by the shift from uncovered to covered African bodies.[43] The description "friends and collaborators" accordingly highlighted the progress made by the Congolese under the care of the company, incarnated by the presence, front and centre of Elso Dusseljé and his underling. This terminology suggested that previously undressed individuals acquired the taste for "decent" clothing such as *pagnes* and shirts once taken under HCB's wing.

Several historians of empires studied how the fluid notion of "nakedness" embodied the "primitiveness" of non-Western "others."[44] Baring one's skin was seen as displaying a lack of shame, exacerbated senses and an absence of the modesty associated with European, Christian values.[45] Social policies destined to enhance the moral status of African workers would therefore comprise a

---

[42] *Basenji* is also the name of a breed of dogs originating from Central Africa. In different Western-Bantu languages, these dogs were known as *mbwa na basenji*, "dogs of the bush people". In the colonial jargon, *basenji* would become a moniker to qualify the Congolese who were considered to have yet to be touched by colonialism. Pierre Ryckmans wrote in 1925 that *"Basenji* is the name with which, all over Congo, we name the savage natives, those leaving in forsaken villages, far from civilization, far from colonial centres, far from the Whites". See: Pierre Ryckmans, *Dominer Pour Servir* (Brussels; Editions Universelles, 1948), 77.
[43] Eric Allina-Pisano, "'Fallacious Mirrors': Colonial Anxiety and Images of African Labor in Mozambique, ca. 1929," *History in Africa*, 24 (1997): 19 – 20.
[44] See for instance: Adeline Masquelier (ed.), *Dirt, Undress;* Hildi Hendrickson (ed.), *Clothing and Difference: Embodied Identities in Colonial and Post-Colonial Africa* (Durham: Duke University Press, 1996).
[45] Philippa Levine, "States of Undress: Nakedness and the Colonial Imagination," *Victorian Studies*, 50:2 (2008), 190 – 4.

132 —— Chapter 5: The concession embodied

Figure 7: "Friends and Collaborators 1.", UA, UAC 2/36/7/1/3, undated, c. 1930

set of strategies aimed at clothing their bodies, rendering visible the transformations occurring in their minds and mores under the patronage of Europeans.

However, the Leverville case calls for nuancing these observations. Although suggested by documents such as "Friends and Collaborators," the concession brought no permanent changes to sartorial uses. Congolese could vest alternative embodiments according to the circumstances in which they found themselves. Moreover, HCB did not necessarily assign only negative meanings to "nakedness." Let us look for instance at an August 1930 letter written by the director of Tango station to Dupont, the then general-director of the Leverville area:

> We demand that on pay day, cutters and their wives dress properly. Because the best cutter is precisely the one that remained the most *basenji*, and so is his wife. At first when they arrive, they look awkward in these costumes to which they are not used, but soon in the hubbub that follows the pay they already blend among the "civilized." I believe that this practice greatly contributes to free our cutters from their inferior position.[46]

Two forms of embodiment are at play here. On the one hand, cutters and their wives were expected to be "properly" dressed when entering the "civilized" enclave of the company office to receive their salaries, a ritual which symbolized their "modern" status as wage workers. On the other, the cutter's nakedness

---

46 L. Van der Eecken à C. Dupont, 14 August 1930, in Vanderlinden (ed.), *Main d'oeuvre*, 10.

Figure 8: "Friends and Collaborators 2.", UA, UAC 2/36/7/1/3, undated, c. 1930

acts as a proof of his professional ability, the best being, allegedly, "the one that remained the most *basenji*." This remark sheds light on Leverville's peculiar business model. As Anna Tsing observed, some commodities are not produced under capitalist control, but through "pericapitalist activities." Skills such as foraging, for instance, are learned outside of standardised environments like industrial plants or workshop. At the same time, these skills could be mobilized in capitalist modes of production.[47] In the concession for instance, fruit cutters have to know how to climb palm trees and cut fruit clusters before entering the company's workforce, skills that they acquire outside of the company's sphere of influence. It paradoxically leads to a situation where their economic value is directly related to their remoteness form colonial modernity, for the "best cutter" is "the one that remained the most *basenji*," which, in return, becomes manifest in his inability to dress "properly."

Three observations can be drawn from this case. First, it shows how concepts such as "anatomo-politics" have to be nuanced in colonial contexts. If the "civilizing" of Congolese bodies could sometimes take the guise of standardisation – as observed with rations – colonial changes brought to embodiments were not always so straightforward. Fruit cutters' productivity immediately depended on the existence of pericapitalist environments in which they could ac-

---

[47] Tsing, *The Mushroom*, 63–6.

quire and pass skills crucial to the company's profitability. Therefore, HCB had to strategically limit its civilizational endeavours – for "uncivilized" embodiments needed to be maintained – even within the enclave of Leverville. Second, it shows how embodiments remained fluid, for the same bodies could alternately assume different guises. Cutters and their wives had to "dress properly" and almost "blend among the civilized" on pay day, yet they had to be *basenji* when they performed their tasks in the palm groves. Finally, it brings to the fore another layer to colonial readings of nakedness. As a marker of otherness, bare skin in colonial contexts has mostly been connoted with immorality, backwardness or sexual proclivity. The present case shows how nakedness could also sometimes be associated with precious labour skills acquired in indigenous surroundings, even within enclaves of capitalist production such as the concession.

From this discussion, it seems clear that imported clothes played an integral role in the process of "civilizing" the native Africans. Imported clothing played a further role as markers of distinction as well. Fruit cutters' pay day experiences showed how they were intimately associated with the "modern" spaces of company outposts, which could hardly be accessed bare-chested. Within these spaces, garments were further used to mark distinctions of rank between manual workers and intermediaries. Oral testimonies pointed out that while fruit cutters wore waistcloths or *culottes* and remained bare chested, *capitas*, *Coastmen* or camp chiefs wore trousers.[48] In Sissi Kalo's mural, an African protagonist can also be singled out by his physical closeness to the HCB representative and by his blazer, while most of the others are bare-chested.

The following images (figures 9 and 10) depict two groups of men dressed in worn-out European garments. In the first one, unidentified individuals are waiting for a *pirogue* to cross the Kwenge river between Leverville and Soa. The second depicts the rowers and the escort accompanying Elso Dusseljé during his tours of inspection in the concession. The escort can clearly be distinguished by their European attire, while the rowers wear a sort of uniform.

The presence of a significant community of West Africans in the concession must also have played an important role in sartorial tastes and display of status. *Coastmen* employed by the HCB were thought to be the first models of African elegance in interwar Léopoldville/Kinshasa. According to Didier Gondola, they "represented for the Congolese youth the final stage of this new status adventure where colonization was taking them. [...] They were described by the Kikongo ex-

---

[48] Georges Zolochi (b.c. 1925–1930), Ifwani/Kakobola, 10 August 2015; Jean Ndeke Lutanda (born c. 1940–1945); Ifwani – Kakobola, 10 August 2015; Lumène Wenge (b. 1931), Nzaji, 11 August 2015; Kunanguka Tungeleko, (b.c. 1930), Nzaji, 11 August 2015.

Figure 9: "Waiting to cross the river, Leverville-Soa, 1926–27", Jesuit Archives, Kinshasa (JAK), B1 J.

pression *mindele ndombi* ('whites with black skin')."[49] It was highly probable that similar displays of distinction from West Africans – and in return similar longings for emulation from the Congolese – did take place in Leverville and its hinterland.

Enmeshing garments and status naturally played into pre-existing social uses. In precolonial Central Africa as in other places around the world, clothing and accessories were key elements used to separate power figures from their underlings.[50] Leaders could also create bounds of allegiance by distributing certain accessories or items of clothing to their close ones, which acted as symbols of distinction.[51] As early as 1916, HCB's management in Kinshasa contemplated the possibility of tapping into these uses to enhance the social status of fruit cut-

---

49 Didier Gondola, "Dream and Drama: The Search for Elegance among Congolese Youth," *African Studies Review* 42:1 (1999): 27.
50 Phyllis Martin, "Contesting Clothes in Colonial Brazzaville," *The Journal of African History*, 35:3 (1994): 401.
51 Martin, "Contesting Clothes," 410.

Figure 10: "My team of rowers and my escort", UA, UAC 2/36/7/1/3, undated, c. 1911–1937.

ters and to overcome the reluctance of recruits. In July of the same year, Sidney Edkins wrote to Lord Leverhulme, "I think the work of cutting can be popularized by appealing to the natives' love of importance. Working upon this line I have instructed the District manager to give each cutter a mark or insignia of his rank. What this is to be has not been decided but it is to take the form of a belt, sash, jersey or special waistcloth."[52] Like the provision of rations, distributing garments to create distinction could also be seen as a way for the company to strengthen its emotional bound with its workforce by acting as the provider of rare and desirable items.

Finally, clothing became a point of contention between the company and the administration. HCB's management rejected public servants' reiterated demands to provide blankets and loincloths to fruit cutters. In his 1923 report, Dr. Emile Lejeune implicitly accused the company of letting its workers contract illnesses by refusing to properly clothe them: "most of the time, recruits receive no blankets or loincloths. Yet, the nights are cold in the Kwilu, and most deaths are caused by respiratory disorders." He concluded, "the Blacks are not dressed by HCB."[53] The company's delegate administrator justified the *Huileries*' position in January 1924 by resorting to financial arguments. "Providing a loincloth and a

---

[52] UA, LB/215, Edkins to Leverhulme, 7 July 1916.
[53] AAB, AIMO 1654, Lettre de l'administrateur-délégué des HCB au gouverneur du Congo-Kasaï, 19 January 1924.

blanket to natives hired for only three months means doubling their salaries, and therefore ruining the company."[54] Once more, HCB limited its social policies for economic imperatives.

Clothing offers a nuanced perspective on how the concession came to be embodied. The seemingly all-encompassing objective of covering bare-skinned bodies was effectively ambivalent, multi-layered, and thoroughly limited. Garments were used to reinforce the distinction between palm groves and villages, where they were deemed unsuited, and company outposts where they were expected. In the latter, they were used to bring further stratification within the company's indigenous workforce, and might have been used to foster bounds of allegiance between employers and employees. These multifaceted limitations were also present in their medical strategies.

Coercive healing

HCB's medical policies were deployed in a climate of public health-related anxiety. Since the late 19th century, Congo underwent a dramatic and multifaceted demographic crisis, fuelled by the colonial expansion. The coerced recruitment of countless young men for portage and labour took its toll on many communities, who lost a significant labour force. Forced migration and the flight of villages attempting to escape colonial agents further contributed to spread diseases such as sleeping sickness (*trypanosomiasis*) far from their basins.[55] Birth rates were also dwindling all over the continent, menacing the economic viability of colonies, who faced potential shortages of indigenous workers.[56]

This health emergency called for a swift answer from colonial authorities. To stimulate fertility and curb mortality rates, the administration set up ambitious plans to tackle issues as varied as unsupervised migrations, venereal diseases or polygamy.[57] Public services zeroed their sanitary efforts on the fight against smallpox, sleeping sickness and malaria.[58]

---

54 AAB, AIMO 1654, Lettre de l'administrateur-délégué des HCB au gouverneur du Congo-Kasaï, 19 January 1924.
55 Jean-Paul Sanderson, *Démographie Coloniale Congolaise: Entre Speculation, Idéologie et Reconstruction Historique* (Louvain-la-Neuve: Presses Universitaires de Louvain), 2018, 20.
56 Vaughan, *Curing*, 141.
57 Nancy Rose Hunt, "STDs, Suffering and their Derivatives in Congo-Zaïre: Notes Towards an Historical Ethnography of Diseases," in *Vivre et Penser le Sida en Afrique*, edited by Charles Becker et al. (Paris: Karthala, 1999), 114.
58 Sanderson, *Démographie Coloniale*, 23.

Sub-Saharan Africa's largest grid of nurseries, midwife schools and orphanages was built in Congo over the course of the interwar.[59] In parallel, a vast network of dispensaries, hospitals and medical mobile teams were progressively founded by public services, missions and private companies.[60] The healthcare budget steadily increased, from 4 million francs in 1920 to 76 million in 1929, to a total of 575 million.[61] According to a 1936 report, "social spending regarding, hygiene, education and subsidies to missions, amount to 20 percent of the colony's administrative spending, and absorb almost the entirety of native taxes."[62]

The massive and diverse efforts to improve the physical standing of the Congolese, lengthen their lifespan and increase their population were inextricably tied to the colony's fortunes. Belgian Congo's prosperity rested on the massive exports of relatively cheap commodities extracted by a considerable workforce. As Dr. Mouchet wrote, "philanthropy put aside, even without taking our moral duties into account towards a race we are using at our benefit, it is an economic necessity, a "good deal" than to preserve and increase if possible the Congo's human capital."[63] In Leverville, as well as in other colonial enclaves, "virtuous" endeavours of care were inseparable from productivity imperatives. It required, in return, the resort to violence in order to submit unruly bodies to mandatory medical practices.

At the opposite of Western bourgeois medical care – individual and curative – colonial medicine was both collective and preventive. This differentiation both stemmed from and contributed to the structural racism of colonial power structures.[64] Just like coercive recruitments were justified on the grounds of the moral benefits of wage labour, force was also deemed necessary to overcome the fears and reluctance of the Congolese towards doctors, nurses, vaccines and screening tests.

Indeed, there were widespread anxieties in sub-Saharan colonies towards European medical practices. According to Luise White, "Africans brought their own epistemologies of causation and cure to European clinics," which often led them to mistrust doctors.[65] Cultural apprehensions related to conflicting interpretations of healing were not their only source of anxiety. Congolese were for-

---

59 Hunt, "Le bébé", 421
60 Poncelet, *L'invention*, 251; Hunt, *A Colonial Lexicon*, 162.
61 Mouchet, *Le problème*, p. 5.
62 RMCA, 54.45.184, La Politique Indigène de la Belgique au Congo, 1er février 1936.
63 Mouchet, *Le problème*, 9.
64 Duncan, *In the Shadows*, 107.
65 Luise White, *Speaking With Vampires. Rumor and History in Colonial Africa* (Berkeley: University of California Press, 2000), 96–7.

cibly pushed into an unknown system of care, founded on drastically different premises, which must have been significantly frightening. This experience was all the more frightening, given that standard sanitary practices such as perfusions or the collection of blood, body parts and bodily fluids played into pre-existing repertoires of malevolent witchcraft.[66]

Coercion was at the very heart of colonial healing policies in Congo, and contributed to both stimulating Congolese medical anxieties and to intensifying the resort to force as a response to refusal. According to Dr. Mouchet in 1930, medical efforts were a totalizing experience which would suffer no delays nor exemptions: "We have to treat in block all of the sick, exert a permanent control on them, looking tirelessly for all the germ-carriers, even if a certain constraint is necessary. The superior interest of the Black race requires it and it would be childish to renounce when facing indolence or prejudice."[67]

Accordingly, healing endeavours could take a martial guise. Medical mobile teams fashioned on the model of military expeditions were sent to the countryside to subject entire populations to screening or vaccination campaigns.[68] Such was the goal of the FOREAMI (*Fonds Reine Elisabeth pour l'Aide Médicale aux Indigènes*), a public institution founded in 1930 to enforce a program of "total care and diagnosis" in the Kwango district.[69] Patients were legally bound to comply: "the law on sleeping sickness gives doctors and aides the right to collective convocation. Chiefs are warned by messengers of the imminent arrival of the medical authority and are required to gather all of their subjects, men, women and children."[70] According to Dr. Mouchet, the menace of confinement was "often sufficient" to "ensure the regular presence" of the sick to "injection centres."[71]

As spaces of concentration for a migrant workforce, enclaves such as Leverville played an ambivalent part in these medical efforts. On the one hand, the authorities were aware that recruitment campaigns played a significant role in depopulation, by taking "able-bodied males" away from their communities.[72] On the other, these enclaves were optimally suited for the implementation of systematic medical efforts. It was easier there to track down, screen, cure and over-

---

66 See: Hunt, *A Colonial*, 7; White, *Speaking*, 90; Bernault, *Colonial Transactions*, 96–118, 168–93.
67 Mouchet, *Le Problème*, 10.
68 Vaughan, *Curing*, 43.
69 Anne Cornet, "Action Sanitaire et Contrôle Social au Ruanda (1920–1940). Femmes, Missions et Politique de Santé" (PhD diss., Université Catholique de Louvain, 2005), 373–4.
70 Mouchet, *Le Problème*, 18.
71 Mouchet, *Le Problème*, 19.
72 Sanderson, *Démographie coloniale*, 51, 55.

all "improve" Congolese bodies mobilized in resource extraction.[73] The concession was accordingly granted with its own medical network. There were two main hospitals – one in Tango and the other in Leverville – where Europeans and Africans were treated in separate wings. Segregation was an essential tool of colonial medicine, deemed to protect white bodies from those of Africans, perceived as a source of contagion.[74] Leverville also further hosted a lazaretto for the *dormeurs*, who had attained the advanced, vegetative stage of sleeping sickness.

Mobile teams were also sent to the concession's camps and villages, to monitor the "sanitary state" of homes and communities. Teams were supposed to fill "hygiene registers" with their observations and subsequent suggestions to improve the living conditions of the visited communities.[75] These teams were usually composed of a doctor, three to four "sanitary agents" trained in the Belgian School of Tropical Medicine, and African male nurses, a social category on which archival information are crucially missing.[76]

However, these ambitious programs proved extremely complex to enforce. Dr. Schweitz, head of the 1920–1921 Kwango-Kwilu's sleeping sickness operation, shared his frustrations in his final report of activity:

> Soon after my return in the Kwilu area, I had to convince myself that in spite of all my pessimism, I had been too optimistic [...] Instead of being able to work simultaneously in three territories, we had to limit ourselves to a single one, where we could barely end the first round of injections [...] after a whole year of hard work. [...] The number of patients to screen, the great number of infected to cure, the difficulties we faced in the treatment, the ill will of the natives, the shortage of nurses and the need to exert a permanent control over their work. [...] The lack of trust one could have in Black nurses and the natives' disobedience have furthermore forced the mission's Europeans to dedicate a significant amount of their time to make the injections themselves, or at least to supervise them.[77]

---

[73] Butchart, *The Anatomy*, 94–5.
[74] Timothy Burke, *Lifebuoy Men, Lux Women: Commodification, Consumption and Cleanliness in Modern Zimbabwe* (Durham: Duke University Press, 1996), 36.
[75] AAB, AIMO 1856, Lettre du chef de la province de Léopoldville au commissaire de district du Kwango, 29 September 1937.
[76] Nancy Rose Hunt, "Letter-writing, Nursing Men and Bicycles in the Belgian Congo: Notes Towards the Social Identity of a Colonial Category," in *Paths Toward the Past. African Historical Essays in Honor of Jan Vansina*, edited by Robert Harms et al, (Atlanta: ASA Press, 1994), 187–8. It is also worth noting that Leslie Sabakinu is currently preparing a PhD thesis on Congolese nurses during the colonial period.
[77] Jacques Schweitz, "Extrait du Rapport de la Mission Médicale Antitrypanosomique du Kwilu-Kwango," 1920–1921, *Annales de la Société Belge de Médecine Tropicale*, 1:3 (1921): 3–4.

Schweitz's disappointment was echoed by other colonial medical workers. During a 1923 medical inspection of the concession, Dr. Lejeune witnessed similar incidents of reluctance on the part of the Congolese workers and their families. "[they] lack trust, and when their illness is somewhat important, disappear to be cured or to die in their villages. Doctors in Leverville only see a very small portion of the sick."[78]

Flight and elusiveness once facing coercive medical care can be read as evident displays of "embodied resistance."[79] If Congolese bodies were sites of power struggles, refusing coercive medicine appear was a way of mobilising one's being against pervasive colonial claims. Furthermore, collectively avoiding doctors and nurses might have contributed to the emergence of shared physical and social experiences among the concession's inhabitants.[80] New forms of embodiment enforced in the Leverville area were therefore not only shaped by the policies put in place by the company and the administration, they could also stem from active and widespread attempts to escape them. Although these vignettes seem to indicate a systematic distrust for doctors, the reality was certainly more complex. Not all of the beds in Leverville's hospital were once occupied by coerced patients. Meghan Vaughan judiciously points out that Africans displayed a vast array of response to colonial medicine, which could range from fleeing to wilfully checking into a hospital.[81] Someone could escape a *trypanosomiasis* screening one day and look for a doctor on the next one. These varied and fluid responses highlight the crucial role individual agency in corporeal experiences, and demonstrate that conceptual readings such as "embodied resistance" should not be oversimplified and uniformly projected on complex sets of attitudes.

Like rations and clothing, HCB's medical policies were also heavily criticised by administrators. As early as 1915, a report pointed out the "alarming" death rate of Leverville's industrial workers – 18 percent – and the uselessness of its 'sanitary brigade,' "mostly assigned to unrelated tasks."[82] In 1923, Dr. Lejeune criticized the company's teams of *injecteurs*, in charge of administering *atoxyl* to those afflicted by sleeping sickness, for some of them "did not know the prop-

---

[78] AAB, AIMO 1654, Hygiène des Travailleurs dans les exploitations des HCB dans le cercle de Lusanga, 1923.
[79] See Covington-Ward, *Gesture and Power*, 3.
[80] See Vaughan, *Curing*, 203.
[81] Vaughan, *Curing*, 43, 52.
[82] AAB, AIMO 1680, Lettre du commissaire de police de Vos au commissaire de district du Kwango, 19 juin 1915.

er dosages and did not pay attention to instructions," while their supervisors used them "as a team of porters and rowers."[83]

Lejeune also made an extensive and far from flattering description of the Leverville medical facilities. The Europeans' hospital, "built in wood and toil, with sad and dark rooms, [...] lack maintenance." African nurses were "negligent, poorly groomed, probably unable to properly take care of a sick European." The Africans' hospital had "three poorly built latrines and a morgue with a dirt floor on which infected liquids are dripping, [...] attracting swarms of flies." There was "an insufficient number of beds. There should be 225 for the 4500 workers of Leverville." Finally, the lazaretto was "old and miserable," a place where patients "are sleeping on the ground with no blankets." His visit left him a "deplorable impression, I was disappointed by the flagrant insufficiency of HCB's medical service. [...] it is regrettable that after so many years of work and so much money spent, the situation was not more satisfying in Lusanga."[84]

In the following months, the rift between Congo-Kasaï's medical authorities and the concession's management only grew wider. In April 1924, Leverville's delegate administrator wrote to the provincial governor to explain that the company lacked the means to prove that it "humanely treated [its] natives, fed them satisfyingly, ensured their medical care" when it remained certain that in an enclave as large as HCB's Kwilu concession, "there will always be room for criticism."[85] In a scathing reply, Lejeune lamented, "instead of thanking us and seizing the opportunity of our recommendations, this prominent company constantly criticizes us," mentioning, for instance, that he "did not find a single nursery with enough medications or sufficient installations and, in several posts, no nursery at all."[86]

In a 22-page letter written in January 1924, HCB delegate administrator Sidney Edkins systematically rebuked the accusations purported by Lejeune on insufficient rations, lacklustre medical care and unsuitable workers' camps. For Edkins, there was a structural imbalance between the costs of legally-binding social programs and the *Huileries*' profitability. Paying a nurse in each HCB's post would, for instance, "strain our company with costs it could not commercially

---

[83] AAB, AIMO 1654, Lettre du médecin provincial Emile Lejeune au médecin en chef de Leverville, 19 November 1923.
[84] AAB, AIMO 1654, Dr. Lejeune, Hygiène des Travailleurs dans les exploitations des HCB dans le cercle de Lusanga, 1923.
[85] AAB, AIMO 1654, Lettre de l'administrateur-délégué des HCB au gouverneur du Congo-Kasaï, 8 April 1924.
[86] AAB, AIMO 1654, Note pr M. le gouverneur du Congo-Kasaï conçernant les protestations des HCB à la suite de mes inspections à Leverville, au Kwilu et à Basongo, March 1924.

sustain." Hiring a third doctor in the concession, as suggested by the medical administration, was not possible, regarding "the current financial situation of the company." [87] The cumulated costs of medical care in the concession would provoke "a 300 franc increase in the price of a ton of palm oil." [88] In conclusion, Edkins sketched out a lengthy scenario where paternalistic obligations resting on private shoulders would drive companies out of the colony:

> The products of Belgian Congo are heavily entailed by the difficulty of evacuating them [...] to compete with similar productions in neighbouring colonies, it is necessary for our prices to be inferior. But the sudden increase in workforce costs destroys the sole advantage of the Congolese product and will make it impossible to efficiently compete with similar goods produced abroad [...] the Black will be the first victim of the ensuing bankruptcies which will halt its ascent towards a superior moral and material life. Therefore, the consequences of protective measures taken in favour of the coloured workforce appear under an unexpected light. [...]
> If at least the legislation imposing to employers such diverse and numerous obligations were compensated by some mirroring obligations purported on the employee, maybe its enforcement would not have [...] endangered the colony's trade and industry. But who does not see that it is socially unfair and economically unreasonable to constrain the employer to properly feed, properly house, properly dress, properly cure, properly transport its workforce and not constraint, at least, the employees to work properly? [...] In the colony, no obligation to work is imposed upon the worker! The employer unhappy with his employee only has a single resource, consisting in ending his contract, while the worker usually wishes nothing more, so few are his needs and so low are his fiscal obligations.[89]

The tensions did not abate with time. In his November 1931 report on the causes of the Kwango revolt, Judge Eugene Jungers accused the company of not fulfilling its obligations. For the magistrate, HCB hid behind the façade of model workers' camps and the state of the art hospitals the bleak living conditions and appalling hygiene of the workforce of what he called – in an attempt to distance Belgian officials from his criticism: "the English colony of the 'Lusanga area': "The government must investigate what happens behind the philanthropic façade showed to distinguished guests, the two splendid hospitals of Tango and Leverville and the magnificent brick-walled camps, exposed to the river banks, able to shelter 4000 men at best while the HCB's workforce is close to 20,000." [90]

---

87 AAB, AIMO 1654, Lettre de l'administrateur-délégué des HCB au gouverneur du Congo-Kasaï, 8 avril 1924.
88 AAB, AIMO 1654, Lettre de l'administrateur-délégué des HCB au gouverneur du Congo-Kasaï, 8 avril 1924.
89 AAB, AIMO 1654, Lettre de l'administrateur-délégué des HCB au gouverneur du Congo-Kasaï, 8 avril 1924.
90 AAB, AE 3268, Rapport d'enquête sur la révolte du Kwango, 29 November 1931.

While crucial for both the concession's benevolent image and productivity, medical care also became Leverville's most bitterly contested paternalist endeavour. Fiery exchanges of letters between public servants and company representatives shed a crude light on the dire state of care facilities. Economic arguments, already mobilized by HCB representatives when the company was criticised for failing to fulfil its other philanthropic duties, were again extensively deployed. Along with rations too small and garments too scarce, dirty hospitals and incompetent nurses embody the unbridgeable gap between paternalist policies and practices in Leverville. Places such as industrial outposts and company hospitals were the most susceptible to be visited, which would render the image of Leverville as a tropical iteration of Port Sunlight. It was these venues that were the primary recipients of the company's attention, leaving smaller facilities largely neglected. Although the concession counted more labour force and infrastructures than most parts of Belgian Congo, discrepancies existed between its main industrialized nodes and marginal outposts, deemed of secondary importance.

Medical care was not only a point of dispute within the colonial power structure; it also became a field of conflict with the concessions' inhabitants. Health and sanitary policies were the object of entangled anxieties. Sickness and barrenness alarmed doctors, managers and public servants. The Congolese were tormented by the experience of medical screenings, injections and the collection of bodily samples. Although their response to colonial medicine was more complex than sheer rejection, coercive medical efforts and frustrated reports on the failures of sanitary campaigns highlight how these streams of anxiety collided with one another. The repressive apparatus surrounding care initiatives reinstated Congolese bodies as fields of power struggles between company and workers, as well as between HCB and the administration.

Conclusion

Studying the complex and contested enforcement of paternalism in the Leverville concession has brought its corporeal dimension to light. The concession was not only a spatial enclave, but also a series of embodied experiences. Participating in these experiences could be intimately felt, both on and beneath the skin. Leverville existed in portions of rice hastily served on banana leaves, in *pagnes* and shirts to be worn on pay day, in the invasive palpation of lymph nodes during screening campaigns. It also materialised in the flight before medical mobile teams and in the rejection of unpalatable rations.

In Leverville, colonial strategies aiming to rationalise Congolese bodies coexisted with a diverse array of embodied resistances. Furthermore, if both administration and company envisioned radical refashions of bodies through their shared paternalist visions, archives shed light on the many fracture lines which separated them. Facing the impossibility of both securing their already meagre profit margins and of pursuing their philanthropic agenda, the company's field managers consciously limited the latter. This issue resulted in small and hardly edible rations and poorly tended medical facilities, which only further fed the discontent of public servants.

Embodied resistances and unbridgeable contradictions between profits and "virtue" also bring to the fore the impotence of colonial actors in Leverville. HCB could not perform its paternalist duties as expected. Beyond the limited scope of its policies of care, the company also failed to resort to them in order attract voluntary workers. To the contrary, some of these very realisations – such as the unpopular rations – could be mobilized by workers as arguments to refuse recruitment. Their lack of attractiveness also meant that strategies of coercion put in place by colonial agents did not stop at the forced recruitment of fruit cutters. They were also mobilised during medical campaigns. Instead of alleviating the concession's "violent" guise, its "virtuous" ambitions only widened its scope of constraint.

Finally, investigating embodiments in Leverville contributes to a better understanding of what the concession actually was. Economically speaking, Leverville stood out as an enclave of capitalism, relatively isolated from Belgian Congo's main colonial strongholds. However, upon closer investigation, the stratified nature of the concession became more evident. Neither HCB nor the administration evenly controlled the concession; rather, it was a patchwork of enclaves characterised by a diverse array of power relations and colonial investment. The main company outposts functioned as nodes of colonial modernity; they were granted with the best medical and industrial facilities. These were places where African bodies were expected to be covered, and where garments played a crucial role in social distinction. Established villages and unsupervised indigenous agglomerations, to the contrary, escaped the totalizing gaze of colonial institutions. This negligence, however, was not only a direct result of colonial impotence, for bare chests and *basenji* behaviours were there deemed normal and even desirable by company managers. HCB's peculiar business model rested on the training of cutters in such zones, where they would acquire body techniques that the company was unable to standardise. African bodies in Leverville could not entirely be reshaped, even as knots and bolts of an industrial machine.

Chapter 6: A war against nature

In the Congo we have really been carrying on a war against nature.[1]

Lord Leverhulme to Max Horn, 15 February 1925

Introduction

Lever Brothers' ambition to turn the basin of the Kwilu river into a tropical utopia amounted to a process of rationalisation and standardisation. As the previous chapter demonstrated, HCB's paternalist policies attempted to mould the bodies of its workers according to its own norms and principles. Similarly, materialising Leverville also implied adapting its environment to the company's needs, a prospect which, in Lord Leverhulme's own words, added up to a "war against nature." The industrial production of palm oil would take the form of a rational triumph on the "unpredictable" Congolese ecosystems described at length by adventurers, missionaries and imperial pioneers (see chapter 1). This chapter focuses on how HCB agents waged this "war", studying the complex, sometimes convoluted and often frustrating attempts at "regulating" and appropriating the Leverville concession's environment. There is a focus on three specific examples, which taken together epitomize the company's multi-layered interventions impact on the Kwilu basin. First, I look at how the company managed to claim ownership of the region's most profuse palm groves through controversial legal constructions. Second, I shed light on the competition between indigenous communities and the company for the use of palm resources. Third, the chapter considers HCB's attempts at improving the concession's productivity through an ultimately unsuccessful plantation scheme.

The concession ecology

The *Huileries*' "war against nature" was tantamount to an attempt at refashioning the concession's ecology; that is, the complex relationships binding human communities with their habitat and the living organisms with which they coex-

---

[1] UA, LBC/230, Leverhulme to Max Horn, 15 February 1925.

https://doi.org/10.1515/9783110652734-010

ist.² Such endeavours were inseparable from the broader context of the accelerating global environmental transformations, emerging in the second half of the 19th century at the crossroads of imperialism and successive industrial revolutions.³ The expansion of capitalism outside of its historic cradle impacted climates and ecosystems alike and brought significant changes to the extraction, transformation and allocation of resources and lands in colonial frontiers.⁴ Increasing amounts of ores and crops, gathered by growing contingents of colonized workers, came to circulate on constantly expanding trade routes. In the interwar, the Kwilu palm oil industry competed with those from West Africa and Southeast Asia. This global contest pushed HCB to improve its comparatively low productivity and quality standards. These endeavours led in turn to profound changes in and around Leverville, impacting both landscapes and the distribution of resources between indigenous communities and the company. The concession's thirst for palm oil triggered new challenges for the Congolese who lived and worked there, and who also relied upon the *Elaeis* as a source of wood, fat, fibres and alcohol. Given that the region remained mostly shielded from capitalist encroachment until the inception of HCB in 1911, ecological transformations brought by the company were both rapid and brutal.

In Europe, colonial interventions in the environment were envisioned as an economic necessity and a moral duty, simultaneously ensuring the commodification of natural resources and the improvement of local populations' living conditions.⁵ However, colonial presence and influence profoundly disrupted the transmission of vernacular knowledge and cultural understanding of sub-Saharan environments.⁶ Existing land uses receded under the implementation of imported techniques of intensive agriculture.⁷ The complete disregard of Western experts, public servants and companies for indigenous uses and practices

---

2 Bruce Winterhalder, "Concepts in Historical Ecology: The View from Evolutionary Ecology", in *Historical Ecology: Cultural Knowledge and Changing Landscapes*, edited by Carole L. Crumley (Santa Fe: School of American Research Press, 1994), 18.
3 William Beinart, Lotte Hughes, *Environment and Empire* (Oxford: Oxford University Press, 2007), 1.
4 Christopher Bayly, *The Birth of the Modern World, 1780–1914* (London: Blackwell, 2004), 444–451.
5 Arun Agrawal, "The Politics of Development and Conservation: Legacies of Colonialism", *Peace & Change* 22:4 (1997): 466–467.
6 Graham Huggan, Helen Tiffin, *Postcolonial Ecocriticism. Literature, Animals, Environment* (London: Routledge, 2010), 2–4.
7 For a case study in Belgian Congo, see: Likaka, *Rural Society*.

often led to their swift replacement by so-called "rational" and "scientific" cropping.[8]

It is nevertheless striking to see that in the interwar Kwango district, such "modernising" efforts took a peculiar form. The forest galleries of the Kwilu basin did not come to host extensive standardised plantations before the mid-1930s. Throughout the first twenty years of Leverville's existence, the company solely exploited *Elaeis* clusters already growing on the river banks. Most fruits were yielded in so-called "managed" palm groves. The concession's forest galleries hosted extensive stands of trees, which covered hundreds of hectares but held a varying density of *Elaeis* (the most prolific did not count more than a hundred oil palms per hectare).[9] To become properly exploitable by fruit cutters, the groves had to first be "managed," which essentially meant they were cleared by the company's workers. All trees and bushes were uprooted except oil palms, while young *Elaeis* trees were planted in the empty spaces left by the clearing.[10]

Given this specific form of resource extraction, the *Huileries* had to rely on indigenous skills and know-how to both exploit its key resources and improve its yields. Fruit cutters and their aides located the richest palm groves; eliminated parasitic vegetation; and harvested fruit clusters thanks to tree-climbing techniques acquired prior to their recruitment by HCB (see chapters 4 and 5). However, "managed" palm groves were also wielded by local communities, which led in turn to a stark competition for resources between the concession's management and its inhabitants.

The exploitation of managed palm groves meant that the transformation of palm fruits into commodities partially occurred outside of the company's grip, in zones which could only be imperfectly supervised by its sentries and messengers (see chapter 4). Anna Tsing conceptualized such liminal forms of capitalist exploitation as "salvage accumulation," which amounted to the possibility of "amassing capital without controlling the conditions under which commodities are produced."[11] The concession's palm groves could be understood as "pericapitalist" zones, which provided key resources valued in the global trade system, yet structurally eluded their full integration in standardised production

---

8 Joseph Morgan Hodge, *Triumph of the Expert. Agrarian Doctrines of Development and the Legacies of British Colonialism* (Athens: Ohio University Press, 2007), 42–45.
9 Edmond Leplae, *Le palmier à Huile en Afrique: Son Exploitation au Congo Belge et en Extrême-Orient* (Brussels: Falk & Fils, 1939), 7–8.
10 Nicolaï, *Le Kwilu*, 283.
11 Tsing, *The Mushroom*, 63.

schemes.¹² The pericapitalist character of the Kwilu river banks constituted a challenge for HCB. The yields and their quality were unpredictable, while its workforce could easily escape the company's oversight. The *Huileries*' "war" against nature equated to a struggle to limit this unpredictability as much as possible by securing land rights; imposing a monopoly on natural resources; and attempting to standardise both oil palms and palm oil. The complex obstacles the company faced in its efforts shed more light on the multifaceted impotence of colonial endeavours.

Owning the palm groves

At the edge of the Congolese rainforest, the basins of the Kwango and the Kwilu rivers were characterised by an intercalation of bushy savannah and dense, wet, subequatorial woods, surrounding its many water streams.¹³ The stark ecological contrast between the forest zones and dry marshes determined the socio-economic fate of the region. The savannah offered few opportunities for agriculture, and did not possess many valuable resources. To the contrary, forest galleries hosted large and dense palm groves, believed to count among the richest in the world.¹⁴

From 1911 on, the Kwilu basin was destined to become an "oil country," devoted to a single economic activity where workforce mobilisation and infrastructure building would be almost solely articulated around the extraction and export of palm oil. Efforts to develop other pastoral activities, or to cultivate alternative crops, were quickly abandoned by colonial authorities. For example, the Kwango district commissioner shared these words in a 1932 report: "there are only commercial opportunities for palm oil and kernels."¹⁵

Securing the right to tap into these resources was therefore of prime importance, both for the company and the colonial administration. However, the *Huileries* faced two major impediments. First, the palm groves coveted by HCB did not grow to be so lush on their own; rather, this growth resulted from the long-term intervention of indigenous communities. Oil palms' continuous exploitation and man-made improvement ran against the idea that the Kwilu *Elaeis* were neglected residues of primeval nature, readily exploitable by colonial capitalism. Second, the *Huileries*' plans to acquire exclusive rights to harvest fruits on

---

12 Tsing, *The Mushroom*, 40.
13 Nicolaï, *Le Kwilu*, 68, 79.
14 UA, UAC 2/34/4/1/1, Diary of T.M Knox, 23 November 1924.
15 AAB, RA/CB 157, Rapport sur la situation de l'agriculture dans le district du Kwango, 1932.

lands already used by indigenous communities ran against the protection of "native lands" enshrined in Belgian Congo's legislation. Tackling those issues required the building of a legal assemblage whose legitimacy was already questioned in the interwar.

One of the key aspects of colonial endeavours was to substitute existing arrangements on the allocation of territory and the division of resources by their own definitions of absolute, individual property rights.[16] Various policies, legal dispositions and ad hoc strategies were implemented in the field to ensure the expropriation of indigenous populations from valuable lands.[17] Since the times of the Free State, Congo laws distinguished three different types of land: 1) "native"; 2) "private"; and 3) "vacant." On paper, native lands were protected against any form of colonial infringement. They were, however, restrictively delimited and only comprised villages and their surrounding fields, a space far smaller than the territories and resources local communities actually used.[18] Legislators were keen on limiting indigenous occupation rights so as to avoid hampering prospective exploitations of yet-to-be discovered resources. A private land would be recognized as such once its would-be owner recorded its property claim in an official registry book.[19] The rest of the colony was considered "vacant," and the state bestowed upon itself the exclusive right to exploit its resources, both above and below ground.[20]

With the inception of Belgian Congo, legal dispositions were redrafted so as to reflect the moral endeavours of the newly appointed colonial power. The separation between private, vacant and native lands was maintained, but the delimitation of the latter would now have to follow a thorough field investigation in order to prevent any "abusive" encroachment of indigenous rights. However, field administrators were reluctant to follow this new policy, which was also impeded by the colony's lack of infrastructures. Public servants did not receive precise instructions on how to properly conduct enquiries leading to land delimitations. Furthermore, they lacked the time, means and human resources to

---

16 Bayly, *The Birth*, 434
17 Bayly, *The Birth*, 439.
18 Henriet, "Colonial Law," 210.
19 Henriet, "Colonial Law," 214.
20 Piet Clement, "The Land Tenure System in the Congo, 1885–1960: Actors, Motivations, and Consequences," in *Colonial Exploitation and Economic Development: the Belgian Congo and the Netherlands Indies Compared*, edited by Ewout Frankema and Frans Buelens (Abingdon: Routledge, 2013): 90.

conduct them. Even when boundaries were effectively set, they were rarely respected, for local communities regularly settled outside of their allotted lands.[21]

In the case of Leverville, determining whether the palm groves were "vacant" or "native" lands was controversial. All over the world, forest landscapes are shaped by geography, climate and the intervention of human and animals.[22] In the Kwilu basin, both the intercalation of forest and savannah, along with the propagation of palm trees, were concomitant with and deeply related to the spreading of settlements.[23] The growth of forest galleries stretching along the region's rivers directly resulted from centuries of human exploitation.[24] Humans and animals disseminated the seeds by eating and processing palm fruits, while *Elaeis* thrived on the slash-and-burn fields tended by local communities.[25] Furthermore, palm groves frequently had an abandoned village site at their centre.[26] Interwar agronomists knew about importance of human influence on the formation of palm groves. Edmond Leplae, director of the department of agriculture at the Ministry of Colonies between 1910 and 1933, noted,

> The Blacks are the main agents of the spreading of palm seeds. [...] Each village harvested palm fruits, often in large amounts, extracted the oil and discarded the seeds in the bush. [...] The seeds gave birth to thousands of trees. [...] The native respected the *Elaeis*, which provided him with oil and wine. He did not cut them. The palm trees benefitted from the disappearance of large trees to thrive.[27]

Inhabitants of the Leverville concession were both well aware of the importance of these resources for HCB and keen to defend their right to use them. As an administrative report on agricultural concessions noted in June 1920, "there are no commercially exploitable palm groves over which some natives won't claim property, with even more vigour for often, elders of the tribe spent several years there, when they don't claim to have planted the trees themselves."[28] The legitimate property of *Elaeis* clusters also became a point of contention between Congolese elders and colonial agents, who protested that the former inflat-

---

21 Clement, "The Land Tenure," 91–92.
22 Carole L. Crumley, "Historical Ecology: A Multidimensional Ecological Orientation," in Crumley (ed.), *Historical Ecology*, 6.
23 Oslisly, "Climatic and Cultural," 4, 7.
24 Nicolaï, *Le Kwilu*, 78.
25 Alain Rival, Patrice Levang, *La Palme Des Controverses: Palmier à Huile et Développement* (Versailles: Quae, 2013), 24.
26 Nicolaï, *Le Kwilu*, 285.
27 AAB, AGRI 335, Les Huileries du Congo Belge, par Edmond Leplae, undated.
28 AAB, AIMO 1403, Quelques reflexions à propos du nouveau régime des concessions, June 1920.

ed their ownership claims far beyond their effective uses, as mentioned in a February 1938 report on HCB circles:

> If during the time when the HCB settled, natives did not immediately realize the interests of their rights on palm groves, their attention was quickly drawn to it. [...] Natives will not only entirely claim their rights, but also make excessive pretences, by trying to assert that their private rights extend to the entirety of natural palm groves, even unexploited, as well as the sub-spontaneous groves emerging from fallow in abandoned villages.[29]

In HCB concessions, issues of land allocation were superficially settled by the 1911 convention (see chapter 1). Article 8 specifically noted, "before exerting its choice, the company could temporarily settle on lands unencumbered with third party rights."[30] This meant, in principle, that the *Huileries* would have to recognize the concession's inhabitants' right to exclusively exploit the palm groves they already tended to prior to Leverville's foundation. However, Lord Leverhulme disagreed with this policy and noted in November 1917, "behind and above all [...] there will always be the menace to the HCB of local interpenetration of native rights and I believe that the HCB can make the native more prosperous and bring within his reach a better system of living than the native can possibly achieve by any other means."[31]

As early as September 1911, Sidney Edkins, the concession's first area manager, asked the colony's General Governor for instructions as to how the company should properly determine which plots of land were effectively unencumbered and how to prevent indigenous communities from impeding upon the company's own chosen palm groves:

> We are asking you to make us know or provide us with the practical means to determine the lands encumbered with third party rights as they existed when the convention was signed [...] It is certain that the natives will claim property over many natural palm groves when they will realize their increased value by our agricultural exploitation. [...] With the convention, we accepted many obligations destined to improve the material and moral conditions of the natives living around our posts. [...] To assume these charges, for the natives to enjoy as much as possible these advantages, we must rely on the just understanding of the rights acquired by each party, and it seems indispensable to us to determine them now.[32]

---

[29] AAB, AIMO 1404, Situation dans les cercles HCB, 9 February 1938.
[30] "Projet de décret approuvant une convention conclue le 21 février 1911 entre le Gouvernement du Congo belge et la Société 'Lever Brothers Limited' et ayant pour objet la concession de terres à une société à constituer sous le nom de: "Société Anonyme des Huileries du Congo Belge," in *Annales Parlementaires 1911*, Document parlementaire n°126.
[31] UA, LBC/229, Lord Leverhulme to Max Horn, 6 November 1917.
[32] AAB, AI 1468, Lettre de Sidney Edkins au GG Fuchs, 25 September 1911.

The impediments of delimitating these lands and the potential hampering of HCB's profits by the protection of "native rights" pushed its management to swiftly change its policy. In March 1912, Edkins directly demanded the suspension of "native rights" over the lands chosen by the company:

> The issue of native rights in the concessions raises many difficulties: villages continuously change places and with them the lands cultivated by their inhabitants. Small groups of three or four huts burn hundreds of oil palms to plant a hectare of corn or manioc, and when they do not burn them, they harvest no more than a hundred fruit clusters a year. [...] It appears to us that the best solution would be not to recognize native rights on the lands we selected under the condition that our company could plant palm trees on their entirety and harvest all the palm fruits.[33]

Belgian Congo's vice-General Governor nevertheless refused to grant such an exception to HCB. "I cannot satisfy your demand of seeing the government fail to recognize native rights on the lands chosen by your company. [...] Native rights to occupy lands is sacred throughout the colony and must be religiously applied."[34] In spite of the existence of a convention created to secure a smooth collaboration between the state and the *Huileries*, both parties found themselves in a legal and moral deadlock in the very first years of the concession's existence. This contradiction led to the elaboration of ad hoc legal dispositions, tailor made to accommodate the *Huileries*' needs while circumventing the spirit of Belgian Congo's land laws.

The colony's registrar of land titles suggested an initial way out of this stalemate as early as 1912. He proposed the auctioning of indigenous *sui generis* rights on land, to which HCB would effectively be the only bidder. According to the registrar, the "native village was a legal entity" whose commons were the collective property of its inhabitants. These rights were inalienable but could nonetheless be temporarily leased to a third party under the approval of the district commissioner, and allocated to the highest bidder in an auction. Per the registrar,

> One of the most justified criticism made towards [HCB] is its desire to eliminate any possibility of competition. The opportunity provided to the village to temporarily alienate its rights in a public option [...] should suppress this criticism [...] There is no doubt that [HCB will try to] obtain this right. Whether it succeeds or not, it would only be at the benefit of the community.[35]

---

33 AAB, AI 1468, Lettre de Sidney Edkins au GG Fuchs, 22 March 1912.
34 AAB, AI 1468, Lettre du vice-GG au Directeur des HCB, 23 May 1912.
35 AAB, AI 1468, Note du conservateur des titres fonciers, 21 July 1912.

This proposal was nevertheless rejected by the General Governor, who found it excessively disadvantageous for the Congolese. The General Governor posed questions regarding the repercussions that might result from implementing this proposal: "Who will take the decision to authorize the natives to deprive themselves of their assets and to prevent themselves of any kind of oil trade? [...] What will the natives do, once they are deprived of their main trading activity?"[36]

In 1934, it became clear for public servants that attempts at separating native lands from those of the company were doomed to fail. In January, the colony's registrar conceded that the main obstacles to HCB's territorial prospects resided "in the dissemination of native villages, for each small village is settled and cultivates lands as scattered as the villages themselves. [...] These plots of land used by the natives act as many nets of resistance against Europeans' land occupation." He concluded, somehow disabused,

> [Natives] always demonstrated a profound antipathy, not to say hostility [towards land delimitation]. Native mores have barely changed, their agricultural and migratory uses stayed the same. Everybody knows that preliminary works performed by geometers were very expensive and were never followed by practical results. [...] Natives never respected these delimitations, [for they] parked them *ex abrupto* within territorial boundaries sometimes designated arbitrarily, this process must have profoundly vexed the natives' spirit of freedom.[37]

In spite of the difficulty of making local communities follow the land allocation envisioned by colonial power holders, jurists already found another way to circumvent the respect of indigenous land rights to ensure the *Huileries'* profitability: the tripartite agreements. Without theoretically infringing on the law, these arrangements were aimed at depriving indigenous communities form their rights over land at the company's benefit. According to the 1911 convention, the colony pledged to lease up to 200,000 hectares to HCB in each of its five circles. The company had until May 1926 to determine which lands it wished to acquire. However, this plan never properly came to fruition because of multiple practical obstacles, such as the disregard of indigenous communities for these boundaries and the company's limited means for determining to whom which land "belonged".[38] In 1922, this original scheme was suspended and replaced by the drafting of those "tripartite agreements."[39]

---

36 AAB, AI 1468 Note du GG Henry, 23 July 1912.
37 AAB, AIMO 1652, Note concernant la délimitation des terres indigenes par le conservateur des titres fonciers, 23 January 1934.
38 AAB, AIMO 1404, Note pour la 4e direction générale du ministère des colonies, 12 May 1933.

These legal arrangements worked as such. A delegation made of surveyors, a representative of the territorial authority, designated chiefs assisted by a magistrate, and a representative of the HCB drafted a contract related to the use of land in a given area situated within an HCB circle. Together, they first delineated blocks of between 250 and 5,000 hectares in which the company intended to harvest palm fruits. Within these blocks, so-called "native" and "vacant" lands were determined with the agreement of all parties. Both types of land were then legally fused into joint ownership under the tutelage of the administration. The representative of the colony then allowed HCB to lease parts of these lands for their own benefits. Within these blocs, indigenous communities were allowed to settle "only under the company's consent" (art. 4). HCB enjoyed the right of exclusive harvest of palm fruits for commercial purpose, while the local communities could continue to collect fruits and produce oil for their own consumption but were strictly forbidden to sell the fruits, kernels or oil to HCB competitors. They were also allowed to freely dispose of other products, such as rubber, ivory and copal.[40]

Both HCB representatives and administrative agents were satisfied with the tripartites, which were renewed in 1938 and 1958.[41] After the implementation of the tripartites, the company boasted in its 1922 annual report that the agreements were "a major event in the history of the company, maybe even in the evolution of the colony."[42] A note circulating in the ministry of colonies suggested that these new laws protected indigenous rights and uses. "Natives would keep on displacing as they wish except on the lands planted by the company or in the managed palm groves, but in those blocks, sufficient lands would be secured for their cultures."[43]

However, not everyone was satisfied with this new arrangement. An article published in the magazine *Notre Colonie* in April 1925 painted the tripartites as an infringement of freedom of trade and detrimental to indigenous communities:

> Tripartite agreements are very complex and very clever. It is certain that they were drafted to safeguard the concessionary's interests. [...] Serious objections can be raised regarding these contracts, both economically and legally speaking. HCB's de facto monopoly, although opposed by several members of the colonial council, is duly extended, [in both space and time], [...] third parties are evicted from the region for another decade [...] Re-

---

39 AAB, AIMO 1404, Memo of meeting with Mr Franck on the subject of native rights, 20 April 1922.
40 AAB, AIMO 1404, Modèle de contrat tripartite, undated.
41 Fieldhouse, *Unilever Overseas*, 528, 533.
42 AAB, AGRI 335, Rapport annuel HCB, 1922–1923.
43 AAB, AIMO 1404, Note pour la 1e direction du ministère des colonies, 22 April 1922.

garding the natives, it is to be feared that [...] as the company enjoys a monopoly on palm oil trade, it would fix a buying price inferior to what could be achieved through free competition.[44]

Other palm oil traders settled in the Kwilu basin saw their business significantly decrease in productivity in the years that followed the implementation of the tripartites.[45] HCB could eliminate competition by claiming rights onto blocs of land that were coveted by other palm oil producers, as underlined by a February 1938 report: "to prevent the settlement of any colonist, planter, trader or industrialist, the company only has to incorporate in a block of 250 hectares grossly determined the area coveted by the third party, and to choose this block at the time of the enquiry."[46] When discussion began in Brussels on the renewal of the tripartite agreements, opposition arose even within the ranks of the colonial council—the deliberative organ in charge of formulating advices on every colonial legislation—who ultimately adopted it at a small majority.[47]

Although the colony's registrar of land titles failed to guarantee an HCB monopoly over land without seeing the administration overtly breaking the law in 1912, both parties found a way to conciliate their respective interests. Overtly complex and opaque, the tripartite agreements were enforced within both private and public spheres in spite of strong opposition of other colonial stakeholders. Their continued presence and enduring influence highlighted the difficulty of bridging the practical needs of colonial actors in the field with the moral standards that were supposed to preside over their deployment.

With the tripartite agreements, HCB managed to secure a relatively strong monopoly over land and palm oil production within its circles. However, the company still had to face another obstacle: local inhabitants' autonomous uses of *Elaeis* and its many resources, which threatened the *Huileries*' ambition to exclusively exploit its concession's riches. Preventing such competition also required casting aside the virtuous ethos, which allegedly imbued the company's activities.

---

[44] AAB, AIMO 1404, Extrait de la revue Notre Colonie, 21 April 1925.
[45] AAB, AIMO 1652, Lettre du commissaire de district du Kwango au gouverneur du Congo-Kasaï, 28 May 1926.
[46] AAB, AIMO 1404, Situation dans les cercles HCB, 9 February 1938.
[47] AAB, AIMO 1652, Contrats tripartites, in *La Libre Belgique*, 24 January 1939.

Competing for palm oil

Before the foundation of Leverville, palm oil was a key resource for the Congo basin's inhabitants. The oil and the flowers of palm fruits were staple ingredients of local cuisines, while the tree's wood and fibres were used in the making of tools and in building construction. Moreover, the fermented sap of *Elaeis* was turned into *malafu* (palm wine), the most frequently consumed spirit in the Kwango district. Calabashes of palm wine were frequently exchanged as gifts or payments and were key elements in the composition of bridewealth.[48] *Malafu* also had important medical applications. As noted by a colonial doctor in January 1935, "palm wine is used in the making of the most varied native drugs: infusions of barks, roots, leaves, some having special properties. [...] It is used to ease the ingestion of medicine, as purgatives or as [...] frictions against body pain."[49]

The consumption of *malafu* raised both economic and moral issues for the authorities. First, making palm wine required significantly weakening or even killing the tree to collect its sap, which limited the resources available for oil companies. Furthermore, the making of wine was a more lucrative and immediately rewarding business than fruit cutting. General commissioner Wauters commented on trading *malafu:* "A *binda* (calabash) of palm oil is worth between two and five francs. Cutters are tempted to make wine instead of cutting fruit clusters."[50]

Second, indigenous consumption of alcohol came to grips with colonial ideals of continence. Inebriation was considered as having two problematic consequences. First, it allegedly led to the "deliquescence" of Congolese mores. Second, it was thought to thoroughly impede upon indigenous workers' productivity. Edmond Leplae summed up their considerations in his undated history of HCB: "drunkenness is generalised and weakens the race, which becomes lazy, meek, unable to work properly. Days and night of drinking inevitably lead to orgies, brawls, murders. Some even fall down adult trees to harvest a few litres of wine and a couple hours of alcoholic insanity."[51] Therefore, the administration tried to significantly curb the making and consumption of *malafu*.

In July 1923, the colony's general government attempted to enforce a decree forbidding its brewing. They issued a statement to this effect: "General Governor

---

48 Nicolaï, *Le Kwilu*, 330–331.
49 AAB, AGRI 335, Le vin de palme, excipient à drogues indigènes, 2 January 1935.
50 AAB, AIMO 1652, Lettre du commissaire general Wauters au gouverneur du Congo-Kasaï, 18 March 1932.
51 AAB, AGRI 335, Les Huileries du Congo Belge, par Edmond Leplae, undated.

Lippens [...] raises attention on the need to react against the natives' tendency to fell palm trees to make palm wine. [...] He proposes to study the measures that would allow authorities to forbid such felling, but also to forbid or reduce as much as possible the making and consumption of palm wine."[52] Functionaries followed the example of neighbouring colonies, Angola and French Equatorial Africa, where it was mandatory for Europeans to destroy calabashes attached to palm trees to collect the sap for making the wine and where the sale of wine was forbidden. The agricultural department of the colonial ministry subsequently advocated for a ban on felling palm trees extended to the entire colony. Nonetheless, field public servants realized the impracticality of such extreme measures:

> There are regions in the Congo where the use of palm wine is so widespread that forbidding its making could not be entirely enforced without generating deep disturbances in native uses and probably foster troubles. [...] In the Kwango for instance, natives are almost permanently drunk on wine, and it has been noticed that their physical vigour is subsequently undermined. It would therefore be rational to limit palm wine consumption, but it can only be achieved gradually, in order to suppress it after a few years, a decade for instance.[53]

If colonial authorities were bent on adapting indigenous mores and uses to their own moral frameworks, many administrators were well aware that such policies would better be enforced on an incremental basis. They feared that imposing an extreme and rapid series of transformations of habits and traditions would be counter-productive and pit the Congolese against the state without improving their "moral standing." An effective example of this cautious stance was the colonial authorities' approach to polygamy. Although the 1908 colonial charter (see chapter 1) contained a pledge to "fight" polygamy, policies implemented in the field attempted to discourage its practice rather than outrightly forbidding it. Many colonial actors feared that too extreme of an authoritarian approach to such a sensitive issue would disrupt the indigenous social fabric, and negatively impact Congo's already dwindling birth rates.[54]

---

52 AAB, AGRI 335, Note au sujet d'un décret sur l'abattage des *Elaeis*, 24 July 1923.
53 AAB, AGRI 335, Note au sujet d'un décret sur l'abattage des *Elaeis*, 24 July 1923.
54 On polygamy in Belgian Congo, see: Amandine Lauro, "'Le Législateur n'Envisage en l'Espèce que le Point de Vue Physiologique': Régulations du Mariage 'Indigène' et Politiques Sexuelles au Congo Belge," in *Le Contrôle des Femmes dans les Empires Coloniaux. Empires, Genre, et Biopolitiques*, edited by Martine Spensky (Paris: Karthala, 2015), 185–192, Nancy Rose Hunt, "Noise Over Camouflaged Polygamy, Colonial Morality Taxation, and a Woman-Naming Crisis in Belgian Africa," *Journal of African History* 32:3 (1991): 471–494.

The making of *malafu* was not the only issue raised by the competition between HCB and the Kwango communities for using the palm groves. The production of palm oil itself was bitterly contested. Inhabitants of Southwest Congo had their own ways of extracting oil out of palm fruits. Fruits were boiled for several hours, and the oil oozing at the surface was then progressively skimmed and set aside. Cooking residues were subsequently pounded and once more mixed with boiling water, which allowed for the collection of oleaginous residues. Until the early 1930s, this artisanal production was then either used for household consumption or sold to HCB.[55]

In the late 1920s, it had already become increasingly clear that the company could not rely on artisanal-processed palm oil, which it considered to be of lower quality. The competition of Congolese palm oil with the standardised, high quality yields of Southeast Asian plantations required a significant improvement of the colony's palm oil output. From 1927 onwards, two business interest groups, the *Association des Intérêts Coloniaux* and the *Association Belge d'Agriculture tropicale et Subtropicale*, began petitioning the government to prevent indigenous communities from disposing of palm fruits.[56] They argued that the significant investments made to build and maintain industrial oil mills had to be protected against the competition of local communities, whose harvesting and production techniques entailed significant losses in quality and output. These business associations submitted two drafts of new legislation to the government, respectively in 1927 and 1928, to secure exclusive rights to exploit the palm groves for private companies. The explanatory statement of their first proposal underpinned their derogatory view of indigenous ways, as well as the discrepancy between Congolese uses of *Elaeis* and the needs of global markets: "Their extraction method by cooking or fermentation are empirical and defective, and extract from the fruit an oil of mediocre quality, far from the output that could be expected from the quality of the pulp."[57]

Their first plan was rejected by the Ministry of Colonies, for it "violat[ed] the natives' freedom of trade" and "lack[ed] precision on the obligations of companies regarding native communities."[58] In response, business owners crafted a second draft, which they deemed more "respectful of the natives," for it "[did]

---

55 Nicolaï, *Le Kwilu*, 350.
56 AAB, AGRI 728, Lettre du secrétaire de l'Association Belge d'Agriculture Tropicale au premier ministre, 9 July 1928. Lettre du président de l'Association des Intérêts Coloniaux au Ministre des colonies, 4 October 1927.
57 AAB, AGRI 728, Exposé des motifs du projet de décret sur la protection des huileries mécaniques, 19 September 1927.
58 AAB, AGRI 728, Note pour la 8e direction du ministère des colonies, 27 October 1927.

not impede on their rights, their freedoms, their customs; their habit of producing oil through rudimentary processes for their own consumption."[59] To strengthen their credibility, its authors underlined the input of key actors in the drafting of their proposal, including "Mr. General-director Leplae," who "honoured us with his presence at our meetings and helped us with his wise advises," as well as the provincial governors of Equateur and the Congo-Kasaï, who "gave us their tentative agreement on the essential clauses of our project."[60]

This second project was submitted to the colonial council in July 1930, but discussions were suspended in November at Edmond Leplae's demand. In his eyes, the protection would impose the economic immobilisation of extensive lands, which was detrimental to the colony's interests in times of economic crisis.[61] Less than a year later, discussions resumed around a renewed disposition, destined to ensure the legal "protection of mechanical oil mills" and their owners. The decree divided palm oil production zones in two distinct areas: 1) "zone A, in which the mill owner is the only one authorized to buy fresh fruits and palm kernels"; and 2) "zone B, in which the government commits not to provide lands to its competitors to settle oil mills or plantations."[62]

The owner of such a zone would be granted an exclusive right for the economic exploitation of the trees growing on vacant lands, which could still be harvested by indigenous communities but only for their own consumption. Under the supervision of the provincial governor, zone owners were authorised to manage and transform the palm groves with the assent of local communities. Competitors who harvested fruits within these protected areas could be fined, and even condemned to penal servitude.[63]

Once enforced, the decree led to disappointing results for palm oil businesses. First, in spite of a congruent law made to increase the production of standardised cash crops in the colony, the new decree paradoxically prevented the creation of oil palm plantations close to the oil mills. From 1933 on, the government also set up a program of compulsory cultivation. Officially speaking, this initia-

---

59 AAB, AGRI 728, Lettre du secrétaire de l'Association Belge d'Agriculture Tropicale au premier ministre Jaspar, 9 July 1928.
60 AAB, AGRI 728, Lettre du secrétaire de l'Association Belge d'Agriculture Tropicale au premier ministre Jaspar, 9 July 1928.
61 AAB, AGRI 99, Rapport du conseil colonial sur le projet de décret réalisant des mesures de protection pour les huileries mécaniques, 1933.
62 AAB, AGRI 728, Note sur le projet de décret accordant une protection aux huileries mécaniques, 1 October 1932.
63 AAB, AGRI 99, Rapport du conseil colonial sur le projet de décret réalisant des mesures de protection pour les huileries mécaniques, 1933.

tive was driven by "the necessity to create and maintain food crops for the alimentation of local communities, and, in an educative objective, to create native resources by the cultivation of cash crops, alimentary goods and forest species for reforestation."[64] On paper, *chefs médaillés* could evaluate their chieftaincy's agricultural needs, which would serve as a blueprint to determine the nature and surface of the crops to be sown. In practice, however, these plans were set up in advance by the administration based on the suggestions made by the district's agronomist.[65] Able-bodied men lacking permanent employment could be mobilized for compulsory cultivation in these fields or plantations for a maximum of 60 days a year.[66] If they refused, they risked having to pay a fine of up to 100 francs, and endure a week of penal servitude.[67]

However, the decree on the protection of mechanical oil mills explicitly forbade all forms of infringement on the mill owner's protected lands. In practice, this meant that the administration was not allowed to set up plantations where they were most needed. "We come to a paradox: no palm tree plantations where there are oil mills, no oil mills where there are palm trees plantations,"[68] noted a functionary of the Ministry of Colonies in 1936. Furthermore, there was no practical means for ensuring that local communities would not harvest palm fruits to sell them to the mill owner's competitors.[69]

Decrees on compulsory cultivation and on the protection of oil mills supplemented the tripartite agreements to further standardise the amount and quality of the colony's outputs in palm oil. However, the *Huileries* and other mill owners' efforts to control *Elaeis* resources ran contrary to the "freedom" of indigenous communities guaranteed by Belgian Congo's law. This tension led to lengthy negotiations between public and private actors, regarding the best way to accommodate the imperatives of *mise en valeur* with the virtuous guise of Belgian rule in Central Africa. In the end, public and private actors still manage to find a working agreement, at the crossroads of profits and morals. Preventing the production and consumption of *malafu* furthered the "civilisational improvement" of the Congolese while side-lining indigenous competitors for palm oil resources. Attempts at compulsory cultivation both responded to the alleged "atavistic idleness" of African men and improved the colony's agricultural productivity.

---

64 AAB, AIMO 1856, Modèle d'arrêté sur les cultures obligatoires, undated.
65 Likaka, *Rural Society*, 47.
66 AAB, AIMO 1856, Modèle d'arrêté sur les cultures obligatoires, undated.
67 Ndaywel, *Nouvelle Histoire*, 363
68 AAB, AGRI 335, Application du décret sur les huileries et plantations obligatoires de palmiers, 18 April 1936.
69 AAB, AGRI 736, Zones Huilières, 6 June 1946.

Even with these changes, laws, rules and decrees could only do so much to strengthen the grip of private actors on the palm groves. The practical enforcement of colonial decrees was proportional to the limited means of field public servants to impose their will in the field. The commodification of fruits growing in the groves was inherently unpredictable, which became increasingly problematic with the passage of time. In the early 1930s, when Southeast Asian palm oil came to flood global markets, it became clear that HCB's only chance of turning a profit resided in shifting from natural groves to standardised plantations as main purveyors of palm fruits.

Fruitless plantations

In early May 1933, the HCB general director signalled to the Belgian minister of colonies that his company envisioned a radical refashioning of its activities. He communicated this vision in a letter to the general director:

> If we do not want the company to be forced into bankruptcy, we must completely reorganize our operations in Congo. [...] We must take swift measures to suppress some disadvantages regarding competing companies in other colonies [...] Congo's disadvantages regarding Sumatra and West Africa [...] can be summed up as follows. A lesser productivity from the Belgian Congo palm tree, resulting from the superiority of the selected oil palm on the wild one, [...] much higher transportation costs from the groves to the factory, caused by the scattering of natural palm groves, [...] social obligations in the form of medical services and schools.[70]

As shown in this letter, the *Huileries*' obsolete business model appeared to be increasingly unsustainable in the early 1930s. The company's dependence on naturally-growing fruits and on the unreliable output of forcibly recruited cutters were no match for the efficiency of the large scale, standardised *Elaeis* plantations of Southeast Asia. At this time, HCB was still following the extractive pattern set up by the Congo Free State's infamous rubber concessions. Furthermore, the propensity for violence that such an economic construction entailed was reined in by a series of costly paternalistic obligations, which also burdened the company's already fickle profitability (see chapter 1). It only took a few years for some colonial actors to realise the unsustainability of yesteryear's giant concession schemes. In 1921, a public servant of the Ministry of Colonies noted, "not one of these concessions has been properly exploited. [...] HCB is far from having selected all of its blocs and already fails to comply with its en-

---

[70] UA, UAC 2/36/1/11, HCB general director to minister of colonies Tschoffen, 1 May 1933.

gagements regarding the valuation of the selected blocs. [...] There is no benefit anymore in delimiting large swaths of territory without prospecting first and without considering the capital one is disposed to invest."[71]

The untenable competition from Southeast Asian palm oil was the final nail in the coffin for Leverville's old business model. The shores of the Kwilu river could no longer remain on the fringes of capitalist encroachment, imperfectly supervised, unreliably harvested and inescapably shared with local communities. In the second half of the 1930s, the company took two main initiatives to safeguard its own existence. First, HCB worked hand in hand with public-funded agronomists to develop new breeds of oil palms. Second, its managers accelerated the development of plantations, destined to ultimately replace the groves as sources of palm oil. The *Huileries* envisioned the planting of 30,000 hectares of *Elaeis* in their five Congolese concessions in less than twenty years; this ambitious goal included planting 12,000 hectares in Leverville.[72]

The plantations of Southeast Asia were not only a topic of anxiety for palm oil producers in Belgian Congo; they also served as a source of inspiration, which was mostly channelled through the Ministry of Colonies. The Belgian government's agronomists participated in an international, closely-knitted network of experts in tropical agriculture and frequently travelled to Java, Ceylon and Sumatra to learn about the latest breakthroughs in colonial cash cropping.[73] These functionaries, working under the supervision of Edmond Leplae, were in turn advising private companies that were active in the Congo on how to improve their yields of cotton, palm oil or coffee. New cropping techniques, mostly inspired by Southeast Asian examples, were tried and tested in the colony's agronomic stations, which were placed under the supervision of REPCO (*Régie des Plantations de la Colonie*).[74] Promising results were then shared with European planters, Congolese farmers and private companies. Out of the Congo's fourteen agricultural stations active in 1931, two were dedicated to the development of new breeds of oil palms: Barumbu and Yangambi. Both stations were located in the Province Orientale in a rainforest ecosystem, which was markedly different from Leverville's patchwork of grasslands and forest galleries.

REPCO agronomists first attempted to create new breeds of oil palms in Yangambi in 1922.[75] Their goal was to foster new types of fruit, which would produce

---

71 AAB, RF 1739, Note sur la concession de terre de la compagnie des Grands Lacs, 1921.
72 AAB, AGRI 736, Rapport annuel Huilever, 1953.
73 Hodge, *The Triumph*, 4.
74 Vellut, "Hégémonies en Construction," 319.
75 Rival, Levang, "La Palme," 28.

more pulp and would contain a smaller kernel.[76] From June 1924 onwards, REPCO began to provide palm seeds to private companies.[77] Furthermore, with the blessing of the colony's agricultural authorities, palm oil producers also bought seeds in Sumatra to start plantations in the Congo.[78]

In 1933, REPCO was replaced by a new organization, INEAC (*Institut National pour l'Etude Agronomique du Congo Belge*). INEAC agronomists approached the colony's fledging palm oil productivity in several ways. They studied *Elaeis* illnesses and parasites; attempted to manually pollinize *Elaeis* blossoms; and studied the optimal ways of refining palm oil and fertilizing *Elaeis* trees. More importantly, INEAC also organised a large-scale distribution of oil palm seeds to planters and private companies. In 1936 alone, it provided more than two million *Elaeis* seeds to its private partners.[79] HCB and INEAC participated in extensive collaboration, which led the company noting in 1935 that the inception of its plantation scheme had been "thoroughly eased by the works of INEAC."[80]

Turning the Kwilu basin's forest galleries into plantations required further collaboration between the company and the administration. According to an undated report on the enforcement of the colony's 1933 decree on compulsory cultivation,

> HCB already created plant nurseries, selected lands and trained agricultural supervisors (*moniteurs agricoles*) to start the plantations, if possible immediately after the dry season. The company counts on the administration's support to proceed to the clearing of the lands selected for the natives, and to organize the necessary propaganda in order for them to plant the selected cuttings put at their disposal.[81]

As with the harvesting of palm fruits in the groves (see chapter 4), setting up plantations in Leverville required the coerced participation of the local workforce. Preparing the land and planting the trees necessitated the mobilisation of men with the help of field administrators; supervision and training of these men was assured by Congolese *moniteurs agricoles*, who acted more as brutal foremen than as instructors. On paper, *moniteurs agricoles* were expected to

---

76 Nicolaï, *Le Kwilu*, 293.
77 AAB, AGRI 335, Lettre du secrétaire général du ministère des colonies au GG Rutten, 16 June 1924.
78 AAB, AGRI 335, DG agriculture to company Palma, 30 April 1925.
79 AAB, AGRI 399, Rapport annuel INEAC, 1936.
80 RMCA, 54.85.183, L'industrie de l'huile de palme au Congo, par l'administrateur-délégué d'Huilever, 1935.
81 AAB, AIMO 1855, Instructions générales sur les modalités d'application du décret du 20 mai 1933, undated.

guide Congolese cultivators and to supervise their work. In practice, however, few had received any kind of agricultural training. They were mostly recruited among veterans of the *Force Publique* and were essentially hired to coercively stimulate production.[82]

In 1934, HCB and the administration set up the guidelines of their collaboration for the realisation of the company's plantation scheme. Public agronomists would supervise land clearings, while HCB would provide stands of selected oil palms to be planted. However, the company struggled to fulfil its commitments. According to a 1934 report on agriculture in the Kwango district,

> Mr. Van Hout, deputy agronomist [cleared] 586 hectares. If Mr Van Hout was unable to plant a single hectare, it is simply because HCB promised to provide plants that it did not possess [...] Kikwit zone: [...] on January 1st 1935, 300 hectares were cleared out and 50 were planted. It is also HCB's fault, for it could not give us more trees than those necessary to plant 50 hectares.[83]

In spite of these issues, public servants and HCB representatives sought to work together on a new plan, which would further their respective interests. They wished to foster Congolese-owned plantations, "of which the natives would be owners and managers."[84] The idea was that if the company would provide local farmers with "selected seeds or plants, technical supervision, even financial help [...], it would furthermore accept to buy to the natives the fruits at a rate determined in agreement with them and the government."[85] The agronomists working for the Ministry of Colonies were enthusiastic about this possibility, as demonstrated in an internal note dated April 1936:

> What do the companies want? To produce fruits, lots of cheap fruits, regularly provided. We offer that to them by ensuring that the natives plant valuable seeds (INEAC seeds) as close as possible from mechanical oil mills and places of economic evacuation. What is the native's interest? What he fails to understand today, but might realize tomorrow: being discharged of the immense, antisocial burden of exploiting natural palm groves, a practice as outdated as it is uneconomic. Palm trees plantations provide him with an important tonnage of fruits of which he can freely dispose, but that naturally, without any pressure whatsoever, he would be invited to sell to the closest honest trader, the owner of the oil zone.[86]

---

82 Likaka, *Rural Society*, 50–51
83 AAB, RA/CB 157, Rapport annuel sur la situation agricole du district du Kwango, 1934.
84 AAB, AGRI 99, Lettre non signée au commissaire de province de Léopoldville, 29 September 1933.
85 AAB, AGRI 99, Lettre non signée au commissaire de province de Léopoldville, 29 September 1933.
86 AAB, AGRI 335, Note pour la 4e direction générale du ministère des colonies, 20 April 1936.

This plan was not only seen in a positive light in Brussels; it was also welcomed by Leopoldville's general government as a way to move forward with the chiefdom regrouping scheme that the administration struggled to implement in the Kwango district (see chapter 3). In early 1934, the colony's General Governor suggested that these Congolese owned plantations could be populated by families grouped in accordance with their "ethnicity" and "racial affinities."[87] The company and administration worked together to devise a plan. They decided to begin by determining the lands on which these plantations could be set before dividing them into small plots, which would each be tended by a Congolese family.[88] In March of the same year, the first contracts were drafted, delimiting the mutual obligations of each partner. Families would be given five hectares of land and had the obligation to plant half a hectare on an annual basis with 50 selected oil palms provided by the company. Fruits had to be sold to the HCB at a government-fixed price, and farmers would be paid in accordance with the number of trees they planted and tended. If they proved to be negligent, the company would seize their parcel. Unruly tenants would be stripped of their rights and any compensation for their labour.[89]

However, this scheme proved to be unpopular among members of local communities. The provincial authorities warned HCB managers that their will to ultimately remain owners of these plots and to potentially reclaim the lands of "disappointing" producers would render the plantation scheme unattractive for potential Congolese producers.[90] In March 1937, an inquiry showed that 31% of the farmers who settled there in November of the previous year had already left their parcel, while potential candidates who could replace them often refused to do so, arguing that they had no guaranteed rights over their outputs. One provincial authority noted, "We are currently powerless to prevent or limit this exodus, which seems to be an expression of the natives' aversion to imposed cultivation."[91]

Ultimately, the plantation program did not reap its expected benefits. In 1956, only 7,350 hectares of selected trees were planted in the Leverville conces-

---

[87] AAB, AIMO 1855, Compte-rendu de la réunion concernant la mise en valeur des rives du Kwilu et de ses affluents, 27 January 1934.
[88] AAB, AIMO 1855, Lettre du Commissaire de district Vandevenne au commissaire de la province de Léopoldville, 8 February 1934.
[89] AAB, AIMO 1855, Contrat d'engagement de planteurs, March 1934.
[90] AAB, AIMO 1856, Lettre du Chef de Province de Léopoldville à l'Administrateur-délégué des HCB, 5 May 1934.
[91] AAB, AIMO 1856, Lettre du Chef de Province A. De Beauffort au Gouverneur Général, 30 April 1937.

sion, far from the goal of 12,000 set by the company twenty years before.[92] Furthermore, the yields of these plantations were disappointing. The selected seeds sent by INEAC were bred in the rainforest in Yangambi and were ill-adapted to the Kwilu's ecosystem. The region's dry seasons slowed down the tree's growth, which limited their output in oil.[93]

HCB's attempts at improving its production were multifaceted; their legal component, embodied by tripartite agreements and the decree on mechanical oil mills was accompanied by a rearticulation of its business model. The company's managers hoped to shift from palm groves to plantations as main sources of raw material. Standardised, supervised and "rationally" organised rows of selected oil palms were thought to bring an end to the unscalable, unpredictable character of extracting fruits naturally growing in the Kwilu basin's forest galleries. However, this radical move did not meet the ambitious goals set by the *Huileries*' management. Plantations were slow to take off, difficult to maintain, and brought disappointing harvests. HCB's plantation scheme shed further light on the difficulty to realize this colonial vision in practice.

Conclusion

HCB waged its "war against nature" on many fronts. They engaged in legal battles to circumvent the laws destined to protect a minimal access to land and resources to the colony's indigenous communities. They fought on behalf of the concession's palm groves to ascertain the company's standing in the exploitation of *Elaeis*. They targeted the unpredictability of managed palm groves by replacing naturally-growing trees with standardised, selected strains in an attempt to shift the company's reliance upon the former. Ultimately, the *Huileries* were engaged in a war of conquest, whose ultimate victory would have been to adapt the concession's ecology to its needs and demands. As with so many power-hungry entities across history, HCB won some battles but lost others. Tripartite agreements had thoroughly limited the competition for palm oil resources. At the same time, the company's plantation scheme did not turn the Kwilu's "pericapitalist" palm groves into overseeable, reliable fruit resources.

This final chapter sheds light on yet another guise of Leverville: a series of interventions on space and resources in an attempt to bring order to an ecosystem where colonial agents thought that chaos originally prevailed. The conces-

---

92 Nicolaï, *Le Kwilu*, 367.
93 Nicolaï, *Le Kwilu*, 368–369.

sion was a physical unit, in which a plethora of groups and individuals competed for access to land and resources. It was a space where the *Huileries*' monopolistic endeavours clashed with the demands of indigenous communities and of the administration. It was a place for which complex and refined legal dispositions were tailored to bridge the gap between economic imperatives and moral principles. It was an environment where agronomic experiments were conducted on hundreds of hectares with disappointing outcomes. It was an ecosystem, which was radically transformed in the early 20th century by the global competition for palm oil resources.

According to Anna Tsing, capitalist modernisation relied on the belief that "everything on earth—and beyond—might be scalable."[94] Investors, entrepreneurs and governments often fostered commodification schemes, resting on the belief that natural resources could be standardised, rationalised, improved through tests and trials. The contrasted outcomes of HCB's "war against nature" testifies to the difficulty of constraining tropical ecosystems and their inhabitants to participate to colonial schemes of commodification. Although *Elaeis* was particularly suited for "scalable" production, Leverville's management systematically struggled to move past its reliance on "unscalable" palm groves. The discrepancy between the strategies of spatial reordering devised by the company and the administration and its practical enforcement brings to the fore another aspect of colonial impotence. Agents of empire not only struggled to impose their will on human communities; they were also confronted by unruly environments.

---

94 Tsing, *The Mushroom*, 40.

Conclusion: The concession experience

This book has taken the Leverville concession as a starting point to study the experience of colonialism in the Kwilu basin, a region which has often been neglected in the historiography of Central Africa. Leverville was positioned on the margins of the great "arteries" through which power, peoples and commodities flowed in Belgian Congo. However, Leverville remained connected to the colony's circulatory system and its skeletal network of strategic enclaves and corridors by its very own vessel, the Kwilu river. HCB steamboats were practically the only ones that navigated this waterway, building a bridge between the remote tropical utopia of Lord Leverhulme and the wider world.

Although relatively isolated and certainly peculiar in its strategies of ruling and exploiting, Leverville can nevertheless be used as a vantage point to (re)consider the deployment of colonialism in sub-Saharan Africa and beyond. The concession was a tropical outpost of Lever Brothers, which was already a prominent player in interwar global capitalism. Furthermore, Leverville can be connected with other early 20th century utopian projects fostered in the global South, where private entrepreneurs attempted to build model, "orderly" societies in what they perceived as "savage" environments. Finally, the daily exercise of governance and capitalist extraction in Leverville epitomises the complex and often conflicted relations of European administrations and private companies in colonial settings.

In this book, I employed the overarching concept of *colonial impotence* in order to articulate Leverville's historical idiosyncrasies with the discernible patterns of colonial intervention it could help illustrate. Colonial impotence forms a red thread, which runs through this book; it is a metaphor that is reflected in the many facets of the daily experience of colonialism I sought to investigate. Colonial impotence speaks of the gap between the virtuous and the violent guises of the Leverville project; of the refusal of Europeans in the field to conform to the behaviours and attitudes demanded from them; of the agency of indigenous communities which hampered HCB's project; and of the impossibility for the company to bend the Kwilu's environment to its designs. Archives and memories collected through this research implicitly spoke of the Leverville concession's impotence by shedding light on the contradictions, frustrations, angers and fears of those who worked and lived in it. However, such conflicted feelings and emotions not only saturated Leverville; they also played a key role in determining the course of many other colonial endeavours. The micro historical study of this enclave can, therefore and hopefully, contribute to a better understanding of the joint deployment of colonialism and capitalism in the field.

The unrealized utopia

In spite of its remoteness, Leverville was the recipient of multifaceted investments. First, it was vested in hopes that it would become the spearhead of a new form of "ethical" colonialism and capitalism, the embodiment of a radical move away from the infamous brutality of the Congo Free State. The forest galleries stretching along the Kwilu river and its tributaries were seen as a blank slate upon which the Belgian state and Lever Brother could write the first chapter of their shared story. Prominent and diverse figures such as Lord Leverhulme, King Albert the 1st, Edmund Morel and Emile Vandervelde, believed in its ambitious promise. They hoped that the implementation of Lever Brothers' English-born paternalism in the tropics of Central Africa would give birth to a benevolent new breed of imperialism.

This sentimental investment had a significant financial counterpart. Leverville absorbed hundreds of millions of Congolese francs for the building of its infrastructures and the deployment of its social engineering endeavours. In spite of this massive influx of cash, HCB yielded few benefits for its shareholders. After Leverville had been in existence for only a decade, it became increasingly clear that its obsolete business model could not match the productivity of its competitors. However, in spite of disappointing results and of belated attempts to correct the concession's economic course in the 1930s, the Port Sunlight mothership continued to support the *Huileries*. The company's long-lasting foothold in Central Africa had to do in part with the affective bounds that its founder, Lord Leverhulme, had fostered with this African project.[1]

However, the long-held hopes of turning Leverville into a benevolent enclave, nested in a model colony, were inalterably tainted by violence. In the interwar, most fruit cutters were forcibly recruited. Small children were seen performing heavy physical tasks in the concession's oil mills. Belgian public servants and their Congolese mercenaries preyed upon local communities; confiscated food and cattle; and raped women they coveted. Medical care was often performed under duress. Forced labour and heavy taxation fuelled the resentment of Pende communities targeted to work in Leverville, which contributed to the 1931 *Tupelepele* revolt. The effective act of colonizing the Kwilu basin, jointly performed by Belgian administrators and HCB representatives, imbued the region with a multifaceted brutality.

The investment of hubris, capital and violence in the Kwilu basin presided over a dramatic reshuffling of pre-existing power structures, social hierarchies,

---

[1] Fieldhouse, *Unilever Overseas*, 509.

extractive practices and settlement patterns. Even with the brutality and hegemony wrought by colonial players, these transformations nevertheless remained limited by the unruliness of the people and environments upon which they were imposed. Schemes of population displacement and the setting up of smallholder plantations, destined to anchor indigenous communities where they could easily be supervised and mobilised, did not meet their goals. The standardisation of palm oil production yielded disappointing results. These shortcomings highlighted the inherent complexity of colonial forms of commodification. Plans could be fostered on the grounds of tried and tested formulas, and yet fail once they were enforced.

When considering the history of Leverville, there is a surprising discrepancy between the concession's grandstanding objectives, the enormous means it mobilised, and the poor results it showed. Like comparable ambitious endeavours in tropical capitalism, Leverville was ultimately an unrealized utopia, unable to fulfil its economic and its ethical designs. This inability to realize this colonial vision for the concession stemmed from its utopian nature, from the fact that the concession's founding forces considered the Kwilu basin from the onset as a disordered blank page. This region was barely studied or charted when the concession was founded. Apart from its extraordinary richness in oil palms, the area was a perceived almost as a non-place, devoid of history and characteristics. It was seen as a space which could – and should – therefore, be easily organised and overseen. The disregard for local traditions, social structures and environmental aspects contributed in no small part to its ultimate demise. In believing that Leverville could be scalable at will, its founders overlooked the issues with which they would be confronted.

The Leverville concession's poor economic downturn can be compared to another key player of colonial capitalism in Central Africa: the *Union Minière du Haut-Katanga* (UMHK). UMHK enforced an even more ambitious paternalist program than HCB to "stabilize" its African workforce around its mines. From the 1920s onwards, the mining company set up workers camps, rations, educational, medical and recreative facilities, creating an all-encompassing disciplinarian structure, which surrounded mineworkers and their families.[2] Both ventures shared a similar ethos: merging large-scale resource extraction with an authoritarian civilisational agenda. However, UMHK proved to be more success-

---

[2] See: Sean Hanretta, "Space and Conflict in the Elisabethville Mining Camps, 1923–1938", in *A History of Prison and Confinement in Africa*, edited by Florence Bernault (Portsmouth: Heinman, 2003), 191–220.

ful at achieving the goals it set for itself. Katanga's mining panopticon was both highly profitable and much less porous than the *Huileries*' Kwilu concession.[3]

To make sense of this discrepancy, it is helpful to go back to Anna Tsing's notion of "salvage accumulation"; that is, "amass[ing] capital without controlling the conditions under which commodities are produced."[4] UMHK could mobilize capital and technology to efficiently exploit the ores which made its fortune. A mineral deposit is fixed and can be clearly delimited. It is therefore possible, although challenging, to build a strategic enclave around it to extract, process and export its resources. Efficiently managing mines also requires a "stabilized" workforce that the company can oversee and mobilize at will through an overarching, paternalist labour policy.

However, the "scalable" nature of copper or cobalt, the possibility to commodify them through a standardized, relatively straightforward process, puts it at odds with HCB's interwar business model. Palm groves were scattered in an extensive, poorly charted "circle" of sub-equatorial wetlands. Exploiting them required the know-how and skills of highly mobile indigenous workers. These very skills could not be acquired through company training, but to the contrary were passed on within local communities. Furthermore, the very mobility necessary for fruit cutting hampered the supervision of HCB workers, which was either non-existent or counter-productive.

Therefore, if UMHK rested on scalability, HCB had to rely on salvage accumulation and could not efficiently oversee a key phase of its commodification process. This key difference put both companies' exploitation models at odds with one another, in spite of cosmetic similarities in terms their paternalist agendas. It helps explain why one was much better than the other at exploiting the colony's resource and at controlling its Congolese workforce.

Finally, it is also worth noting that the troubles faced by the Leverville concession after Congo's independence in 1960 were mostly similar to those already present in the interwar period. The then renamed company, *Plantations Lever au Congo* (PLC), remained inefficient; was resented by its workers; and lacked transparency in its relations with public authorities. First, the company was still unable to effectively compete with Southeast Asian producers, and endured further losses in the post-war era. PLC's value dropped by 35% between 1959 and 1965, while its palm oil production was cut in half in the same time span of time.[5] Second, the long-established resentment against the palm oil economy in the Kwan-

---

3 Guy Vanthemsche, *Le Congo*, 200.
4 Tsing, *The Mushroom*, 63.
5 Fieldhouse, *Unilever Overseas*, 541.

go would burst out again thirty years after the *Tupelepele* uprising. Between 1963 and 1966, a rebellion led by Pierre Muelele, a former Minister of the Lumumba cabinet, used the Gungu-Idiofa area as a base to kickstart an ultimately failed revolution.[6] This region was both the historical recruitment basin of Leverville and the cradle of the 1931 uprisings. The brutality of the *Tupelepele* repression was outmatched by this protracted guerrilla. Mulelist rebels and governmental forces tortured, raped and murdered local inhabitants.[7]

Third, the company remained embroiled in shady political arrangements. In 1973, the newly renamed company, *Plantations Lever au Zaïre* (PLZ), fell prey to the process of *zaïrianisation*, the forced nationalisation of foreign-owned companies decided by then president Mobutu. PLZ was given to a loyal supporter of the regime with no business acumen, which only deepened its economic woes. In September 1977, *zaïrianisation* was reverted in light of its dramatic outcome, and PLZ was repossessed by its former owner. This marked the moment where Lever's Zairian branch decided to fall back on local markets instead of trying to keep up with global competitors.[8] However, even within Zaïre, PLZ struggled to compete with artisanal palm oil producers. Although their products were of inferior quality, their extremely low prices were more adapted to the buying power of the population. In the beginning of the 1990s, confronted to the lack of profitability of its Kwilu installations, Unilever ultimately sold PLZ to a local businessman and politician, Henri-Désiré Takizala. As of today, the company is in an effective state of bankruptcy. Leverville's oil mills and industrial plants have been progressively stripped off by local communities and sold as scrap metal. Former employees still harvest palm fruits in discarded oil palm plantations and sell their hand-pressed oils to neighbouring clients.

The post-colonial downfall of PLC/PLZ can be better grasped in the light of the present study. Far from only being a victim of post-colonial turmoil and poor governance, the *Huileries* were already marred by issues of solvency, corruption and violence decades before the end of colonisation. A *longue durée* take on the history of capitalism in Africa helps with understanding how North/South economic inequalities are rooted in the very structure of resource extraction and workforce mobilisation, rather than resulting from short- to mid-term conjunctural impediments.

---

6 Mark Traugott, "Economic Origins of the Kwilu Rebellion," *Comparative Studies in Society and History*, 21:3 (1979), 472.
7 Emery Kalema, "Scars, Marked Bodies, and Suffering: The Mulele 'Rebellion' in Postcolonial Congo," *Journal of African History*, 59:2 (2018): 263–282.
8 Nicolaï, "L'Huile," 2013.

The protean enclave

Throughout this research, I attempted to demonstrate that concessions were multifaceted and comprised multiple guises. The opening chapter began with an overview of the concession's inception as a capitalist utopia. The following one approached Leverville as an impotent machine, hampered by its inability to fulfil the goals set by its founders. Then, the concession was studied as a field of social tensions, where the multifaceted agency of indigenous communities hampered the hegemonic designs of colonial actors. After that, Leverville was considered as space of saturated violence, where the enforcement of HCB's agenda inextricably relied on the exercise of constraint. The concession was also grasped as a bodily experience, where company and administration attempted to determine what the Congolese should eat; what they should wear; and how they should be medically treated. Finally, Leverville was considered as a physical environment, altered and transformed by a series of legal and agricultural interventions.

The concession therefore existed – and continues to exist – in many forms. Its ambitious objectives were put on paper in 1911 as a legally-binding contract signed between Lever Brothers and the Belgian government. Its inscription in the networks of global capitalism was materialised in the Sunlight soap made out of its oil yields, which were used by millions of people all over the world. Leverville also offered a series of very diverse experiences for its employees. The concession provided its reluctant workforce with the experience of eating rations, receiving medical treatment and attempting to evade recruitment; being clothed and unclothed according to circumstances; climbing trees, cutting fruit clusters and transporting them to the buying station. Memories of the concession's physicality continue to circulate in and around the now disbanded enclave, passed down by relatives of long-deceased HCB workers.

These intimate experiences were also inextricably entangled with Leverville's existence as a field of tensions and power struggles. Disputes arose between field agents and their superiors when the former overlooked their responsibilities. Resentment festered from the abuses performed by territorial agents, recruiters, messengers and sentries. These individuals regularly used their fraction of the colonial capacity for violence to improve their own personal standing. Inhabitants distrusted the company; more often than not, they also refused to take part in its plantation scheme. Chiefs and elders deceived colonial functionaries in order to avoid the coerced displacement of their communities, or to disguise the circulation of *Lukusu*.

Leverville also embodied two different physical guises. On a symbolic plane, it was represented as a perfect circle built around its main station, which suggested an even control and mastering of the large zone put under the *Huileries'* care in 1911. In practice, however, the concession was closer to a sort of patchwork, formed out of industrial enclaves, plantations and managed palm groves. Outside of this relatively well-controlled grid, HCB had little grip on its "perfect circle." Palm trees were still felled by its inhabitants to produce *malafu* or were burned to leave place to subsistence crops. The loose supervision that the company held on its sphere of influence paradoxically constituted one of its main powers of attraction. Fruit cutters could travel in and out of informal settlements known as *villages doublures*, where they were able to partially escape from the administration's supervision while harvesting palm fruits on behalf of the company.

Although relatively isolated, Leverville remained profoundly vulnerable to outside influences. It was not secluded from its surrounding environment, but rather remained physically and culturally porous, constantly traversed by fruit cutters and their families, influenced by the spiritual agency and healing practices they fostered to make sense of the dramatic changes they experienced. Leverville was also subject to changes wrought by the overarching forces of global capitalism. The emergence of fierce competitors in oil palm markets triggered a radical refashion of the concession's business model. The Great Depression led to an intensification of practices of coerced recruitment.

Finally, Leverville did not constitute a "reset" of imperialism in Central Africa. The concession was envisioned as a fresh start, a new form of colonial venture. At the same time, many of its daily routines were fashioned out on the obsolete practices of the Congo Free State, such as its reliance on naturally-growing palm fruits and on the brutality of sentries and messengers as production incentive. The intimate correspondence between Leverville and the rubber concessions of old was strikingly embodied in the "Congo Atrocities!!!" tableau vivant which was shared in the opening chapter of this book.

In conclusion, Leverville was a liminal space rather than a fully-formed enclave of colonial hegemony. It embodied, on a smaller scale, the fields of tension traversing the colony in general. These tensions wove an uneven tapestry of European control, which was illustrated by the contradicting agendas of its economic and administrative actors; its vulnerability to outside influence; and the determining role played by indigenous communities in determining its historical trajectories.

Impotence, in Leverville and beyond

Impotence was the overarching framework traversing the different components of this book. I used this metaphor to tie together the inability to materialize the virtuous enclave envisioned by Leverhulme and the Belgian government. Furthermore, the structural impotence of the Leverville experience also contributed to further observations on the nature of colonial rule beyond interwar Central Africa.

The inability to realise the utopian agenda laid out by the concession's founders in 1911 originally stemmed from the structural discrepancy between their objectives and field realities. The makers of Leverville overestimated the willingness of the Congolese to take part in the *Huileries*' holistic project. They failed to see that their business model was already obsolete in the 1910s, and did not envision that producing palm oil would require resorting to the coercion of workers of all genders and ages. They did not envision that land laws protecting "native rights" would have to be circumvented to allow the company to find a sliver of profitability. In short, Lord Leverhulme and the Belgian government believed that paternalism would provide an answer to the violent guise of colonial capitalism, while violence was in fact inherently necessary to impose the virtuous vision they devised. The unbridgeable gap between the "mission to civilize" and the structural violence of imperialism has long been exposed by historians of colonialism.[9] It constitutes a first aspect of colonial impotence, namely the frequent impossibility for Europeans to fulfil their expected goals in the field.

This deficiency also had much to do with the agency displayed by indigenous communities. Reluctance, elusiveness, protest, secrecy and open violence steered the concession experience in directions that were not part of the original vision of Leverville's founders and power holders. The capacity of Africans to weigh upon the course of colonial affairs has also been previously and extensively demonstrated.[10] The conceptual framework of impotence allowed for the consideration of indigenous agency alongside the inner contradictions of colonial endeavours as widening together the gap between the virtuous and violent guises of colonialism. As detailed in the book's introduction, impotence is inherently relational; it supposes an intimate contact where one partner cannot perform

---

9 See for instance: Alice Conklin, *A Mission to Civilize. The Republican Idea of Empire in France and in West Africa* (Stanford: Stanford University Press, 1997); Tiquet, *Travail Forcé*; Frederick Cooper, *Colonialism in Question: Theory, Knowledge, History* (Berkeley: University of California Press, 2005).
10 See for instance, for Belgian Congo: Jean-Luc Vellut, *Congo: Ambitions et Désenchantement, 1880–1960* (Paris: Karthala, 2017), 165–211; Likaka, *Rural Society*; Hunt, *Nervous State*, 61–135.

accordingly. In the late 19th and early 20th century medical literature, the causes of such an affliction were often pinned on an inadequacy on the part of the ailing male's sexual companion.[11] Metaphorically speaking, impotence therefore referred not only to the relative powerlessness of European actors, but also encompassed the inherently relational nature of colonial power relations in the field. If sexual impotence was believed to be rooted in the inappropriate behaviours of women, colonial impotence was also explained as resulting from the unruliness and alleged "backwardness" of Africans, who refused to follow the behavioural patterns expected of them by colonial powers.

Impotence speaks of inadequacy more than it alludes to powerlessness. In its sexual guise, impotence was a problem, for it embodied a gap between social ideals of masculinity and the inability of some men to conform to them in their most intimate contacts. Resorting to the framework of colonial impotence constituted an attempt to transcend the paradigm of "helpless" or "anxious" colonial states. What made a colonial endeavour impotent was less its structural weaknesses than its inability to follow its own objectives. As this book demonstrated, private and public agents active in Leverville were anything but powerless. HCB built extensive infrastructures; forcibly recruited thousands of workers; and produced enormous amounts of palm oil. The company managed to do all of this even in challenging circumstances. However, the company's output did not match its economic nor its moral goals. Similarly, public field servants and their aides were also able to command significant authority. Nevertheless, they often did not mobilise their power in the ways that were expected of them. Many functionaries shunned the "prestige" vested in their function and used their privileges to amass wealth and to satisfy their lust. Governing and exploiting Leverville in the interwar was characterised by a constant and multifaceted disjunction between an inescapable "ugliness" described by some of the concession's visitors and the elevated ideals in the name of which HCB's flagship endured in spite of its lack of profitability.

According to Achille Mbembe, colonialism was akin to a form of phallic violence. As this book suggested, the "phallic" act of colonizing could also lead to forms of impotence. In spite of Leverville's manifold peculiarities, the discrepancy between principle and practices which presided over its interwar history are echoed in other colonial endeavours.

---

11 McLaren, *Impotence*, 112.

Bibliography

Archival sources

AFRICAN ARCHIVES, FEDERAL PUBLIC SERVICE FOR FOREIGN RELATIONS, BRUSSELS (AAB)
Affaires Etrangères (AE) 3268
Agriculture (AGRI) 99, 335, 360, 728, 736
Affaires Indigènes (AI) 4739
Affaires Indigènes/Main d'Oeuvre (AIMO) 1403, 1404, 1415, 1598, 1599, 1624, 1625, 1644, 1652, 1654, 1855, 1856, 3547, 3548
Main d'Oeuvre Indigène (MOI) 1820, 3602, 3607
Rapports Annuels AIMO (RA/AIMO) 190
Rapports Annuels Congo Belge (RA/CB) 157
Régime Foncier (RF) 1428, 1437, 1739

AFRICAMUSEUM ARCHIVES, TERVUREN (RMCA)
Private archives of Sidney Edkins: RMCA EA 54.85.171, RMCA, 54.45.184, RMCA, 54.85.183

UNILEVER ARCHIVES, PORT SUNLIGHT (UA)
Leverhulme Business Correspondence (LBC): LBC/215, LBC/229, LBC/230
United Africa Company (UAC): UAC 2/34/4/1/1, UAC/2/36/7/1/2, UAC 1/11/14/3/12, UAC 2/36/7/1/3

JESUIT ARCHIVES, KINSHASA (JAK)
Pictures of the Leverville-Soa Mission: B1 J

Published sources

"Projet de décret approuvant une convention conclue le 21 février 1911 entre le Gouvernement du Congo belge et la Société "Lever Brothers Limited" et ayant pour objet la concession de terres à une société à constituer sous le nom de : "Société Anonyme des Huileries du Congo Belge". In: *Annales Parlementaires* 1911, Document parlementaire n°126.
Congo Belge: Bulletin Officiel 1910. Brussels, Hayez, 1910
Durieux, André. *Institutions Politiques, Administratives et Judiciaires du Congo Belge et du Ruanda-Urundi*. Brussels: ed. Bieleveld, 1955.
La Compagnie du Kasaï à ses Actionnaires. Réponse à ses Détracteurs. Brussels, 1906.
Leplae, Edmond. *Le palmier à Huile en Afrique: Son Exploitation au Congo Belge et en Extrême-Orient*. Brussels: Falk & Fils, 1939.
Mouchet, René. *Le Problème Médical au Congo*. Liège: H. Vaillant-Carmanne, 1930.
Piron, Pierre and Jacques Devos (ed.). *Codes & Lois du Congo Belge*. Brussels: Larcier, 1954.
Raingeard de la Bletière, Paul. "La Main d'Oeuvre au Kwango." *Revue de Médecine et d'Hygiène Tropicale* 24 (1932): 21–48.
Recueil à l'Usage des Fonctionnaires et des Agents du Service Territorial au Congo Belge. Brussels: Weissenbruch, 1925.

Recueil à l'Usage des Fonctionnaires et des Agents du Service Territorial au Congo Belge.
Brussels: Weissenbruch, 1930.
Ryckmans, Pierre. *Dominer Pour Servir.* Brussels: Editions Universelles, 1948.
Schweitz, Jacques. "Extrait du Rapport de la Mission Médicale Antitrypanosomique du Kwilu-Kwango 1920–1921." *Annales de la Société Belge de Médecine Tropicale* 1:3 (1921): 339–65.
Trolli, Giovanni. "L'alimentation Chez les Travailleurs Indigènes dans les Exploitations Commerciales, Agricoles, Industrielles et Minières du Congo". *Africa: Journal of the International African Institute* 9:2 (1936): 197–217.

Interviews

Pemba Dimamaso (born 1961), Lusanga, 4 August 2015
Christophe Mwazita (born 1946), camp Kalamba, Lusanga, 4 August 2015
Gaston Willia Fetsi (born 1923), camp Avion, Pindi, 6 August 2015
Fabien Kalaki (born 1933), Ifwani – Kakobola, 10 August 2015
Jean Ndeke Lutanda (born c. 1940–1945), Ifwani – Kakobola, 10 August 2015
Georges Zolochi (born c. 1925–1930), Ifwani-Kakobola, 10 August 2015
Lumène Wenge (born 1931), Nzaji, 11 August 2015
Kunanguka Tungeleko, (born c. 1930), Nzaji, 11 August 2015

Reference works

Adams, Julia. "Principals and Agents, Colonialists and Company Men: the Decay of Colonial Control in the Dutch East Indies." *American Sociological Review* 61:1 (1996): 12–28.
Aderinto, Saheed and Paul Osifodun. "500 Children Missing in Lagos': Child Kidnapping and Public Anxiety in Colonial Nigeria." In: *Children and Childhood in Colonial Nigerian Histories*, edited by Saheed Aderinto, 97–121. New York: Palgrave-Macmillan, 2015.
Agrawal, Arun. "The Politics of Development and Conservation: Legacies of Colonialism." *Peace & Change* 22:4 (1997): 463–482.
Allina-Pisano, Eric. "'Fallacious Mirrors:' Colonial Anxiety and Images of African Labor in Mozambique, ca. 1929." *History in Africa* 24 (1997): 9–52.
Allina-Pisano, Eric. "Resistance and the Social History of Africa." *Journal of Social History* 37:1 (2003): 187–98.
Allina-Pisano, Eric. *Slavery by Any Other Name: African Life Under Company Rule in Colonial Mozambique.* Charlottesville: University of Virginia Press, 2012.
Allman, Jean, and Victoria Tashjian. *"I Will Not Eat Stone": A Women's History of Colonial Asante.* Portsmouth: Heinemann, 2000.
Arzel, Lancelot. "Des Chasseurs en Guerre : Imaginaires et Pratiques Cynégétiques dans les Pacifications de l'Etat Indépendant du Congo 1885–1908." In: *Coloniser, Pacifier, Administrer. XIXe-XXIe siècles*, edited by Samia El Mechat, 141–161. Paris: CNRS Editions, 2014.

Auerbach, Jeffrey. *Imperial Boredom: Monotony and the British Empire.* Oxford: Oxford University Press, 2018.

Austen, Ralph, and Rita Headrick. "Equatorial Africa Under Colonial Rule." In: *History of Central Africa*, vol. 2, edited by David Birmingham and Phyllis Martin, 27–94. New York: Longman, 1983.

Bayart, Jean-François. "Hégémonie et Coercicion en Afrique Subsaharienne. La 'Politique de la Chicotte.'" *Politique Africaine* 2:110 (2008): 123–152.

Bayly, Christopher. *The Birth of the Modern World, 1780–1914.* London: Blackwell, 2004.

Beinart, William, and Lotte Hughes. *Environment and Empire.* Oxford: Oxford University Press, 2007.

Benton, Lauren. *A Search for Sovereignty. Law and Geography in European Empires, 1400–1900.* Cambridge: Cambridge University Press, 2009.

Berman, Bruce, and John Lonsdale. *Unhappy Valley: Conflict in Kenya & Africa. Book One: State & Class.* London: James Currey, 1990.

Bernault, Florence. *Colonial Transactions: Imaginaries, Bodies and Histories in Gabon.* Durham: Duke University Press, 2019.

Berry, Sara. "Hegemony on a Shoestring: Indirect Rule and Access to Agricultural Land." *Africa* 62:3 (1992): 327–355.

Bisschof, Eva. "Tropenkoller: Male Self-Control and the Loss of Colonial Rule." In: *Helpless Imperialists: Imperial Failure, Fear and Radicalization*, edited by Maurus Reinkowski, and Gregor Thum, 117–137. Göttingen: Vandenhoeck & Ruprecht, 2013.

Blanchard, Emmanuel, and Joël Glasman. "Le Maintien de l'Ordre dans l'Empire Français : une Historiographie Emergente". In : *Maintenir l'Ordre Colonial. Afrique et Madagascar (XIXe-XXe siècles)*, edited by Jean-Pierre Bat, and Nicolas Courtin, 11–41. Rennes: Presses Universitaires de Rennes, 2012.

Branche, Raphaëlle. "La Violence Coloniale: Enjeux d'une Description et Choix d'Écriture." *Tracés* 19 (2010): 29–42.

Burke, Timothy. *Lifebuoy Men, Lux Women: Commodification, Consumption and Cleanliness in Modern Zimbabwe.* Durham: Duke University Press, 1996.

Butchart, Alexander. *The Anatomy of Power: European Constructions of the African Body.* London: Zed Books, 1998.

Callaway, Helen. *Gender, Culture, and Empire. European Women in Colonial Nigeria.* London: Palgrave-MacMillan, 1987.

Cardoso de Mello, Louise, and Sven Van Melkebeke. "From the Amazon to the Congo Valley: A Comparative Study on the Violent Commodification of Labour During the Rubber Boom (1870s-1910s)". In *Commodity Frontiers and Global Capitalist Expansion*, edited by Sabrina Joseph, 137–181. London: Palgrave, 2019.

Clement, Piet. "The Land Tenure System in the Congo, 1885–1960: Actors, Motivations, and Consequences." In: *Colonial Exploitation and Economic Development: the Belgian Congo and the Netherlands Indies Compared*, edited by Ewout Frankema and Frans Buelens, 88–109. Abingdon: Routledge, 2013.

Conklin, Alice. *A Mission to Civilize. The Republican Idea of Empire in France and in West Africa.* Stanford: Stanford University Press, 1997.

Cooper, Frederick. "Conflict and Connection: Rethinking Colonial African History." *The American Historical Review* 99:5 (1994): 1516–1545.

Cooper, Frederick. *Colonialism in Question: Theory, Knowledge, History*. Berkeley: University of California Press, 2005.
Cooper, Frederick. *Decolonization and African Society. The Labor Question in French and British Africa*. Cambridge: Cambridge University Press, 1996.
Coquery-Vidrovitch, Catherine. *Les Africaines. Histoire des Femmes d'Afrique Noire du XIXe au XXe Siècle*. Paris: Desjonquères, 1994.
Cornet, Anne. "Action Sanitaire et Contrôle Social au Ruanda (1920–1940). Femmes, Missions et Politique de Santé," PhD diss., Université Catholique de Louvain, 2005.
Covington-Ward, Yolanda. *Gesture and Power: Religion, Nationalism and Everyday Resistance in Congo*. Durham: Duke University Press, 2016.
Crumley, Carole L. "Historical Ecology: A Multidimensional Ecological Orientation." In: *Historical Ecology: Cultural Knowledge and Changing Landscapes*, edited by Carole L. Crumley, 1–17. Santa Fe: School of American Research Press, 1994.
Cunningham Bissell, William. "Engaging Colonial Nostalgia." *Cultural Anthropology*, 20:2 (2005): 215–248.
De Boeck, Filip. "Être un Danger, Être en Danger: Exclusion et Solidarité dans un Monde d'Insécurité Spirituelle." In: *Sorcellerie et Violence en Afrique*, edited by Bruno Martinelli, and Jack Bouju, 85–105. Paris: Karthala, 2012.
De Roo, Bas. "The Trouble with Tariffs: Custom Policies and the Shaky Balance between Colonial and Private Interests in the Congo (1886–1914)." *Low Countries Journal of Social and Economic History* 3 (2015): 1–21.
Dembour, Marie-Bénédicte. "La Chicote Comme Symbole du Colonialisme Belge?" *Canadian Journal of African Studies* 26:2 (1992): 205–225.
Donovan, Stephen. "Congo Utopia." *English Studies in Africa*, 59:1 (2016): 53–75.
Duncan, James S. *In the Shadows of the Tropics: Climate, Race and Biopower in Nineteenth Century Ceylon*. Aldershot: Ashgate 2007.
Dunn, Kevin. *Imagining the Congo: The International Relations of Identity*. New York: Palgrave-MacMillan, 2003.
El Mechat, Samia. "Introduction." In : *Les Administrations Coloniales, XIXe-XXe Siècles: Esquisse d'une Histoire Comparée*, edited by Samia El Mechat, 13–25. Rennes: Presses Universitaires de Rennes, 2009.
Emirbayer, Mustafa, and Ann Mische. "What is Agency?" *American Journal of Sociology* 103:4 (1998): 962–1023.
Ferguson, James. *Global Shadows. Africa in the Neoliberal World Order*. Durham: Duke University Press, 2006.
Fieldhouse, David. *Unilever Overseas: The Anatomy of a Multinational*. London: Croom Helm, 1979.
Fischer-Tiné, Harald (ed.), *Anxieties, Fear and Panic in Colonial Settings: Empires on the Verge of a Nervous Breakdown*. Cambridge: Cambridge University Press, 2016.
Foucault, Michel. *Histoire de la Sexualité I: La Volonté de Savoir*. Paris: Gallimard, 2010 (1976).
Fraiture, Pierre-Philippe. *La Mesure de l'Autre. Afrique Subsaharienne et Roman Ethnographique de Belgique et de France (1918–1940)*. Paris: Honoré Champion, 2007.
Gardner, Leigh. *Taxing Colonial Africa: The Political Economy of British Imperialism*. Oxford: Oxford University Press, 2012.

Geschiere, Peter and Cyprian Fisiy. "Domesticating Personal Violence: Witchcraft, Courts and Confessions in Cameroon." *Africa* 64:3 (1994): 323–341.

Gondola, Didier. "Dream and Drama: The Search for Elegance among Congolese Youth." *African Studies Review* 42:1 (1999): 23–48.

Gordon, David M. *Invisible Agents: Spirits in a Central African History.* Athens: Ohio University Press, 2012.

Gordon, David M. "Reading the Archives as Sources." Oxford Research Encyclopedia of African History (2018), accessed 13 August 2019, doi: 10.1093/acrefore/9780190277734.014.227

Grandin, Greg. *Fordlandia. The Rise and Fall of Henry Ford's Forgotten Jungle City.* New York: Metropolitan Books, 2009.

Grant, Kevin. "The Limits of Exposure: Atrocity Photographs in the Congo Reform Campaign." In: *Humanitarian Photography: A History*, edited by Heide Fehrenbach and Davide Rodogno, 64–88. Cambridge: Cambridge University Press, 2015.

Grier, Beverly. "Invisible Hands: The Political Economy of Child Labour in Colonial Zimbabwe, 1890–1930." *Journal of Southern African Studies* 20:1 (1994): 27–52.

Halen, Pierre. *'Le Petit Belge Avait vu Grand': Une Littérature Coloniale.* Brussels: Labor, 1993.

Hanretta, Sean. "Space and Conflict in the Elisabethville Mining Camps, 1923–1938". In: Florence Bernault (ed.), *A History of Prison and Confinement in Africa*, 191–220. Portsmouth: Heineman, 2003.

Hardin, Rebecca. "Concessionary Politics: Property, Patronage, and Political Rivalry in Central African Forest Management." *Current Anthropology* 52:3 (2009): 113–125.

Henderson, Janice, and Daphne Osborne. "The Oil Palm in All Our Lives: How this Came About." *Endeavour* 24:2 (2000): 63–88.

Hendrickson, Hildi (ed.). *Clothing and Difference: Embodied Identities in Colonial and Post-Colonial Africa.* Durham: Duke University Press, 1996.

Hendriks, Thomas. "Erotics of Sin: Promiscuity, Polygamy and Homo-Erotics in Missionary Photography from the Congolese Rainforest." *Visual Anthropology* 26:4 (2009): 355–382.

Hendriks, Thomas. *Rainforest Capitalism: Ecstasis and Extraction in a Congolese Timber Concession.* Durham: Duke University Press, forthcoming.

Henriet, Benoît. "'Elusive natives'": Escaping Colonial Control in the Leverville Oil Palm Concession, Belgian Congo, 1923–1941." *Canadian Journal of African Studies* 49:2 (2015): 339–361.

Henriet, Benoît. "Colonial Law in the Making: Sovereignty and Property in the Congo Free State (1876–1908)." *The Legal History Review* 83 (2015): 202–225.

Henriet, Benoît. "Des Ethnographes Anxieux : Pratiques Quotidiennes du Pouvoir au Congo Belge, 1930–1940." *Vingtième Siècle* 140:4 (2018): 41–54.

Henriet, Benoît. "Facing the Talking Snake: Witchcraft, Anxiety and Sense-Making in Interwar Belgian Congo." *International Journal of African Historical Studies* 51:2 (2018): 219–241.

Higginson, John. *A Working Class in the Making, Belgian Colonial Labor Policy and the African Mineworker, 1907–1951.* Madison: University of Wisconsin Press, 1989.

Hobsbawm, Eric. "Peasants and Politics." *The Journal of Peasants Studies* 1:1 (1973): 3–22.

Huggan, Graham, and Helen Tiffin. *Postcolonial Ecocriticism. Literature, Animals, Environment.* London: Routledge, 2010.

Hunt, Nancy Rose. "Colonial Medical Anthropology and the Making of the Central African Infertility Belt." In: Helen Tilley et Robert Gordon (eds.), *Ordering Africa: Anthropology, European Imperialism and the Politics of Knowledge*, 252–281. Manchester: Manchester University Press, 2007.

Hunt, Nancy Rose. "Letter-writing, Nursing Men and Bicycles in the Belgian Congo: Notes Towards the Social Identity of a Colonial Category." in *Paths Toward the Past. African Historical Essays in Honor of Jan Vansina*, edited by Robert Harms et al., 187–210. Atlanta: ASA Press, 1994.

Hunt, Nancy Rose. "Noise Over Camouflaged Polygamy, Colonial Morality Taxation, and a Woman-Naming Crisis in Belgian Africa." *Journal of African History* 32:3 (1991): 471–494.

Hunt, Nancy Rose. "STDs, Suffering and their Derivatives in Congo-Zaïre: Notes Towards an Historical Ethnography of Diseases." In: *Vivre et Penser le Sida en Afrique*, edited by Charles Becker et al., 111–131. Paris: Karthala, 1999.

Hunt, Nancy Rose. *A Colonial Lexicon: Of Birth Ritual, Medicalization and Mobility in the Congo*. Durham: Duke University Press, 1999.

Hunt, Nancy Rose. *A Nervous State. Violence, Remedies and Reverie in Colonial Congo*. Durham: Duke University Press, 2016.

Jackson, Will. "The Private Lives of Empires: Emotion, Intimacy and Colonial Rule." *Itinerario* 42:1 (2018): 1–15.

Janzen, John. "Ideologies and Institutions in Precolonial Western Equatorial African Therapeutics." In: *The Social Basis of Health and Healing in Africa*, edited by John Janzen and Steve Feierman, 317–26. Berkeley: University of California Press, 1992.

Jewsiewicki, Bogumil. "A Century of Painting in the Congo: Image, Memory, Experience and Knowledge." In *A Companion to Modern African Art*, edited by Gitti Salami, Monica Blackmun Visonà, 330–349. New York: John Willey and Sons, 2013.

Jewsiewicki, Bogumil. "Political Consciousness among African Peasants in the Belgian Congo." *Review of African Political Economy* 19 (1980): 23–32.

Jewsiewicki, Bogumil. "The Great Depression and the Making of the Colonial Economic System in the Belgian Congo." *African Economic History* 4 (1977): 153–176.

Kalema, Emery. "Scars, Marked Bodies, and Suffering: the Mulele 'Rebellion' in Postcolonial Congo." *Journal of African History* 59:2 (2018): 263–282.

Kalman, Samuel. "Introduction: Colonial Violence." *Historical Reflections* 36:2 (2010): 1–6.

Lachenal, Guillaume. *Le Médecin Qui Voulut Être Roi : Sur les Traces d'une Utopie Coloniale*. Paris: Seuil, 2017.

Laumann, Dennis. "A Historiography of German Togoland, or the Rise and Fall of a 'Model Colony.'" *History in Africa* 30 (2003): 195–211.

Lauro, Amandine. "'Le Législateur n'Envisage en l'Espèce que le Point de Vue Physiologique': Régulations du Mariage 'Indigène' et Politiques Sexuelles au Congo Belge." In: *Le Contrôle des Femmes dans les Empires Coloniaux. Empires, Genre, et Biopolitiques*, edited by Martine Spensky, 183–200. Paris: Karthala, 2015.

Lauro, Amandine. "'Une Oeuvre d'Étaiement et de Reconstruction.' Notes Sur la Fabrique du Droit Coutumier, le Pouvoir Colonial et l'Ordre du Mariage dans Le Congo Belge de l'Entre-Deux-Guerres." In: *Droit et Justice en Afrique Coloniale: Traditions, Productions et Réformes*, edited by Bérengère Piret, 165–188. Brussels : Presse de l'Université Saint-Louis, 2013.

Lauro, Amandine. "Maintenir l'Ordre dans la 'Colonie-Modèle' : Note sur les Désordres Urbains et la Police des Frontières Raciales au Congo Belge." *Crime, Histoire & Sociétés* 15:2 (2011): 97–121.

Lauro, Amandine. *Coloniaux, Ménagères et Prostituées au Congo belge (1885–1930).* Brussels: Labor, 2005.

Levine, Philippa. "States of Undress: Nakedness and the Colonial Imagination." *Victorian Studies* 50:2 (2008): 189–219.

Lewis, Brian. *So Clean: Lord Leverhulme, Soap and Civilization.* Manchester: Manchester University Press, 2008.

Likaka, Osumaka. *Naming Colonialism: History and Collective Memory in the Congo.* Madison: University of Wisconsin Press, 2009.

Likaka, Osumaka. *Rural Society and Cotton in Colonial Zaïre.* Madison: University of Wisconsin Press, 1997.

Loffman, Reuben, and Benoît Henriet. "'We Are Left with Barely Anything': Colonial Rule, Dependency, and the Lever Brothers in the Belgian Congo, 1911–1960." *The Journal of Imperial and Commonwealth History* 48:1 (2020): 71–100.

Loffman, Reuben. *Church, State and Colonialism in Southeastern Congo, 1890–1962.* London: Palgrave-Macmillan, 2019.

Lowenhaupt Tsing, Anna. *The Mushroom at the End of the World: On the Possibility of Life in Capitalist Ruins.* Princeton: Princeton University Press, 2015.

Lynn Osborn, Emily. *Our New Husbands Are Here. Households, Gender, and Politics in a West African State from The Slave Trade to Colonial Rule.* Athens: Ohio University Press, 2011.

MacGaffey, Wyatt. "African Objects and the Idea of Fetish." *RES: Anthropology and Aesthetics* 25 (1994): 123–131.

MacGaffey, Wyatt. "Fetishism Revisited: Kongo "Nkisi" in Sociological Perspective." *Africa* 47:2 (1977): 172–184.

MacGaffey, Wyatt. *Kongo Political Culture: The Conceptual Challenge of the Particular.* Bloomington: Indiana University Press, 2000.

MacLachlan, Malcolm. *Embodiment: Clinical, Critical and Cultural Perspectives on Health and Illness.* Maidenhead: Open University Press, 2004.

Martin, Phyllis. "Contesting Clothes in Colonial Brazzaville." *The Journal of African History* 35:3 (1994): 401–426.

Maß, Sandra. "Welcome to the Jungle: Imperial Men, 'Inner Africa,' and Mental Disorder in Colonial Discourse." In: *Helpless Imperialists: Imperial Failure, Fear and Radicalization*, edited by Maurus Reinkowski, and Gregor Thum, 92–117. Göttingen: Vandenhoeck & Ruprecht, 2013.

Mashini, Jean-Daniel. *Le Développement Régional en République Démocratique du Congo de 1960 à 1997: L'Exemple du Kwango-Kwilu.* Paris: L'Harmattan, 2013.

Masquelier, Adeline. *Dirt, Undress and Difference: Critical Perspective on the Body's Surface.* Bloomington: Indiana University Press, 2006.

Mauss, Marcel. "Les Techniques du Corps," *Journal de Psychologie* 32 (1936): 1–23.

Mbembe, Achille. *On the Postcolony.* Berkeley: University of California Press, 2001.

McClintock, Anne. *Imperial Leather. Race, Gender and Sexuality in the Colonial Context.* London: Routledge, 1995.

McLaren, Angus. *Impotence: A Cultural History.* Chicago: University of Chicago Press, 2007.

Meredith, David. "Government and the Decline of the Nigerian Oil-palm Industry, 1919–1939" *The Journal of African History* 25:3 (1984): 311–329.
Messi Me Nang, Clotaire. *Les Chantiers Forestiers au Gabon. Une Histoire Sociale des Ouvriers Africains*. Paris: L'Harmattan, 2014.
Monaville, Pedro. "A Distinctive Ugliness: Colonial Memory in Belgium." In: *Memories of Post-Imperial Nations: The Aftermath of Decolonization, 1945–2013*, edited by Dietmar Rothermund, 58–75. Cambridge: Cambridge University Press, 2015.
Morgan Hodge, Joseph. *Triumph of the Expert. Agrarian Doctrines of Development and the Legacies of British Colonialism*. Athens: Ohio University Press, 2007.
Mudimbe, Valentin. *The Idea of Africa*. Bloomington: Indiana University Press, 1994.
Mumvwela, Clément. *Le Développement Local au Kwango-Kwilu (RD Congo)*. Brussels: Peter Lang, 2004.
Muschalek, Marie. "Honourable Soldier-Bureaucrats: Formations of Violent Identities in the Colonial Police Force of German Southwest Africa, 1905–18." *The Journal of Imperial and Commonwealth History*, 41:4 (2013): 584–599.
Muschalek, Marie. *Violence as Usual: Policing and the Colonial State in German Southwest Africa*. Ithaca: Cornell University Press, 2019.
Ndaywel E Nziem, Isidore. *Nouvelle Histoire du Congo. Des Origines à la République Démocratique*. Brussels: Le Cri, 2010.
Nicolaï, Henri. "Le Congo et l'Huile de Palme. Un Siècle. Un Cycle?", *Belgeo*, 4 (2013), Accessed October 25, 2020. doi: 10.4000/belgeo.11772
Nicolaï, Henri. *Le Kwilu: Étude Géographique*. Brussels: Centre Scientifique et Médical de l'ULB en Afrique, 1963.
Noland, Carrie. *Agency & Embodiment. Performing Gestures/Producing Cultures*. Cambridge: Harvard University Press, 2009.
Northrup, David. *Beyond the Bend in the River: African Labor in Eastern Zaïre, 1865–1940*. Athens: Ohio University Press, 1988.
Oslisly, Richard et al. "Climatic and Cultural Changes in the West Congo Basin Forests Over the Past 5000 Years." *Philosophical Transactions of the Royal Society* 368 (2012), accessed August 29, 2019, doi: 10.1098/rstb.2012.0304.
Pandey, Gyanendra. "Voices from the Edge: The Struggle to Write Subaltern Histories." In: *Mapping Subaltern Studies and the Postcolonial*, edited by Vinayak Chaturvedi, 281–300. London: Verso, 2012 (2000).
Pavlakis, Dean. *British Humanitarianism and the Congo Reform Movement, 1896–1913*. Farnham: Ashgate, 2015.
Pierce, Steven, and Anumpama Rao (eds.). *Discipline and the Other Body. Correction, Coroporeality, Colonialism*. Durham-London: Duke University Press, 2006.
Polasky, Janet. *Emile Vandervelde: Le Patron*. Brussels: Labor, 1995.
Poncelet, Marc. *L'Invention des Sciences Coloniales Belges*. Paris: Karthala, 2009.
Pratt, Mary Louise. *Imperial Eyes: Travel Writing and Transculturation*. London: Routledge, 1992.
Ranger, Terence. "The Invention of Tradition in Colonial Africa." In: *The Invention of Tradition*, edited by Eric Hobsbawm, and Terence Ranger, 211–262. Cambridge: Cambridge University Press, 1983.

Reinkowski, Maurus, and Gregor Thum. "Helpless Imperialists: Introduction." In: *Helpless Imperialists: Imperial Failure, Fear and Radicalization*, edited by Maurus Reinkowski, and Gregor Thum, 7–21. Göttingen: Vandenhoeck & Ruprecht, 2013.
Rival, Alain, and Patrice Levang. *La Palme Des Controverses: Palmier à Huile et Développement*. Versailles: Quae, 2013.
Rodet, Marie. "C'est Le Regard qui Fait l'Histoire. Comment Utiliser des Archives Coloniales qui Nous Renseignent Malgré Elles sur l'Histoire des Femmes Africaines." *Terrains & Travaux*, 10 (2006): 18–35.
Sanderson, Jean Paul. *Démographie Coloniale Congolaise: Entre Speculation, Idéologie et Reconstruction Historique*. Louvain-la-Neuve: Presses Universitaires de Louvain, 2018.
Schatzberg, Michael. *Political Legitimacy in Middle Africa. Father, Family, Food*. Bloomington: Indiana University Press, 2001.
Scott, David. "Colonial Governmentality." *Social Text* 43 (1995): 191–220.
Scott, James C. "Everyday Forms of Resistance." *The Copenhagen Journal of Asian Studies* 1:4 (1989): 33–62.
Scott, James C. *Weapons of the Weak: Everyday Forms of Peasant Resistance*. Bloomsbury: Yale University Press, 1985.
Seibert, Julia. "More Continuity than Change? New Forms of Unfree Labor in the Belgian Congo, 1908–1930." In: *Humanitarian Intervention and Changing Labor Relations: The Long-Term Consequences of the Abolition of the Slave Trade*, edited by Marcel Van der Linden, 369–386. Leiden: Brill, 2011.
Shoemaker, Nancy. "Whale Meat in American History." *Environmental History*, 10:2 (2005): 269–294.
Sikitele, Gize. "Histoire de la révolte des Pende de 1931". PhD Diss. University of Lubumbashi, 1986.
Sipho Simelane, Hamilton. "Landlords, the State and Child Labor in Colonial Swaziland, 1914–1947." *The International Journal of African Historical Studies* 31:3 (1998): 571–93.
Smith, Robert Eugene. "Les Kwilois Parlent de l'Epoque Coloniale." *Annales Aequatoria*, 26 (2005): 165–217.
Stanard, Matthew. *Selling the Congo: A History of European Pro-Empire Propaganda and the Making of Belgian Imperialism*. Lincoln: University of Nebraska Press, 2011.
Stanard, Matthew. *The Lion, the Leopard and the Cock: Colonial Memories and Monuments in Belgium*. Leuven: Leuven University Press, 2019.
Stoler, Ann Laura Stoler, and Frederick Cooper. "Between Metropole and Colony. Rethinking a Research Agenda". In: *Tensions of Empire: Colonial Cultures in a Bourgeois World*, edited by Ann-Laura Stoler and Frederick Cooper, 1–56. Berkeley: University of California Press, 1997.
Stoler, Ann Laura. *Along the Archival Grain: Epistemic Anxieties and Colonial Common Sense*. Princeton: Princeton University Press, 2009.
Stoler, Ann Laura. *Carnal Knowledge and Imperial Power: Race and the Intimate in Colonial Rule*. Berkeley: California University Press, 2002.
Stoler, Ann Laura. *Race and the Education of Desire. Foucault's History of Sexuality and the Colonial Order of Things*. Durham: Duke University Press, 1995.
Strother, Zoé. "Eastern Pende Construction of Secrecy." In: *Secrecy: African Arts that Conceals and Reveals*, edited by Mary Nooter, 67–86. New York: Center for African Art, 1993.

Tiquet, Romain. *Travail Forcé et Mobilisation de la Main d'Oeuvre au Sénégal. Années 1920–1960*. Rennes: Presses Universitaires de Rennes, 2019.
Tiquet, Romain. "Maintien de l'Ordre Colonial et Administration du Quotidien en Afrique." *Vingtième Siècle*,140:4 (2018): 3–13.
Tiquet, Romain. "Rendre Compte Pour ne pas Avoir à Rendre des Comptes: Réflexion sur l'Écrit Administratif en Situation Coloniale (Sénégal, Années 1920–1950)" *Cahiers d'Histoire* 137 (2017): 123–140.
Tower Sargent, Lyman. "Colonial and Postcolonial Utopias." In: *The Cambridge Companion to Utopian Literature*, edited by Gregory Claeys, 200–222. Cambridge: Cambridge University Press, 2010.
Traugott, Mark. "The Economic Origins of the Kwilu Rebellion". *Comparative Studies in Society and History* 21:3 (1979): 459–479.
Turner, Tom. "Images of Power, Images of Humiliation: Congolese "Colonial" Sculpture for Sale in Rwanda." *African Arts* 38:1 (2005): 60–96.
Van Walraven Klaas, and John Abbink. "Rethinking Resistance in African History: An Introduction," in *Rethinking Resistance: Revolt and Violence in African History*, edited by Jon Abbink, Mirjam de Bruijn and Klaas van Walraven, 1–40. Leiden: Brill, 2003.
Van Wolputte, Steven. "Hang on to Your Self: Of Bodies, Embodiment and Selves." *Annual Review of Anthropology* 33 (2004): 251–269.
Van Yve, Françoise. "Une Communauté Missionnaire au Kwango. Les Soeurs de Sainte-Marie de Namur à Leverville (1923–1940)." *Enquêtes et Documents d'Histoire Africaine*, 7 (1987): 56–87.
Vanderlinden, Jacques (ed.). *Main d'oeuvre, Eglise, Capital et Administration dans le Congo des Années Trente*. Brussels: ARSOM, 2011.
Vanderstraeten, Louis-François. *La Répression de la Révolte des Pende du Kwango en 1931*. Brussels: ARSOM, 2001.
Vansina, Jan. "Les Mouvements Religieux Kuba (Kasaï) à l'Epoque Coloniale." *Etudes d'Histoire Africaine* 11 (1971): 155–187.
Vansina, Jan. "Lukoshi/Lupambula: Histoire d'un Culte Religieux Dans les Régions du Kasaï et du Kwango (1920–1970)", Études d'Histoire Africaine, 5 (1971): 51–97.
Vansina, Jan. *Oral Tradition as History*. Madison: Wisconsin University Press, 1985.
Vansina, Jan. *Paths in the Rainforest: Toward a History of Political Tradition in Equatorial Africa*. Madison: University of Wisconsin Press, 1990.
Vanthemsche, Guy. *La Belgique et le Congo : L'Impact de la Colonie sur la Métropole*. Brussels: Le Cri, 2007.
Vaughan, Meghan. *Curing their Ills: Colonial Power and African Illness*. Stanford: Stanford University Press, 1991.
Vellut, Jean-Luc. "Hégémonies en Construction: Articulation entre État et Entreprises dans le Bloc Colonial Belge (1908–1960)," *Canadian Journal of African Studies* 16:2 (1982): 313–330.
Vellut, Jean-Luc. *Congo: Ambitions et Désenchantement, 1880–1960*. Paris: Karthala, 2017.
White, Luise. *Speaking with Vampires. Rumor and History in Colonial Africa*. Berkeley: University of California Press, 2000.
Wilson, Charles. *The History of Unilever: A Study in Economic Growth and Social Change*. London: Cassel, 1970.

Winterhalder, Bruce. "Concepts in Historical Ecology: The View from Evolutionary Ecology". In: *Historical Ecology: Cultural Knowledge and Changing Landscapes*, edited by Carole L. Crumley, 17–43. Santa Fe: School of American Research Press, 1994.

Young, Crawford. *Politics in Congo: Decolonization and Independence.* Princeton: Princeton University Press, 1965.

Index

ABIR, Anglo-Belgian India Rubber Company 107
Africa 3, 11f., 15f., 19–22, 26, 28f., 32f., 38f., 41, 54, 70, 74, 77, 80–82, 86–88, 91f., 97, 101, 114–116, 124, 130f., 136, 138f., 148, 159, 162f., 170–172, 174, 176f.
Agency 8, 11, 13, 23, 26, 70f., 73f., 80, 92, 94, 122f., 130, 141, 170, 175–177
Alberta, circle of 37
Amazon 7, 30f., 43
Angola 16, 159

Balot, Maximilien 67f.
Boma 50, 52
Brabanta, circle of 37, 117
Brazil 7
Brussels 3, 15, 17, 19f., 22, 34, 38, 41, 48, 50f., 60, 68, 76f., 79f., 91, 131, 149, 157, 167
Bula Matari 55f.
Bulungu 44, 50, 107
Bwanga 87–90

Cameroon 30, 88
Capitalism 6f., 11–13, 25, 27, 29, 36, 39, 43, 65, 80, 85, 116, 122, 133f., 145, 148–150, 164, 169–172, 174–177
Capitas 96, 106, 110f., 118, 134
Ceylon 121, 164
Chefs médaillés 18, 77, 81, 102
Chicotte 1, 104
Chiefs 91
Chieftaincy 63, 74, 76f., 79, 82f., 85, 92, 115, 162
Children 24, 26, 77, 88, 96, 98, 112f., 116–119, 127, 140, 171
CK *See* Compagnie du Kasaï
Clothing 119f., 122f., 131f., 134, 136, 142
Colonial Charter 34f.
Compagnie du Kasaï 3, 17f., 67
Concession 7, 8, 75

Congo basin 7, 15, 32f., 47f., 54, 71, 87, 158
Congo Free State 2–5, 7, 17, 29, 33–35, 38f., 41, 43–45, 50, 85, 96f., 107, 111, 119, 151, 163, 171, 176
Congo-Kasaï, province of 47, 50, 52, 54, 60–64, 71, 76, 79, 82, 91, 110f., 118, 126–129, 137, 142f., 157f., 161
Congo Reform Association 38
Conrad, Joseph 32
Copal 156
CRA *See* Congo Reform Association

Democratic Republic of Congo (DRC) 8
Dusseljé, Elso 1, 42, 44, 64, 67, 79, 107–109, 114f., 131, 134
Dutch Indies 18

Eating 18f., 24f., 76, 115, 119–121, 123–130, 162, 171
Edkins, Sidney 22f., 40, 44, 136, 143, 153f.
Elaeis 15, 18, 148–150, 152, 157–160, 162–165, 168f.
Elisabetha, circle of 37
Embodiment 36, 43, 45, 51, 55f., 59, 69, 99, 111, 119–122, 130f., 133, 137, 141, 145, 168, 171, 175f., 178
Ethnicity 80, 82f., 167

Fiji Islands 33
First World War 34
Flandria, circle of 37
Force Publique 3, 6, 17, 19, 47, 61, 102, 166
Forced labour 100
Ford, Henry 7, 30f., 36, 43
Fordlandia 7, 25, 29–32, 36, 40, 43
Franck, Louis 51, 82, 129, 156
Free State *See* Congo Free State
French empire 17, 31
French Equatorial Africa 39, 80, 159

Fruit cutters   50, 64, 66f., 71f., 74–77, 79f., 93, 95f., 100f., 105f., 108–111, 113, 116, 119, 130, 133f., 136f., 145, 149, 171, 176

Gabon   11, 75, 80, 93
General Governor   34, 50, 62–64, 79, 102, 105, 153–155, 158, 167
Gungu   24, 76, 83, 174

Healing   15, 72, 86f., 91f., 94, 120, 122f., 137, 139, 176
Honour   48f., 56, 72

Idiofa   66, 129, 174
Imperialism   9, 29, 38, 69, 97, 107, 148, 171, 176f.
impotence   8f., 12–14, 23, 27, 46, 48f., 58f., 61, 63, 68–70, 74, 106, 111, 123, 145f., 150, 169f., 177f.
Institut National pour l'Etude Agronomique du Congo Belge   21, 165f., 168
Ivory   156

Java   164
Jesuits   22
Jungers, Eugene   47, 57, 62–64, 66f., 68, 95, 103, 106, 110, 144

Kalo, Sissi   99f., 102, 109, 134
Kamtsha-Lubue, territory of   71, 86, 90
Kikwit   19, 44, 50, 54–57, 60, 107, 166
Kilamba   47, 67f., 70
King Albert the 1st   34, 41
Kwango district   15–25, 47–50, 52–68, 70f., 74f., 77–83, 85f., 90–93, 95, 101–103, 105, 108–111, 116, 118, 123f., 127, 139–142, 144, 149f., 157–160, 166f., 174
Kwango-Kwilu   15–17, 19, 24f., 58, 101, 116, 123, 140
Kwenge river   28, 37, 56, 82f., 129, 134
Kwilu river   2, 15, 17, 24, 28, 37, 44f., 64, 75, 80, 82–85, 93, 102, 114, 117, 124, 128, 137, 141–143, 147–150, 152, 157f., 160, 164f., 167f., 170–174

Leopold II   2f., 34, 38, 44
Léopoldville   47, 50, 52, 60, 66, 77f., 135, 140, 166f.
Leplae, Edmond   149, 152, 158, 161, 164
Lever Brothers   5, 7, 22, 25f., 28, 33, 35–37, 39f., 42f., 45, 66, 123–125, 147, 153, 170f., 175
Leverhulme, Lord William Esketh Lever   22, 35–38, 41–44, 52, 64, 75, 80, 95, 112, 125, 136, 147, 153, 170f., 177
Lower Congo   91
Lukusu   19, 71–74, 86–93, 175
Lusanga   18, 37, 44, 98f., 102, 104, 108f., 114, 128f., 141f., 144

Malafu   15, 63, 110, 158f.
Malaysia   18
Messengers   18f., 96, 102, 106, 108–111, 118, 139, 149, 175f.
Migration   15, 19, 80, 83, 85, 137
Minister of Colonies   34, 42f., 51, 62, 82, 101, 105, 129
Ministry of Colonies   50, 152, 160, 162–164, 166
Mise en valeur   18, 35, 51, 101, 113, 116, 118, 162, 167
Missions   4, 17, 22f., 92, 138
Mobutu, Joseph-Désiré   174
Morel, Edmund D.   38f., 171
Moseley, HCB manager   52
Mouchet, René   126, 138–140
Mozambique   8, 131

Neurasthenia   49, 66
Niadi   44, 50, 107, 118

Palm oil   2, 15, 17–19, 27, 36f., 42, 60, 75, 96, 98, 103, 112, 114, 116, 128, 143, 147f., 150, 157f., 160–165, 168f., 172–174, 177f.
Palm wine   *see:* Malafu
Paternalism   7, 25, 27, 80, 95f., 100, 111, 119, 145, 171, 177
Périer, Gaston-Denys   32
Plantations   18, 37, 40, 97, 105f., 149, 160–168, 172, 174, 176
Plantations Lever au Congo   24, 173

Port Sunlight 22, 36–38, 42, 48, 80, 144, 171
Prestige 13, 47–49, 51, 53, 56–59, 63 f., 69, 92, 111, 178
Province Orientale 65, 164

Raingeard de la Bletière, Paul 103 f., 117
Recruitment 5, 7, 19–21, 24, 26, 34, 50, 65, 67, 71, 96–98, 100–106, 109, 111 f., 119 f., 127, 129, 137, 140, 145, 149, 174–176
Régie des Plantations de la Colonie 164 f.
Renkin, Jules 34
Resistance 8, 19, 63, 72 f., 93, 122, 141 f., 155
Rubber 3, 5, 7, 17, 19, 30 f., 35, 43–45, 97, 106 f., 119, 156, 163, 176
Ryckmans, Pierre 60, 102 f., 105, 107–110, 113 f., 124, 131

Second World War 30, 44
Sentries 3, 96, 106–108, 111, 118, 149, 175 f.
Sleeping sickness 30, 40, 137–140, 142
Société Anversoise du Commerce au Congo 107
Stanley, Henry Morton 32, 44, 55
Sumatra 163–165

Takizala, Henri-Désiré 174
Tango, HCB station of 95, 118, 132, 140, 144
Taxes 18 f., 49, 51, 53, 57–61, 65, 68, 77 f., 91, 117, 143
Territorial agents 19, 51, 57, 59, 62, 65–68, 74 f., 77 f., 103 f., 111, 117 f., 175
Tilkens, Auguste 19, 62 f., 101 f.
Tupelepele 19, 47, 53 f., 56 f., 61–63, 65, 67 f., 71, 88, 90, 103, 171, 174
Twain, Mark 32

unfreedom *See* Forced labour
Unilever 18, 22, 39, 42 f., 99, 156, 171, 173 f.
Union Minière du Haut-Katanga 78, 172

Vandervelde, Emile 38 f., 171
Villages doublures 75 f., 77–80, 85, 92, 176

Wahis, Théophile 43
Wauters, general commissioner 19, 47, 53 f., 56–58, 62, 102, 158
Witchcraft 19, 71, 86, 88 f., 139
Women 13 f., 19, 26, 67 f., 77, 87, 90, 96, 110–119, 131, 139, 171, 178

www.ingramcontent.com/pod-product-compliance
Lightning Source LLC
Chambersburg PA
CBHW020232170426
43201CB00007B/399